THE EARLY CORRESPONDENCE OF JABEZ BUNTING 1820–1829

edited for the Royal Historical Society
by
W. R. WARD
M.A., D.Phil., F.R.Hist.S.

CAMDEN FOURTH SERIES
VOLUME 11

LONDON
OFFICES OF THE ROYAL HISTORICAL SOCIETY
UNIVERSITY COLLEGE, GOWER ST., W.C.1
1972

© Royal Historical Society

ISBN 0 901050 09 1

Printed in Great Britain by Butler & Tanner Ltd.
Frome and London

CONTENTS

PREFACE

I WOULD like to thank the Royal Historical Society for undertaking the publication of this portion of the Bunting correspondence, especially at a moment when the Methodist Conference (*Methodist Recorder*, July 13, 1972, p. 11) is seriously considering the public vending of its archives to the United States, the kind of transaction hitherto practised by its Book Stewards only surreptitiously and piecemeal. My best thanks are due also to the connexional archivist, Dr. J. C. Bowmer, and his committee, for making their holdings available to me for study on generous terms; their kindness made possible the discovery (amongst other things) that the surviving Bunting correspondence was far more extensive than had been supposed. I am grateful to Mrs. Brenda Farish and Mr. F. Scollan for assistance with the transcribing, and to the Society's Joint Literary Director, Mr. K. V. Thomas, for valuable suggestions at a late stage. My wife and colleagues have no doubt had their fill of Bunting in the last few years; their forbearance has been duly noted and appreciated.

Durham, August 1972.   W. R. W.

TABLE OF DATES

1779 Birth of Jabez Bunting

1795 Plan of Pacification

1797 Foundation of Methodist New Connexion by Alexander Kilham: Wesleyan Conference adopts the Form of Discipline

1799 Jabez Bunting becomes Wesleyan Preacher

1811 Formation of Primitive Methodist Connexion

1814–1820 Jabez Bunting Secretary of Conference

1820 Jabez Bunting President of Conference (first time)

1821–1824 Jabez Bunting connexional editor

1824 Mark Robinson forms the Society of Church Methodists

1827–1828 Leeds organ case

1828 Jabez Bunting President of Conference (second time)

1833 Jabez Bunting settled permanently in London as Secretary for foreign missions

1835 Expulsion of Dr. Warren from Wesleyan Methodist Connexion: Jabez Bunting President of Theological Institution

1836 Jabez Bunting President of Conference (third time)

1844 Jabez Bunting President of Conference (fourth time)

1849 Expulsion of Everett, Dunn and Griffith from Wesleyan connexion

1850 Wesleyan Reform secessions begin

1851 Jabez Bunting retires from the full time work of the ministry

1858 Death of Jabez Bunting

INTRODUCTION

(1) THE BUNTING CORRESPONDENCE

(a) *Principles of Selection*

WHEN work for the present edition began, it was believed that the surviving portion of the Bunting correspondence ran to some 700 letters, about half of which justified publication. A combing of the holdings of the Methodist Church Archives and Research Centre at 25–35 City Road, London E.C.1, revealed the existence of more than 4,000 letters to and from Jabez Bunting, which have now been catalogued, and arranged, alphabetically by correspondents, in the boxes containing the general correspondence of the archive. Four other collections which have deviously reached the United States of America have been traced, photocopies of which have been united with the main collection in City Road; some of these letters appear below. Every letter may be traced by the card catalogue at the Centre. The selection which follows has been arrived at by a process of elimination. That part of the *Life of Bunting*[1] completed by Jabez's third son Percy ends early in 1829, but long before the end the author was aware that the work had got out of control. 614 of his 700 pages were expended on the period before his father had been raised to the Presidential chair for the first time in 1820, most of them filled with transcriptions from the correspondence on a scale which would now be prohibitively expensive. Percy Bunting was a careless editor, and in silently omitting portions of documents he occasionally went well beyond carelessness. Nevertheless he provides a reasonably representative selection of the correspondence, and includes a great many letters which are now lost. The present collection therefore excludes letters before 1820, except those required for editorial purposes, and a few dating from late in 1819 which help to introduce the problems of Bunting's first Presidential year.

Reaching the year 1820, Percy Bunting realized that he must drastically reduce his scale of treatment, and ceased almost entirely to publish the correspondence. This was particularly unfortunate because the early letters, though very valuable, are not the chief manuscript source for Methodist history in that period. But from Bunting's first Presidency his correspondence is much more important than all the other unpublished sources put together. The present

---

[1] T. P. Bunting, *The Life of Jabez Bunting, D.D.* (London, 1858–1887) [cited below as *Life of Bunting*].

collection therefore includes everything of importance for domestic connexional policy for the period embracing Bunting's first two years as President, 1820 and 1828, and the years between. (For the years of Bunting's greatest influence from 1829 onwards, the corpus of documents, virtually none of which has been published, is enormous, and it is hoped to edit the core of the collection elsewhere.) From the present edition 279 letters of the following categories have been excluded: (1) those which are intrinsically worthless, or are of merely small, local or personal interest; (2) those concerned with missions overseas (letters concerning the impact of missionary organization on English Methodism have been retained); (3) those concerned with Scottish Methodism, which was always a law unto itself; (4) a very small number of letters which duplicate others included in the collection.

(b) *The Character of the Correspondence; its Historical Value*

In this correspondence the number of in-letters greatly exceeds Bunting's own out-letters, of which some 600 survive in draft or final form. For reasons which are not clear, Bunting always kept many of the letters he received, and made a point of keeping important letters addressed to him as President (together with his replies) for future reference. But the ministry as a body came from social levels at which there was no tradition of keeping letters, and the itinerant life discouraged the accumulation of paper, even when it was in the holograph of Jabez Bunting. The loss of many of Bunting's letters may be of no great importance, for although he would deal with questions of law, administration or moral casuistry, with economy and incisiveness, he was often uninformative on general matters. It is possible, however, that his letters have suffered selective destruction since the collection was constituted. Bunting never carried out his original intention to destroy papers of biographical importance, but in his will he instructed his elder sons to destroy whatever they thought expedient.[1] The impression left with the editor after transcribing the entire corpus is that Percy Bunting removed everything he could find written to or by himself (he did not find everything), and also whatever he thought might be construed to his father's discredit in the most explosive episode of his career, the great conflict with Dr. Warren (1834–1835), which arose from the establishment of a seminary for training preachers, and which gave rise to a substantial separation and the formation of the Wesleyan Methodist Association. These papers seem to be lost and may have been early destroyed.

---

[1] *Life of Bunting*, i, p. v.

Otherwise the collection seems to have suffered no more than random losses since Percy Bunting took it over with a view to writing the *Life*.

In many respects the value of the collection as an historical source is enhanced by the great number of in-letters. Received from all parts of the country, they provide an invaluable social commentary in the terms of the Wesleyan preachers themselves, as distinct from those which have often been thrust upon them by critics and historians, and distinct occasionally from those which they themselves publicly affirmed. The confrontation in the north between popular radicalism and the discipline of the connexion; the administrative problems created by high-pressure revival in Cornwall or the Isle of Man; the problems of financing a heavily indebted voluntary body in a time of falling prices; the difficulties of keeping order in large-town circuits; the mutual jealousies of itinerant and lay preachers; questions of liturgical change and moral casuistry; the relations between the Wesleyan preachers and other ministries, and between the connexion and non-ecclesiastical agencies of religious action, such as Sunday schools, at a time when the tone of churchmanship among the preachers was rising rapidly: the impact of Irish evangelicalism upon the Protestant cause in England; the way the connexional administration sought to deal with the first great secession of the age of Bunting, the kind of doctrine with which they underpinned their action, and the mechanisms through which agitation reverberated through the connexion; all these and other questions in the social history of religion in the period are illuminated with great vividness and circumstantial detail.

(c) *Editorial Practice*

In the text of the letters punctuation and the use of capitals have been modernized, and abbreviations have been expanded. The often eccentric spelling has been left unchanged, since it gives some indication of the varied levels of literacy among the Wesleyan preachers of the 'twenties. A few passages have been omitted on the same principles which have governed the omission of letters from the collection, and the subscriptions to the letters, none of which are of any significance, have also been omitted; the omissions are indicated by points (. . .). Editorial additions to the text appear in square brackets ([ ]) or, in the case of emendations where the manuscript has suffered damage, in pointed brackets (⟨ ⟩). Brief biographical details are provided for all the preachers and most of the laymen mentioned in the letters, and there are notes on the principal *explicanda;* these are contained in the footnotes on the first occasion of mention, and may be traced through the index. This device has been adopted to save an inordinate number of cross references, and it is hoped that it will prove convenient. In the period of this volume, as today, the Methodist connexional year began on 1 September; a note that a preacher served in a particular station, 1826–1827 for example, implies one year's service from 1 September 1826 to 31 August 1827. The Methodist Conference, however, met later than it now does, assembling for up to three weeks, late in July and early in August. A note that a preacher was President in 1826 or 1826–1827 implies, therefore, a period beginning late in July and continuing for a year.

(2) METHODISM IN THE AGE OF BUNTING

IT would be no great exaggeration to say that the Methodism of Bunting's boyhood was almost without government. Wesley's daily personal oversight over the whole connexion perished with his death, and while he provided for the Conference of itinerant preachers to continue as a sovereign legislature after him, it speedily proved that an assembly meeting for not more than three weeks in the year, with a President changing annually, could not govern a large and growing community. There is reason to think that Wesley intended to establish a form of episcopal government like that which he set up in America, but there was no unequivocal testimony of his intentions (like the Deed of Declaration (1784), which laid down the constitution of Conference and bestowed on it the power to appoint preachers to all the pulpits in the connexion), and several attempts in the 1790's to establish hierarchical rule foundered on the mutual animosities of the preachers. In its place District Meetings (there were nineteen in England, composed of all the preachers within their bounds) steadily developed both administrative and disciplinary functions, but District Meetings could suffice no more than the Conference for daily management and the generation of policy. It was Bunting's achievement to turn Methodism into a very actively governed community; partly by new central institutions, of which the Methodist Missionary Society (1813) and the Theological Institution (1834) were the most notable; partly by standing and *ad hoc* committees of Conference (on which prominent laymen were invited to serve) to control the raising or expenditure of funds; partly by the exertion of the corporate power of the pastorate in Conference locally, through pressing Superintendents to puruse common policies, or through Presidential deputations or Special District Meetings to enforce discipline or administrative changes. Bunting further shifted the balance from the fringes to the centre by bringing the connexional management into more continuous negotiations with government than it had ever been before, on public order or slavery, foreign missions or education.

The practical problems which were the spur to these changes were in part pastoral and political, in part financial and administrative.[1] In the first twenty years of the century not only the peace of congregations, but the supremacy of the Wesleyan understanding of the spiritual life, were jeopardized by the spread of revivalism. The reawakening of popular radicalism in the Luddite movement began a generation in which the Methodist flock were bitterly divided on social issues. In the large towns these questions came to a head first. It was here that the revivalists were at their most class-conscious; here that the chapels were related more or less closely to great Sunday schools, often quite independent of Methodism in their origin, and open to gusts of popular radicalism; here that class division was early translated into geographical separation. Steady growth in the size of town circuits led Conference to enforce circuit divisions in Manchester, Leeds, Liverpool and other towns during the 'twenties, which aroused serious opposition. The new arrangements could not fail to acknowledge the importance of the new suburban chapels, built by the affluent, and they involved the dismemberment of the old circuit Leaders' Meetings amongst the various societies, and the division of extra-circuit institutions like the Sunday schools and organizations for cottage prayer meetings in which lay democracy had reigned supreme. In every case there were upheavals in decayed town-centre chapels; ministerial authority unsupported by the influence of substantial laymen who had migrated to the suburbs was confronted with problems of discipline beyond its power to solve.

In Methodism, as in society at large, peace and order were much affected by the trade cycle, and conditions of economic difficulty tended not only to kill the evangelistic appeal of the movement and raise problems of internal discipline, but to aggravate its financial problems. These were at their worst between the end of the war and Bunting's first Presidential year in 1820. Before 1815 difficulties were arising from the fact that the number of preachers had been rapidly multiplied without calculation of the future liability of the allowance for wife and family to which they would become entitled. After the war the fall in prices multiplied the real burden of the debt which encumbered almost every chapel in the connexion, made two thirds of the home circuits insolvent even by 1815,[2] and destroyed financial

---

[1] For a fuller account see W. R. Ward, 'The religion of the people and the problem of control, 1790–1830', in *Studies in Church History*, viii (1972), pp. 237–257, and my book *Religion and society in England, 1790–1850* (London, 1972), pp. 75–104.
[2] *Life of Bunting*, ii, p. 96.

control. Finding that they were not absolutely committed to their obligations, circuits bid for preachers by offering allowances they had no intention of paying, and, via the District Meetings, the accumulated deficiences of the circuits fell upon the Contingent Fund, administered by Conference and viewed 'somewhat in the light of a sick-club box or a parish fund to which all sick and needy subscribers may make application'.[1] The Fund, supported in the first instance by a Yearly Subscription from members, was basically intended to support home missions (and for this purpose was re-inforced by an annual July congregational collection in 1815), and also by grants from the profits of the Book Room, the connexional publishing house. Business recession had a directly crippling effect on the evangelistic work of the connexion by reducing the yield of all three sources of revenue to the fund, and greatly multiplying the preachers' claims to unpaid allowances to be charged against it. In 1818 deficiencies to the sum of £5000 could not be met at all and were born by the preachers, half in the shape of unpaid allowances, half by taking up the unsold stock of the Book Room.

In 1820 at the Liverpool Conference Bunting recalled the preachers to their evangelistic mission, but his main answer to an accumulation of difficulties lay in the re-establishment of discipline in the flock and in the ministry by the determined exercise of the collective authority of the pastorate. The financial problem was inseparable from that of urban pastoral reorganization, for the great northern towns were the financial mainstay of the connexion. Financial stringency clinched the alliance of the preachers with the propertied laymen of the con-nexion which had come into being at the time of the Luddite troubles, an alliance which inflamed radical sentiments and evoked bizarre suspicions in the flock. Bunting was brought to the front rank of the ministry in 1820 by his simple answer to unmistakable difficulties, and the toughness with which he confronted them. Later crises again made him the first choice of his fellows in 1828 and 1836. Nor is there any doubt that Bunting inspired the doctrinal development with which the exercise of ministerial authority was to be underpinned,[2] and which bore fruit in 1829 in the formulation of the high Wesleyan doctrine of the Pastoral Office by John Beecham and Richard Watson (see nos. 64, 123, 134, *infra*). Appealing to the New Testament and to Wesley, they held that Christ, who occupied the whole Pastoral

---

[1] J. Crowther, *Thoughts upon the finances or temporal affairs of the Methodist connexion* . . . (Leeds, 1817), pp. 5, 16.
[2] On this subject see my forthcoming paper on 'The legacy of John Wesley' in *Essays presented to Lucy Stuart Sutherland*, ed. J. Bromley, P. Dickson and A. Whiteman.

Office himself, had committed the government of His Church to a distinct and separated order of pastors, whose function was (in Wesley's words) to feed and guide, to teach and rule the flock. Hence Bunting sought to have the preachers' reception into full connexion acknowledged as ordination and if possible accompanied by imposition of hands (see nos. 10, 64), and pressed the plan for a Theological Institution in 1834 which at a late stage was challenged by Dr. Warren.

Since the death of Wesley (who had not regarded his preachers as ministers) nothing had been heard of the teaching and ruling, and the new emphasis portended trouble in three areas. Unecclesiastical agencies of religious action like Sunday schools or cottage prayer meetings must be brought under pastoral control. Then by the Plan of Pacification (1795) and the Regulations of 1797 important rights had been ceded to the local and predominantly lay courts of the connexion. By a majority of the Leaders and Trustees, a Society might petition Conference to receive the sacrament from its preachers; under certain conditions the Leaders might put the preacher on trial; without the consent of the Leaders a Superintendent might not admit persons into, or expel them from Society membership. According to the high Wesleyan doctrine these could only be procedural provisions designed to prevent the abuse of the indivisible plenitude of pastoral power; when that plenitude of power was exercised in expulsions without trial, the local courts were to feel robbed of their rights. It also portended difficulties with local preachers. Because, according to the high doctrine of the Pastoral Office, local preachers were not separated from worldly employment, they could not be pastors, and hence, however valuable their spiritual services, they could not participate in government. There was in any case friction between the two sides especially in the Manchester area, because of ministerial suspicions of local preachers' repeated efforts to provide for their mutual charitable assistance with congregational support. This was due partly to dislike of extra-constitutional combinations amongst members, partly to the fear that it might injure the funds from which the itinerants were supported;[1] and when the Local Preachers Mutual Aid Association was founded in 1849 it at once attracted the fire of the connexional leaders. A full scale clash between local and itinerant preachers never came, but in Bunting's time it was constantly feared, and their mutual suspicion entered into the great Leeds organ crisis which forms the largest single topic discussed in the letters which follow, and which embraced all the sources of friction mentioned above.

[1] George Morley to Jabez Bunting, March 23, 1807. Holograph at Emory University Library, Atlanta, Ga.

In 1826 the Leeds circuit was divided, and there was great ill-feeling over the division of the Sunday school, which was not in origin a circuit or even a Methodist institution, and from the radical leaders of which serious trouble was expected. The explosion in fact came over the proposal to install an organ in the Brunswick chapel which was new, fashionable, and reputed the largest in the connexion. The law was clear that the organ might be introduced only with Conference consent after an investigation and approval by a District Meeting, and clear on almost nothing else. The Brunswick Trustees applied for the organ by a majority of 8 votes to 6 with one neutral; the Leaders' Meeting, viewing the organ as a middle-class status symbol, and thoroughly irritated by the new arrangements in the circuit and by the itinerants' refusal to entertain any representations from the local preachers, opposed it by a majority of more than twenty to one, and were upheld by the District Meeting. Bunting nevertheless persuaded a Conference committee largely composed of the same preachers who had met in the District Meeting to reverse their verdict. When serious opposition developed in Leeds, Conference sovereignty was demonstrated by the summoning of a Special District Meeting (attended by Bunting as President's special adviser) to settle the affairs of the circuit. This court expelled members in large numbers without trial before a Leaders' Meeting from which palatable verdicts could not have been obtained. This exercise of central authority and personal influence turned the radicals into inveterate defenders of circuit rights, led in 1828 to the formation of a secession connexion, the Leeds Protestant Methodists, and established their view of Bunting as the Methodist Pope. What kind of a man was he in fact?

(3) JABEZ BUNTING

Jabez Bunting was *born* at Manchester, May 13, 1779; and through the tender mercy of God his Saviour, *born again* at the same place in the year 1794. In 1799 he felt it his duty to quit the study of medicine, in which for four years he had been engaged, under the truly paternal direction of Dr. Thomas Percival; and to devote himself to the Christian Ministry among the Wesleyan Methodists, in serving whom, 'for Jesus's sake', he has now spent twentynine busy and laborious, but happy years.

> O may I every mourner cheer,
> And trouble every heart of stone;
> Save, under God, the souls that hear,
> Nor lose, in seeking them, my own;

Nor basely from my calling fly,
But for thy gospel live and die.[1]

THIS autograph, composed by Bunting in 1828 as he entered upon
the Presidency of the Wesleyan Conference for the second time,
neatly poses the two-fold biographical problem presented by his
career. The Bunting of Methodist historiography was an indispensable adjunct to the high Wesleyan doctrine of the Pastoral Office,
and was invested with an appropriate aura of legend by both the
champions and the opponents of that doctrine. The difficulty of
penetrating to the man behind the legends—the legend of the child
blessed by John Wesley himself, the young man who could not take
home his bride without their being 'privileged to have Mr. Wesley's
own bed for their use',[2] or on the other hand the Methodist Pope and
ruthless practitioner of caucus politics—is doubled by Bunting's own
willingness to sink himself in his office; not merely never basely to fly
from his calling, but to regard a career principally devoted to administration and public affairs as one which was in authority pastoral,
given over to saving 'under God, the souls that hear'. 'I feel that I
am *public* property,' he confessed in 1824;[3] and the evidence of a
huge correspondence confirms that by then the personality of Jabez
Bunting had been completely encapsulated by the public persona of
the ecclesiastical statesman, and made only one brief reappearance,
upon the death of his first wife in 1835.

The evidence, both of silence and of solid fact, of Bunting's
early career suggests that in origin he was something different from
what he speedily became. The late Dr. Scott Lidgett is said to have
claimed his own place in the Wesleyan succession by affirming that as
a child he had been blessed by the great Dr. Bunting, as the young
Jabez had been blessed by John Wesley. In his autograph, however, it
is noteworthy that Bunting makes no such claim for himself, convenient as it would have been on the morrow of the Leeds secessions,
and, in the sermon he preached for Bunting's funeral, Thomas
Jackson was quite silent about the matter. Bunting's mother, a
country girl from Monyash in the Peak of Derbyshire, admirably

---

[1] M[ethodist] C[hurch] A[rchives] MS. Autograph by Jabez Bunting, August
30, 1828.
[2] *Life of Bunting*, i, p. 21; M.C.A. MS. notes of the life of Jabez Bunting, July
18, 1877. In fact the newly married pair were given hospitality in the homes of
substantial laymen for some months, being allotted only the room at City Road
normally taken by the junior preacher and 'the use of the large drawing room . . .
on the second floor'. M.C.A. MSS. Jabez Bunting to George Marsden, April 21,
1804.
[3] No. 58, *infra*.

B

fitted the pattern of Wesleyan piety, and is said to have been converted by a sermon from a Methodist itinerant on his way to America, on the text 'And Jabez was more honourable than his brethren; and his mother called his name Jabez' (1 *Chron.* iv. 9). But his father was a different matter, and more than Jabez's son and biographer, Percy Bunting, could account for. William Bunting was a radical Manchester tailor who sent his son to not one but two unitarian preachers for his education, and finally apprenticed him to Thomas Percival, a leading unitarian doctor in the town; moreover Percival's great kindness (not only to Jabez, but to other Methodist preachers and their families)[1] which Bunting commemorated in his autograph and in the baptismal names of his third son, did not fit the established polemic of the high Wesleyan case. It could only be suggested that 'the lapse from orthodoxy of many of the Presbyterians in England was, at that time, neither so great nor so well understood as it afterwards became', an unlikely story in Manchester in the 1790s, and that Dr. Percival was in a measure redeemed by 'very moderate' opinions in secular and ecclesiastical politics, and and by the fact that almost all his descendants returned to the communion of the Established Church.[2] Still worse, one period of Methodist education which Jabez gave his own son and namesake was too embarrassing to bear mention, for it took place in the Leeds academy of James Sigston, the notorious radical and revivalist, the constitution-maker to the Leeds Protestant Methodists, whom Bunting drove from the connexion in the great clash of 1827.[3]

To the outward eye the young Bunting was himself a revivalist. His first public ministry was exercised in the Manchester cottage prayer-meetings, the spear-head of revival. He first preached in the streets in the doorway of an enthusiastic mechanic who thrust his hand into the fire to prove his ability to burn for Christ; the recollection of his sponsor was so embarrassing to the mature Bunting that he related how he had been ultimately hanged for murder, making a false profession of innocence on the scaffold. Jabez's trial sermon as a local preacher was preached in the Manchester Band Room, a centre of revivalism, maintained by Broadhurst, the celebrated draper, whose following Bunting was to help turn out of the connexion in 1806.

[1] M.C.A. MSS. Joseph Entwisle to Jabez Bunting, February 29, 1804. After Dr. Percival's death Jabez Bunting arranged his papers. M.C.A. MSS. Jabez Bunting to [Rd. Reece] November 28, 1804.

[2] *Life of Bunting*, i, pp. 11, 25, 51.

[3] It was clearly affirmed in Bunting's life-time by William L. Thornton, preacher and classical tutor at Didsbury College, who later edited Bunting's sermons, that he and young Bunting had been pupils at Sigston's academy at the same time. M.C.A. MSS. W. L. Thornton to Dr. Melson, June 20, 1845.

Bunting's own former minister, John Barber, wrote him a word of encouragement as he entered the ministry, which in retrospect could hardly have been more ironical:

> I am fully convinced that what our friends at Manchester call the spirit of the revival is the spirit in which we shall all live, if we wish to be useful.

> But you will find that many of the rich, and all the lukewarm Methodists, will be against it, because they want a religion and a mode of worship that will meet the approbation of the world. If our ancestors had regulated their opinions and conduct according to the judgement of the world what would the Methodists have been at this day?[1]

Almost all that is known of Bunting's first ministry at Oldham (1799–1801) is that he arranged dinner parties in which he and his superintendent enjoyed religious fellowship and theological conversation with the Congregational and Baptist ministers of the neighbourhood, in full accord with the denominational openness of his upbringing, and the revulsion against sectarian exclusiveness which characterized so much of the evangelical world of that day. On his next station in Macclesfield as late as October 1802, he could still write, 'We have considerable expect[atio]ns of a gracious revival; and many think they "hear the sound of abundance of rain". May our hopes be blessedly realized.'[2]

Within a year Bunting's whole outlook had changed, and had taken a form which was hardened, deepened and made more sophisticated by the passage of time, but not again fundamentally altered. Before he arrived in Macclesfield the local revivalists had begun to separate from the Methodist Society; in 1803 they published their rules as Christian Revivalists, and, still worse, prepared to unite with Sigston's revivalists who separated in Leeds, and the Band Room men in Manchester, the whole body to be led by William Bramwell, a Methodist preacher with revivalist ambitions, who now resigned his ministry. In the event the scheme went off at half-cock. The Manchester men would not separate, Bramwell succumbed to great personal pressure to withdraw his resignation, and Bunting was infuriated.

---

[1] *Life of Bunting*, i, p. 115. This MS. copy of this letter in M.C.A. seems to have been made from the printed version here quoted.

[2] M.C.A. MSS. Jabez Bunting to [Disney Alexander], October 14, 1802. The argument of this paragraph seems confirmed by a sentence in Jackson's funeral sermon that 'Jabez Bunting belonged to the class of revivalists, but not to that class only'. T. Jackson, *The Character and dismission of the Prophet Daniel* (London, 1858), p. 29.

Divisions *from* the Church, though awful, are perhaps less to be dreaded than divisions *in* the Church, which, I fear, would have been perpetuated, if these men had remained among us . . . Revivalism, as of late professed and practised, was ⟨likely if⟩ not checked, to have gradually ruined genuine Methodism. ⟨I am⟩ glad, however, that they have been the first to draw the sword. But as they have drawn it, I earnestly wish that our Preachers would take the opportunity of returning fully to the spirit and discipline of ancient Methodism, and with that resolve to stand or fall . . .[1]

From this time forth he could think of no terms too severe for the challenge to order and decency the revivalists presented; indeed, in the anti-Anglican moods which came upon him periodically in his youth (as in his old age), it seemed that the only thing worse was in the Establishment.

I have witnessed many extravagancies in the Prayer-meetings, etc. of the persons called Revivalists amongst us; but I never saw or heard anything there so irreverent, so irrational, so unscriptural, as these proceedings in St. Paul's [Cathedral]. The Clergy of the Establishment have no right to throw stones at us for tolerating Ranterism, whilst such things are practised by themselves in their own Cathedrals.[2]

The charge, defect of discipline, is characteristic. Few Methodist preachers would have spoken of their community as a church in the unqualified terms used by Bunting in 1803. But the rest of his life was dedicated to 'that proper ministerial *pastorship* and *oversight* of the flock which the N. Testament enjoins as universally necessary'.[3]

Bunting, the church administrator, was already in evidence in his early ministry at Macclesfield (1801–1803) where he was full of schemes for reorganizing the circuit to make it one of the most eligible in the connexion.[4] His talent in this line was immediately recognized by his appointment to a prestige station in London, with special responsibility for sorting out the muddled accounts of the foreign missions and the connexional Book Room.[5] Yet this opening was made possible only by the fact that Bunting was an immediate and tremendous success in the pulpit, and the Bunting legend is not in error in seeing this as the triumph that opened every other

[1] M.C.A. MSS. Jabez Bunting to Richard Reece, July 15, 1803. For Bunting on Bramwell, cf. his letter to George Marsden, December 13, 1803.
[2] *Life of Bunting*, i, p. 186.
[3] M.C.A. MSS. Jabez Bunting to George Marsden, December 13, 1803.
[4] M.C.A. MSS. Jabez Bunting to George Marsden, June 10, 1803.
[5] M.C.A. MSS. Notes of the life of Jabez Bunting, July 18, 1877.

door. From his very first year as a probationer he received pressing invitations from the wealthiest and most important circuits in the connexion, and though he took the sanctimonious line that the voice of Conference was the voice of God,[1] whose dictates he would passively await, his brethren did not fail to note that he received the very best stations in succession. In a system weighted as heavily in favour of seniority as the Wesleyan connexion of that day this meteoric ascent was made possible only by preaching gifts of a quite unusual order; Bunting's later pulpit career lends some credibility to the opinion of his lifelong friend James Wood[2] that he never preached a better sermon than his first.

Not much is known about Bunting's reading in sermon preparation, but at the beginning, it lacked nothing in breadth or catholicity. At the end of the eighteenth, and early in the nineteenth, century, English translations were appearing of the great French preachers of the seventeenth century, Catholic and Protestant—Bourdaloue, Massillon, Fénelon, Bossuet, Saurin—indeed one of the translators actually labouring in Macclesfield during Bunting's ministry there was one of his bugbears, Melville Horne, the ex-Methodist evangelical incumbent of Christ Church. And as Bunting noted 'from the monthly lists for foreign publications [in 1802], . . . a great variety of foreign sermons have been recently imported, chiefly by Genevese preachers'. These sermons were exchanged and discussed with his friend Disney Alexander, a Yorkshire doctor, at this time a Methodist local preacher in the course of evolution from scepticism into unitarianism and moves were set on foot to get Saurin printed in the *Methodist Magazine*.[3] Bunting also had some volumes of Simeon's skeleton sermons,

[1] M.C.A. MSS. Jabez Bunting to J. Dutton, February 3, 1809 (Draft endorsement to J. Dutton to Jabez Bunting, January 30, 1809). Cf. Bunting's endorsement to Jonathan Barker to Jabez Bunting, April 6, 1807.

[2] James Wood (1777–1849) entered the same Methodist class with Bunting in September 1794. In 1796 he became one of the first members of a religious improvement society founded by Bunting, along with Edward Westhead, with whom he formed a successful partnership in the cotton trade. First President of the Manchester Chamber of Commerce, opponent of free trade and tory politician, he was a lifelong local preacher and class leader, and acutely divided Manchester opinion. Esteemed by tories for venerating 'church order and discipline as an ordinance of God for the maintenance of religion' (*Manchester Courier*, May 9, 1849, p. 293), he was an especial target of radical abuse. 'Of all men amongst us who have acquired wealth, without an accompanying enlargement of the intellect, there is none . . . more conceited and self-important, and less able to comprehend a liberal principle in commerce or politics, than Mr. James Wood.' *Manchester Times*, July 15, July 22, 1837. Cf. *Manchester Guardian*, June 1, 1833.

[3] M.C.A. MSS. Jabez Bunting to [Disney Alexander], October 14, 1802 [partly printed in *Life of Bunting*, i, p. 144]: Disney Alexander to Jabez Bunting, January 30, 1802; July 25, 1802; February 28, 1803; Joseph Entwisle to Jabez

but claimed never to use them.[1] Admitting at the outset that he was 'too declamatory' in his preaching manner,[2] he allowed his approach to the pulpit to be governed by his revulsion against revivalism. If an 'oratorical stile' was not for him, he would have no truck with the stock-in-trade of the popular preachers; if he could be tempted at all to a Sunday school anniversary it would be by the prior promise that 'everything shall be conducted Methodistically according to your wish, no parade, no bands of music etc.'; and he had no use for 'some very popular preachers in our day [who] are never happy in the pulpit except when they are trying to make some unhappy hearer believe that they know the deepest secrets of his particular conscience, and can warn him of his personal and inevitable doom.'[3] The great defence of church order and preservative against the revivalists was to unite sound learning with vital religion. Bunting's assessment of the Sheffield society in 1808 is quite candid.

> The Society at large . . . are more deeply pious than any we have before seen; and, at the same time, what I hardly expected, more free as a Body, than most others from the extravagancies and follies of enthusiasm. At this I am the more surprized, because few of them have attained to any considerable degree of mental improvement, or possess much general intelligence.[4]

It was Bunting's hope that the *Eclectic Review*, launched on an undenominational basis in 1805, would 'unite the pair, so long disjoined, Learning and vital piety', but his disillusionment with the outcome was sealed by the editors' refusal to insert a pseudonymous letter of his own,[5] and, the anti-slavery movement apart, he refused to enter any new interdenominational organizations until the mid-'forties, when his political policies were falling to pieces, and the Evangelical Alliance was seeking to salvage something from the

Bunting, December 20, 1803. Thomas Jackson claimed that Bunting 'studied the best sermons in the English language'. *Character . . . of Prophet Daniel*, p. 30.

[1] M.C.A. MSS. W. H. L. Eden to Jabez Bunting, June 25, 1812; Jabez Bunting to W. H. L. Eden, July 3, 1812.

[2] *Life of Bunting*, i, p. 182.

[3] M.C.A. MSS. Jabez Bunting to James Wood, March 25, 1823: R. Johnson to Jabez Bunting, September 25, 1804 (cf. W. E. Miller to same, [1805]): W. H. L. Eden to same, October 31, 1809, with Bunting's pencilled endorsement. (This letter is very inaccurately printed in *Life of Bunting*, i, p. 345 n.)

[4] U[nited] M[ethodist] C[hurch] A[rchives, Lake Junaluska, N.C.] MSS. Jabez Bunting to James Wood, March 15, 1808. (A garbled version of a portion of this letter is printed in *Life of Bunting*, i, p. 310.)

[5] M.C.A. MSS. B. Sadler to Jabez Bunting, January 24, 1804: Jabez Bunting to [Richard Reece], November 28, 1804: same to George Marsden, June 24, 1805. (This letter is partly printed in *Life of Bunting*, i, pp. 258–261.)

shambles of the Protestant onslaught on Maynooth. There remained, however, the pulpit. In 1805 Bunting professed himself 'no friend to Colleges or Academies', but felt that 'some regular systematic plan ought to be adopted with respect to the young preachers . . . which . . . would make them more accurately and thoroughly acquainted with *Divinity as a science*'. At the Conferences of 1811 and 1812 a series of sermons was begun in which the leading preachers of the connexion were to expound the principal heads of Christian doctrine as preached among Methodists, with a view to meeting precisely this need. The series made little progress, but it established Bunting among the official doctors of his church with the publication of his most famous sermon, upon *Justification by Faith*, preached at the Conference of 1812, and barely retouched thereafter.[1]

If there was any development at all in Bunting's preaching, this was its apogee. The immense administrative burden which he gradually shouldered channelled his creative energies in another direction; his books went unread (and on his last appointment to Manchester, for months unpacked[2]), his sermon-writing dried up, his ability to carry his congregation eventually declined. And Bunting knew it.

I have a very strong and growing dislike to preaching and speaking on any public occasion whatever [he confessed in 1827] and shall soon be obliged wholly and absolutely to decline that department of service, being convinced that *my* call is now in another way.[3]

The biggest drain of all came with the dependence of a great part of the ministry upon him to screw up their corporate courage for the fight, first against financial collapse and social radicalism, 1818–1821, and then against continued dissidence in the ranks. For Bunting the climax of these contests came in 1835, when he fought day and night to defeat Dr. Warren and his allies, and in the crisis suffered the death of his wife, much-loved and blessed with a personal effervescence and elasticity which Bunting himself lacked. The decline was a sad one. Always prone to vehemence, Bunting's preaching came to depend increasingly upon the fighting qualities which made him formidable in debate. He relied on forcefulness; he preached too long; without apology he could be late in the pulpit, and preach till it was impossible to meet the Society after the service. And when the Warrenite crisis exhausted his reserves, Bunting preached less and less frequently, and less and less effectively. Congregations began to walk

---

[1] *Life of Bunting*, i, p. 259; ii, pp. 24–28. It is noteworthy that a projected course of 17 sermons included nothing on the doctrine of the ministry.
[2] M.C.A. MSS. Jabez Bunting to Thomas Marriott, November 25, 1824.
[3] No. 96 *infra* contains another portion of this letter.

out before the end.[1] After Bunting's death the Book Room refused on financial grounds to undertake publication of his sermons.[2] Equally unhappily for the ageing Jabez, his eldest son William was a pulpit caricature of what he had been in his prime.[3]

The decline of Bunting, the preacher, which coincided with the supremacy of Bunting, the ecclesiastical statesman, had been long preceded by the disappearance of Jabez, the private personality. His earliest letters, particularly to his lifelong friend James Wood, are open affectionate.

> . . . there are two inexhaustible topics concerning which I can easily scribble over my sheets. [He writes] The first is *myself;* a subject this, (*one's self*) which one never wants inclination or materials to expatiate upon when writing to a friend . . . The second topic . . . is my love and affection for you. This would indeed be an inexhaustible subject. You know that you are literally *my most intimate* earthly friend, and I have the satisfaction to be assured that the esteem & attachment I feel towards you are reciprocated.[4]

What attracted the young Jabez was the opportunity not for egotism but for free personal exchange.

> I account your acquaintance and intimacy to be one of those mercies which the God of Mercy has poured upon me in such rich abundance, and for which I shall for ever bless him.[5]

They discussed the issues in dispute between the Calvinists and Arminians, and it was in entire accord with the supposition that Bunting began life much closer to the revivalists than he was later willing to admit, that he confessed his 'need of a revival of personal religion',[6] begged Wood to 'point out my faults, reprove my errors, and correct my mistakes, whether as a preacher or as a Christian', and reported that Richard Reece's preaching was 'much improved with the spark of Bramwellian fire and vehemence which he has caught'. Nor was it to James Wood alone that the young Bunting gave himself, receiving unbounded affection in return.

> I am lately returned from Saddleworth, [writes Disney Alexander] . . . James Ratcliffe's mother . . . spoke of you, and the tears

---

[1] M.C.A. MSS. David Watson to Jabez Bunting, October 14, 1824; Robert A. West, *Sketches of Wesleyan Preachers* (London, 1849), p. 17.

[2] M.C.A. MSS. John Mason to Elijah Hoole, February 6, 1861.

[3] *Memorials of the late Rev. William M. Bunting,* ed. G. Stringer Rowe (London 1870), pp. 15, 24–25, 34–35, 36.

[4] U.M.C.A. MSS. Jabez Bunting to James Wood, September 26, 1801.

[5] U.M.C.A. MSS. Jabez Bunting to James Wood, December 11, 1801.

[6] M.C.A. MSS. Jabez Bunting to James Wood, October 14, 1802.

gushed from her eyes. Three weeks ago I saw likewise your friends Messrs. Platt, Greenwood etc. You are literally engraven on their hearts. Your very name is precious to them. O how pleasing a thing it is to love and to be loved![1]

Bunting's popularity with the children of Joseph Entwisle, his superintendent at Macclesfield, had a deeper source than presents of books.

I read to the children that part [of your letter] which concerned them [wrote Entwisle after Bunting's departure to London]. They were mightily pleased. After a considerable pause, Jo. said, very expressively, 'I love him'; Mary, 'Bless him, he is sweet, I give him a kiss.'[2]

Yet already Bunting was hoisting the warning signs to both himself and his fiancée in Macclesfield, Sarah Maclardie.[3]

I think I shall be quite charmed with the London Methodists, when I can become more familiar with them. I believe it is one of my faults to form attachments too strong and tender for a man who is literally a sojourner only . . .

The man must bend to the Pastoral Office. It was much the same with his engagement. Sarah Maclardie was a lively and attractive girl, evidently a great favourite with Joseph Entwisle, and the prospect of his wedding and the journey back to London kept the spark of ordinary humanity alive in Jabez.

If the weather, though as fine as this, be also as cold, in the month of January, I shall not much like to travel all night. At least we shall be obliged to squeeze as close to each other as we can.[4]

But the great effort of his engagement period, foreshadowed in the paper on which he assessed his mind beforehand,[5] was to make Sarah conform to the pattern of a minister's wife he had in mind, a process to which she was too strongly marked an individual to submit lightly. Recriminations followed, Jabez attacking her

affected jealousy and affected indifference . . . all who know your talents in that line will allow, that they are such as must render any attempt of yours to seem suspicious and unkind tolerably successful . . . I overlook for this time the sarcasm conveyed in the

[1] M.C.A. MSS. Disney Alexander to Jabez Bunting, January 30, 1802.
[2] M.C.A. MSS. Joseph Entwisle to Jabez Bunting, September 6, 1803.
[3] Life of Bunting, i, p. 169.
[4] M.C.A. MSS. Jabez Bunting to Sarah Maclardie, November 5, 1803.
[5] Life of Bunting, i, pp. 150–156, esp. pp. 154–55.

Address and Conclusion of your letter . . . I am very doubtful
indeed whether you can with propriety appear in habit-shirts . . .[1]

Jabez conquered Sarah's affections but not her character, and when
provisions were dear, or Leaders' Meetings troublesome, she was
always likely to tease him playfully by threatening to turn Calvinist.
'Sometimes,' Percy Bunting was assured, 'your dear Mother's
uncontrollable wit suddenly disturbed our gravity; but he was never
seen otherwise than in his own proper character as a Minister of the
Gospel of Christ.'[1] Sarah possessed personal qualities on which
Jabez turned his back, and the home they created out of their dis-
similarities retained for them the life-long affections of all but one of
their children.

Bunting's fencing with his fiancée was nevertheless prophetic of a
future in which he altogether repressed his own individuality to meet
the demands of the Pastoral Office, or, as his son quaintly put it in
the *Life*, 'he avoided the snare, into which some great men have
fallen, of maintaining an extensive miscellaneous correspondence'.
Disney Alexander was hurt when Bunting came north early in 1805.

I felt not a little mortified at seeing so little of you, and when I
did see you at that want of openness and friendship which I
discovered . . . in you . . . , so different from the sentiments with
which you had been before accustomed to regard me.[2]

The most extensive correspondence to survive, that with James Wood,
tells its own tale, Affection and esteem united them to the end.
Bunting baptized Wood's children, and preached his funeral sermon;[3]
Wood in his turn sent barrels of black beer,[4] became a political and
financial pillar of Bunting's policies in the 'thirties, and was Treasurer of the Centenary Fund, launched to commemorate the formation of the United Societies in 1739, which in a time of unexampled
commercial depression provided Bunting's missions and ministerial
training schemes with the buildings they needed, and publicly demonstrated that the Warrenite revolt had not disrupted the old connexion.
But the correspondence between them became so trivial as hardly
to appear at all in the following selection. There could be none of the
mutual confession for which Bunting had asked at the outset; a

---

[1] *Life of Bunting*, i, pp. 157, 338.
[2] *Ibid*. i, p. 223: M.C.A. MSS. Disney Alexander to Jabez Bunting, November
18, 1805.
[3] U.M.C.A. MSS. Jabez Bunting to James Wood, November 8, 1810: *Manchester Courier*, May 9, 1849, p. 293.
[4] U.M.C.A. MSS. Same to same, September 29, 1807. (Partly and inaccurately
printed in *Life of Bunting*, i, pp. 300–301.)

layman, even as eminent and as pliable as James Wood, could not be encouraged to lay bare the faults of those whom God had appointed to the oversight of the flock.

Of course the discipline which Bunting imposed upon himself before proposing to others had its admirable side. When he moved to Sheffield in 1807, his predecessor, Peter Haslam, was too casual to come back from Conference in time and assist his expectant wife to vacate the manse. While Bunting's children were cooped up in the same room in cramped temporary accommodation, they gave each other whooping-cough and erysipelas and his daughter died.[1]

No person can vindicate the extraordinary conduct of Mr. H. [wrote John Gaulter.] Such an instance . . . of inattention and neglect, I never heard of before, and I dare predict that any recurrence of that, even without great caution on your part, will revive those acute feelings which you have endeavoured to suppress.

Bunting was desolate but did not complain. Mrs. Robert Newton[2] thought she 'could perceive in him a natural warmth of temper, and secretly admired the power of grace in its subjection',[3] and Bunting's last confession to James Wood was that[4]

my *constitutional* disposition is more *ardent* than is perhaps at all times consistent with the meekness and gentleness of Christ. I am prone to think and speak with an excess of decision and energy.

It was unhappily the case that however Bunting disciplined himself in personal relations, he used his natural vehemence as an instrument of policy in Conference and committee to a degree at times deplored even by his admirers. It was a friend who held that in the Leeds case 'he allowed personal friendship to unduly bias his judgement . . . [to] say nothing about his cutting remarks (. . . his sword had a keen and double edge)',[5] and, as we have seen, vehemence had to carry his preaching till it could carry it no more. As a young man Bunting saw the superiority of Arminianism over Calvinism in the fact that 'it neither shackles our affections, nor fetters our tongues'.[6] The regimen he applied to himself shackled the one but not the other.

[1] M.C.A. MSS. Jabez Bunting to John Gaulter, February 24, 1808: Emory University, Atlanta, Ga. MS. John Gaulter to Jabez Bunting, May 4, 1808. For a posthumous attempt to put a good gloss on Haslam's conduct, *Life of Bunting*, i, p. 336.

[2] On Robert Newton, see n. 1, p. 93.

[3] *Life of Bunting*, i, p. 338.

[4] U.M.C.A. MSS. Jabez Bunting to James Wood, April 1, 1805.

[5] M.C.A. MSS. John P. Haswell to [T. P. Bunting], September 7, 1868: J. Hocken to Dr. Leppington, July 29, 1841.

[6] U.M.C.A. MSS. Jabez Bunting to James Wood, March 16, 1802.

The cost of Bunting's policies in personal terms has never been assessed, and it was paid by his friends as well as himself. John Riles won the first round of the battle in Liverpool, at the cost of having to resign his ministry and dying soon afterwards. The special District Meeting which descended on Leeds in 1827 was summoned when the doctor of the superintendent, Edmund Grindrod, told him he had only six weeks to live if he did not obtain relief.[1] Not only was more being asked of the ministry as an institution than it could perfome, but an intolerable strain was being put on the key individuals. The exponents of the doctrine of the Pastoral Office claimed Wesley for their father, though that great man had not exercised his ministry in a situation of ideological conflict nor built an administrative machine. As a politician Bunting was uncannily acute in estimating which way the cat would jump down to the early 1840s,[2] but from then onwards, as he aged and British politics slid gradually into acrimonious confusion, the general success of his administrative schemes was offset by the failure of almost all his public policies. As the Methodism of Bunting shed its old empiricism in an heroically doctrinaire attempt to do what could not be done, it not only became narrower, but damaged the constituency from which it recruited. This process can be traced in the letters which follow.

[1] M.C.A. MS. Journal of proceedings of Conference, 1828.

[2] As a very young man Bunting spotted (generations ahead of historians) 'that Mr. Pitt's integrity as a statesman is by no means equal to his extraordinary talents'. M.C.A. MS. Jabez Bunting to Sarah Maclardie, November 5, 1803. Percy Bunting characteristically omits this sentence without notice. *Life of Bunting*, i, p. 210.

THE EARLY CORRESPONDENCE OF
JABEZ BUNTING

1. *From Robert Pilter*[1]   North Shields, October 23, 1819

I take the liberty of addressing you on a subject which appears to myself and friends of very great importance. I shall impartially state the case, and leave you to judge of the propriety of laying it before your brethren in town or calling together the Committee of Priviledges.

On Monday the 11th instant a meeting of reformers was held at Newcastle for the purpose of expressing their opinion on the Manchester Murders as they call them. 50 or 60,000 people attended, amongst whom were a great number of our people, several of our Leaders and some of our Local Preachers. One of the latter William H. Stephenson, a young man who teaches a school at Burton Colliery in this Circuit went upon the hustings and made a speech, condemning in strong terms the conduct of the Manchester magistrates: this has given very great offence to most of the Travelling Preachers and respectable friends in this neighbourhood and to none more than myself, and I have been advised at all events to *put him off the plan.* I have had repeated interviews with him and *advised him as a friend on public grounds to give up his plan.* He replied that he would never give up his plan until he was compelld, that he would be *tried by his peers* and did not fear the result, that if they expell him he will publish the cause to the world, that I had better let it quietly pass as three quarters of our people are radical reformers, that if he be tried so must hundreds more, that he only went to plead the cause of suffering humanity, that he believed it his *duty* to go, that he never joined himself to the reformers, nor attended any of their private meetings. I fixed on Friday the 22nd as the day of his trial. I will tell you in a parenthesis how I acted in the interim. (Conceiving that the *Body* might be seriously implicated and not feeling disposed to push matters to extremities on my own responsibility I wrote to the President[2] for his advice. After stating the case as above I asked him the following questions—'Shall I do all I can to influence the meeting to expell him? Or if the meeting resolve that his offence is not of a nature so atrocious as to justify his expulsion, shall I by my own authority leave him off the plan; and look to a District [Meeting]

---

[1] Robert Pilter (1784–1847), superintendent, North Shields circuit, 1817–1820.
[2] Jonathan Crowther (d. 1824, *aet.* 64), President of Conference, 1819–1820.

for an act of indemnity (this I am advised to do by our chairman) or shall I act according to the decision of the meeting?' And I also stated what might probably be the consequences of his being expelled etc. The substance of Mr. President's reply is as follow[s]. 'I do not believe that we are called either to pull down Governments or to prop them up. Our business is of a higher and more spiritual nature. We are called to promote the salvation of souls. We should, therefore, as far as possible avoid exasperating or hardening any description of men against us, and especially on grounds merely political. It was Mr. Wesley's opinion and advice, that the Methodists should never appear in politics as a body. The doing this in the affairs of America had like to have ruined Methodism there.[1] I do not see why we should *volunteer* our services in support of the Government, more than any other body of people, whether Dissenters or Churchmen. I do not hear of any of these expelling or punishing their people on account of their politics. Respecting the case of your local preacher, I think as he said nothing but what related to the magistrates of Manchester, so much ado need not have been [made] about it, more especially as he never did join himself to the reformers. My opinion and advice is this, that you give him a serious admonition, including in this your thoughts on his recent conduct, and your advice that he keep out of such matters in future. I verily believe this will be the best line of conduct you can pursue. If you expell such men, the Kilhamites and Ranters will greedily gather them up. In politics I think our present duty is neutrality. In *stillness and quietness will be our strength*. Stand still and see the salvation of the Lord. Such is my opinion and advice to obtain which you wrote. You must, however, do as you think best.' My writing to the President was a profound secret and I did not inform any person, except my worthy colleague of the reply). Last night the meeting was held, and the trial or altercation lasted from 7 to halfpast 10 o' clock. We positively interdicted the discussion of politics, the question whether reform was a good or bad thing abstractedly considered was not the business of the meeting, but whether Brother Stephenson as a Methodist preacher had done right in attending and speaking at the Meeting. He insisted on arguing the necessity of a radical reform, contended that he had done right as a Christian and a preacher in speaking, that his conscience impelled him to the duty, that im-

---

[1] Originally sympathetic to the American cause, Wesley in 1775 published a short and popular version of Samuel Johnson's pamphlet *Taxation no Tyranny*, under the title of *A calm address to our American colonies*, strongly supporting the British government. This pamphlet brought on him great obloquy, but he reaffirmed its main position in *A calm address to the inhabitants of England* (1777).

mense mischief would result from his expulsion and that he relied on
the justice of his Brethren for his acquittal. The question was then
proposed whether it was expedient for Brother S. as a Methodist
preacher to attend and speak at those meeting[s]. The consequence[s]
to the Circuit and the Connexion were mentioned, particularly his
being called in the London papers 'The Rev. G. Stephenson who we
understand is a preacher in the Methodist Connexion'. Two thirds
of the meeting pronounced it inexpedient but 4 Brethren thought
he was justified in so doing. I then asked if he would promise his
Brethren never to attend another public meeting? But he said he
would not *pledge* himself. He was an Englishman and would not
give up his liberty and his conscience. I then submitted it to the
meeting, how I could especially after such an avowal plan the
Brother. Several however thought that expulsion were too severe a
punishment and that such an act would be fatal to the interests of
the circuit. They laboured in vain to extort a promise for him. It was
then proposed 'that as our decision might on the one hand *injure*
the whole *connexion*, or on the other ruin the circuit and subject
themselves, but especially ME, to *assassination* it would be well to
pause and consult you gentlemen at the fountain head of information before we came to a final decision. We accordingly agreed to
adjourn the meeting untill Friday the 5th November.

Now my dear Brother what must I do? If my own Circuit alone
was concerned, I should know how to act. But Mr. Grindrod[1] and
others think we shall, unless we exclude him, bring down the vengeance of government upon the whole connexion. But is it probable
that the government would attend more to the conduct of one in-
significant individual, than to the loyal address of Conference and
the loyal conduct of the Body at large? If so I think he should at all
events be expelled. If he be expelled we have reason to apprehend
the following consequence. Many of our members will leave the
Society, 20 in one place have resolved on this. Some of our Local
Preachers will give up their plans. A great and general ferment
⟨will be⟩ excited as he is already considered a persecuted man. A
⟨col⟩league and I will be in no small danger of being mu⟨rdered⟩.
You are no doubt apprized of the state of the public ⟨m⟩ind in
these parts. During a riot at Shields on the 14th instant a man was
shot. The jury after sitting 4 days brought in their verdict 'Justifiable
Homicide'. Some of the people were so exasperated that they assailed
the houses of three of the jurymen and actualy fired into their

---

[1] Edmund Grindrod (1786–1842), superintendent, Newcastle circuit, 1817–1820.
Grindrod's old saw had embodied real substance in the 1790's, but was now part
of a political operation.

parlour windows. However no personal considerations shall deter me from the performance of my duty. But amidst so many conflicting considerations and interests, I am at a loss how to act. I would just observe that the Brother is a great stickler for law and right and some of our local Brethren are jealous of their prerogatives. Anxiously waiting your reply. . . .

2. *From Robert Pilter*   North Shields, November 6, 1819
                                 [*Postmarked Nov. 5*]

. . . I read the unanimous resolution of the Committee of Priviledges, and did the best I could to convince them of its propriety. Stevenson [*i.e.* Stephenson] then delivered a long defence, justifying his conduct, and deprecating the severe sentence of expulsion for an act which the meeting had only pronounced *in*expedient. In opposition to the various evil consequences which I pointed out to the meeting, which either *had* or probably would occur if he were continued, some of the Brethren enumerated all the evils which they were sure would take place if we silenced him. He having repeatedly intimated that it was very probable he never would attend another meeting, but at the same time declared that he would not bind himself by a pledge. His friends who appeared determined at all events to drag him through, laid hold of his intimation and stated that the meeting might rely upon Stevenson's *honour* that he would not in future act against the declared opinion of his Brethren and moved that, with this understanding, he should not be put off the plan. The ballot, for I judged it prudent that we should vote by ballot, was 7 for his continuance and 4 for his being silenced. The meeting was partly induced to come to this resolution in consideration of what he has already suffered, the owners of the colliery having dismissed him from his school. Thus stands the case. How would you, my dear Brother, advise me to act under existing circumstances. . . .

3. *From J. B. Holroyd*[1]   Haslingden, December 23, 1819

I cannot refrain from acknowledging the gratitude I feel for the timely encouragement afforded by the address from the committee for guarding our privileges. The state of the public mind in these parts exceeds all description. The country for a few miles round here may with propriety be called the hot-bed of radicalism. I believe I shall be within compass in saying that two-thirds of the population

[1] James Briggs Holroyd (1777–1862), superintendent, Haslingden circuit, 1818–1820.

in this circuit are reformers, and having no magistrate or chief constable within 8 miles, every man seems as if left to do that which is right in his own eyes. We have had them parading the streets almost every night by 200 or 300 together, singing their favourite songs of Hunt and Liberty, with lighted torches, flags and a Cap of Liberty hoisted upon a high pole with a lanthorn suspended with it. At the houses of the Radicals they stop and salute them with three cheers, and at the houses of the *marked kings-men* they give three horrible groans. They make no hesitation at calling by name the *marked* ones, who are to be killed the first day the orders come for them to break out. There are five in this town openly spoken of. The church minister and myself are of the number. They have regular organized societies that meet weekly, where they read the *Manchester Observer*, Cob[b]ett's *Register*, *Black Dwarf*, etc., the leader asks them personally if they are still resolved to observe the resolutions of the *Union* and then receives their subscriptions, part of which goes to support the general cause of reform, and part to purchase pikes and pistols. There have been great numbers of pikes made in this town. One evening a few weeks since, just as I came out of my door to go into the chapel, the procession was just drawing up in front of the house, I did not judge it prudent to go through the croud but stood inside the garden gate; they gave three of the most horrid groans I ever heard, and with each groan a young man brandished a pike within a yard of my breast accompanied with such dreadful oaths, enough to make one's blood run chill. I believe there is no part of the kingdom where the distresses of the poor are more general than in this neighbourhood. They are principally cotton weavers, who by working hard six days cannot earn above 7s. or 8s. per week, for the support of a family, this having been the case for sometime past they now seem quite impatient for relief and are ready to adopt the most desperate means to obtain it. It is with grief I say that our society is not free from the contagion. Some have left us this quarter, and assign this as their reason. They do not think it right to give anything towards the support of those who encourage and pray for a number of tyrants.

The Address[1] is very unpopular in some parts of the circuit, the

---

[1] The Committee of Privileges, a Conference standing committee created in 1803 to guard its religious privileges, published an Address (drawn up by the connexional solicitor Thomas Allan [M.C.A. Thos. Allan's MSS. T. Allan to Joseph Allan, November 27, 1819]) which, while acknowledging the right of members of religious societies to diversity of political judgment, strongly condemned tumultuous gatherings, and recommended preachers to expel members who, after admonition, persisted in identifying themselves with the factious and disloyal, *Methodist Magazine*, n.s. xvi (1819), pp. 942–7.

c

sentiments of the *Manchester Observer* are prefered where I am informed they charge the committee with assuming an authority they were never invested with. The above are not the sentiments of our leading friends in Haslingden, quite the reverse, but they can render the preachers no efficient support in opposing the general impetus.

I fear we shall have a considerable decrease both in numbers and collections this year. It is painful in the extreme to see the change which this spirit of reform has made in some places where a few months back they were all alive to God, and the work spreading, but now you can scarcely prevent them introducing reform into the House of God. On Sunday last I had but just got out of the Chapel before I was attacked by 3 Leaders, 2 Local Preachers, 1 Steward and several private members on t⟨he⟩ subjects of Lord Castlereagh's bills, and the Address from the Committee, when they told me in plain terms that ⟨the⟩ Methodist Preachers were as bad as the Church ministers in supporting government, but it was asked, 'Will Lord Castlereagh support you?' To the troubles without I have some severe family affliction . . . if we are spared till the ensuing Conference I shall beg the indulgence of having an appointment some w[h]ere in the South. . . . Begging the favour of a line at some convenient season . . .

4. *From J. B. Holroyd*   Haslingden, January 26, 1820

It is impossible to express the grateful feelings produced by the perusal of your affectionate letter of the 15 instant for which I beg you to accept my most sincere thanks. In reply to your enquirey, if I have any objections to an extract of my letter being published, I have to say you are at perfect liberty to make what use of it you think proper; only you will see the propriety of keeping me out of sight, though hundreds here would attest the truth of what is there stated. I do not remember weather I informed you that the night when the pike was brandished at me was the 15th November after their return from a public meeting at Burnley, and that they have never gone about in that formidable way since. For the last month we appear as if sunk into a dead calm. The taking up several of the head radicals in the neighbourhood has very much lowered the tone of the rest. Some maintain a sullen silence, while others in low murmurs say, their cause is going on well and will shew it by and by when least expected.

I yesterday called to see a sick woman who is one of our occasional hearers at a place about 4 miles hence. Her husband, who appears an honest artless man, asked me if if I knew how they (the Radicals) were coming on at Haslingden. I replied, 'I hear very little of them now, and I expect it is all over'. He said, 'Not so, I believe it is gaining strength faster now than ever, but in a quieter way—that their agents are continually going from place to place carrying inteligence, as they will not trust anything by post for fear of being detected.' He informed me that a doctor who has lately left Haslingden, chiefly on account of his principles, told him above two months since, that he has seen a list of upwards of 400,000 names, all members of the Union, who are bound to appear at an hour's notice and must either fight or die. I asked him by what means they were to be supported, supposing they were to be called out, as I could see no way but plunder. 'No,' said he, 'they will pay for everything.' I asked how? 'They can make paper money,' said he, 'as well as the Government, and I know tradesmen who would rather take it just now'. I asked him, what is their real object? Is it to relieve the suffering poor? 'Yes,' said he, 'but not in the way you have pointed out in your pamphlet'; they say 'that would be but a partial relief; there are many corruptions in the state which must be purged out, and there is no way by which it can be effected but for one evil to destroy another'. He declared he had never attended either public or private meeting among them, but that his information had been chiefly brought into his own house. I learned from his wife that he had been often urged to join the Union, as no person's life would be safe who did not, but weather he has joined I cannot say.

I do not know that there are any radical schools[1] in this place. They have rented rooms for holding their meetings at, but not for youth in perticular. The one they had in Haslingden was given up a few weeks since, also a large one at another of our principle places. That there have been no backwardness among them in expressing their sentiments you may infer from the following extract from my memorandum book; 'Tuesday Octr. 12th 1819. I this day called at the shop of Mr. ——. He gave me a newspaper, and began to talk about the affair at Manchester on the 16th of August. Among other things he said was, that the cause of reform had acquired much strength through it; that many of the nobility had joined the reformers, and that people would no longer be kept out of their *rights*; that there is no justice in this land now; that the Prince Regent is a *blood-thirsty tyrant*, and ought to be brought to *public justice*, and every one of his *ministers*, for supporting and commending those *hireling* magistrates, and *butchering yeomanry*, and that the stain could never be wiped from the British character till they were every

---

[1] Union (or undenominational) Sunday Schools were begun by the radicals in Manchester, Oldham and other places.

one *hanged.*' The Doctor before alluded too and the person who uttered the above have both left the town, chiefly on account of their principles. The Doctor to America, the latter it is not known where. I believe I should not have made the above memorandum, but from hearing so frequently that I was a *marked man.*

I expect one of our friends coming to London next month, and I purpose sending you by him a few copies of the pamphlet I have published on the subject of reform, in two letters addressed to a gentleman in the cotton trade, made under the borrowed name of a friend to the poor. The principle objects aimed at are, First to turn the attention of the suffering poor to their employers, instead of the government, and the second is, to induce the manufacturers and merchants to take the subject into consideration, and I know it has been of real use to some.

[His wife is much better] . . . I hope through mercy I shall be able to abide at my post, I feel I am in the Lord's hands, and am willing to do or suffer his righteous will. . . .

5. *To Jonathan Edmondson*[1] (Birmingham)

London, February 10, 1820

. . . They have need of patience and good humour, who have to do with Methodist preachers in general, in matters of accounts. Many of our brethren are not men of business, and do not feel inclined to be taught the art of strict and stern regularity. They think it enough to be upright and brotherly. This, however, *in public life*, is a mistaken and defective view of the subject. . . .

6. *From Edmund Grindrod*   Newcastle, March 11, 1820[2]

. . . Much of my time for several months past has been taken up in assisting our friends here to commence building a chapel in lieu of the Orphan House. The Chancery suit is at length concluded, and the title declared good to the Trustees; each party to pay their own costs.[3]

---

[1] Jonathan Edmondson (d. 1842, *aet.* 75), superintendent, Birmingham circuit, 1819–1821.

[2] The holograph is at Southern Methodist University, Dallas, Texas.

[3] The Orphan House, built at Newcastle by Wesley in 1743, was the third Methodist chapel property, and the second specially built. The lower part of the house formed a chapel with pulpit, on the first floor were classrooms, and, on the second floor, apartments. These seem to have been intended for the education and accommodation of orphans, but the orphanage never began operation, and the upper rooms were occupied by the preachers and their families, the House becoming the headquarters of Methodism in the north. The trust deed under

We are going to build on the plan and dimensions of the large chapel at Hull, with the exception of the vaults and some of its ornaments. If the chapel produce a surplus one half of it is to be given to the New Road, untill that chapel is brought into easy circumstances; and on this plan both sets of Trustees have united and are perfectly harmonious. Our subscription list now stands at £1100, and we hope to get 300 more. We are waiting for our plans from Hull and shall commence building as soon as they come. The Trustees have ingaged to settle the chapel on the form of the last copy of a deed issued by the Book Committee. Mr. Blanshard[1] will probably have informed you, that his Grace the Duke of Northumberland has subscribed £50. In his letter his Grace observes that he has numerous applications to assist dissenting places of worship, which he thinks proper to decline; but, in consequence of the loyalty of the Wesleyan Methodists of Newcastle, recently displayed in their opposition to principles subversive of all religion, he is induced to make them an exception. This is gratifying to those of us who made a firm and open stand against radicalism. . . .

I hope we shall see you in the chair at the next Conference. Many of the junior brethren, I am persuaded, intend to give you their votes: and, I hope, if spared so long, Mr. George Marsden[2] will follow you: but that is looking into futurity. It would be well if those who take the lead in our affairs would understand each other, and not be so divided as they were last year. . . .

7. *From John Mercer*[3]   Peeltown, March 14, 1820

. . . as you have travelled upward of twenty years in the richest of the rich circuits, and I have travelled upward of nineteen in the poorest of the poor circuits, I conceive that we are prepared to meet half way. My object in writing what I gave to you at Conference, and what I am now about to offer, is to make it appear that our Connexion hath resources within itself sufficient to pay the preachers' salaries according to Conference allowance, with the help of the profits arising from the Book Room. The number in Society in

---

which the property was vested occasioned persistent litigation after Wesley's death, as did a new deed executed in 1813. Disputes between Church Methodists and others at the Orphan House were healed, however, and the reconciliation created a need for more substantial premises. The present Brunswick chapel, the planning of which is here described, was opened in 1821.

[1] Thomas Blanshard (d. 1824, *aet.* 49), connexional Book Steward, 1808–1823.

[2] George Marsden (1773–1858) succeeded Bunting as President, 1821–1822.

[3] John Mercer (1770–1839), superintendent, Peel circuit, and chairman of the Isle of Man District, 1819–1820.

Great Britain, this year, is 196,605. One penny per week and one shilling per quarter for the above number amounts to the sum of £81,918. 15. 0. per year. The July Collection £2500, the yearly Collection £5500. From the Book Room £5000, making a total of £94,918. 15. 0. The number of travelling preachers in Great Britain is 647. Divid[e] the above sum among them, and it makes the sum of £146. 14. 1½. for each Preacher married or unmarried. Now I am persuaded that all the circuits in Great Britain (with the exception of the Isle of Man) either does, or might, raise upward of one penny per week and one shilling per quarter per member. I think it must be allowed that Hexham, Whitehaven, Brough, Barnard Castle and Carlisle are among the poorest circuits in the Connexion. I travelled two years in each of them and therefore speak from personal knowledge. In Brough, at the end of the first year, we had about £20, and at the end of the second year £21 19. 5. more than 1d. per week and 1s. per quarter per member. . . . In Barnard Castle, at the end of the first year, we had £25. 19. 1. and at the end of the second year £32. 0. 7½. more than 1d. per week and 1s. per quarter per member. . . . In Carlisle at the end of the first year we had £39. 13. 0. and at the end of the second year £48. 11. 1½. more than 1d. per week and 1s. per quarter per member. . . . And I am almost certain that Carlisle is one of the poorest circuits in England. If the above circuits raise so much more than 1d. per week and 1s. per quarter per member, I think all the circuits in England might do likewise. And were the money so raised distributed in any measure according to equality, then those who gather much would have nothing to spare, and those who gather little would have no want. However, I rejoice that one step is taken toward equality, I mean the stationing the children according to the number of members;[1] and hope it will soon be followed by another step, viz. the stationing the wives in the same way, and so by little and little remove those objections which the preachers in general make against going to poor circuits, and at the same time remove those objections which the poor circuits make against married preachers. Yet as the best laws which were ever framed by the wisest human legislator; and the best rules which were ever made by the most pious bodies of Christian ministers have been and still are liable to be abused; I have my fears that the rule made last Conference, allowing each circuit a definite sum, and no more, will be abused. I certainly highly approve of the rule, and hope it will be productive of much good to the Connexion. I hope it will

[1] In 1819 Conference established the 'Children's Fund', under which the cost of maintaining preachers' children was divided among Districts in proportion to the number of their members.

have a tendency of making the Quarterly Meetings more careful how they allow their preachers more than Conference allowance. And also I hope it will make some of the preachers more careful of the weekly and quarterly contributions. Yet I see two ways by which the above rule, excellent as it is, may be abused. The first is by those preachers who are in the constant habit of leaving debt in their circuits. And I am sorry to say that there are too many among us of this discription. I consider poor circuits which cannot support the Preachers stationed on them to be something like poor labouring men who have so much per week, and receive their wages every Saturday. If they run into debt this week, if it is but one shilling, how are they to pay it next week? Just so with those poor circuits that cannot pay their preacher's salaries without help from the Contingent Fund. If a preacher does but leave five or ten pounds of debt in a circuit, how is his successor to pay it? Unless he get it from the Contingent Fund. But as the rule now stands this way is blocked up; and consequently the evil of leaving debt in poor circuits becomes the more serious. For my part I have been tormented in most of the circuits where I have travelled with the debts of those who were before me. . . . In August 1816 I was appointed to Ramsey Circuit and Mr. Burgess Jun.[1] with me. And we soon found it out that the old method of leaving bills unpaid and borrowing money had been resorted to by our predecessors for a considerable number of years. So that the Circuit debt amounted to the awful sum of £84. 7. 2. And notwithstanding all the exertions which myself and colleague were able to make, yet our quarterage for the whole year only amounted to £80. 5. 1½, so that we laboured hard the whole year for £4. 2. 0½. less than nothing. Under the remains of this debt we are still groaning; and whether we shall be able to rise, or it will sink us altogether, I cannot tell. . . . Now if any method could be adopted to prevent the preachers who travel in poor circuits from leaving debt behind them; or any mode of punishment inflicted for doing so, I am certain our Connexion would rise in point of money matters, and we should soon be able to pay our way honourably. For my part I see no way of curing the evil but the one proposed in the manuscript which I gave you at Bristol, viz. that every Superintendant produce at his respective District Meeting an exact account of all the money raised in his circuit; and also an account of the ways in which the money so raised has been expended; and that the accounts so produced at the District Meetings be taken to Conference and examined by a Committee appointed for that purpose.

---

[1] Joseph Burgess, Jnr. (1785–1859), preacher, Ramsey circuit, 1816–1818.

At any rate let this, or something like it, be attended to with all those circuits which make any claim on the Contingent Fund.

The second way by which the rule which allows a definite sum to every circuit is liable to be abused, is in respect to furniture. Conference allows £20 toward furnishing every aditional house. And you know, my dear Sir, that this will go but a very little way towards necessary articles even, for a man and his wife. What is the poor fellow to do? Perhaps he buys a few things, and borrows a few more; and so makes out as well as he can. At the end of the first or second year he removes. And perhaps a preacher with a large family is stationed in his place. And what are they to do? Those who had had the goodness to lend a few things to his predecessor want them home again. And ⟨the⟩ new articles which were bought with the £20 are the worse for wearing. So that he finds the house almost emty, though it may be both swept and garnished. He is forced to buy twenty or thirty pounds worth more. But how is he to get paid for them? Say he begins to make a private subscription. Nine out of ten are so poor they *can* give nothing. And almost nine out of ten of the rest will tell him that they never went to beg for their furniture, and *will* give him nothing. He then makes complaint to the Quarterly Meeting, and meets with little better reception there than while making his private subscription. But by giving them good words and telling them that they can take, or send a little more to Conference, perhaps he gets it. But on the present plan a certain sum is allowed and no more. I have been in this situation also. . . .

I would also further observe, in reference to the rule which allows a certain sum to every circuit, that it will be necessary to consider the state of the chapels in every circuit, as this will make a considerable difference in paying the preacher's salaries. Some chapels can spare a little toward supporting the preachers, but others are so burdened with debt, that they are not able to support themselves. We have several of the latter discription in this island, but not one of the former. But the one which affects us most is Ramsey Chapel. The seat rents come considerably short of paying the interest of the money borrowed upon it; and consequently it keeps sinking in debt every year in spite of all we can do to prevent it. And in consequence of this the Ramsey Society cannot do much toward supporting the Preachers as they otherwise would do. Ramsey itself is only like a country village in point of size; has about one hundred in society, and most of them very poor. All they have been able to do for several years towards paying the preacher's board, and all they are now able to do, is to pay 3/9 per week to the married man. A few friends have kept the single man gratis for several years. However about two years ago some of those friends who had kept the single preacher while in Ramsey, became less able to do it; and one of them removed from the place, so that last year we had to provide board and lodging for the single preacher as well as for the married preacher. This we did last year by a private subscription. But now the single man is married, and is to provide for as such. So that you may see that we are in a very poor situation as it respects money matters. If Conference had only laid ten children upon us instead of fifteen, and allowed us £200 instead of £180, perhaps we might have been able to make ends meet, or nearly so. But how we shall do as we now stand, God only knows. . . .

Before I lay down my pen I beg to say a few words on the state of discipline in this island. It is well known to the preachers in general that the late Mr. Crook[1] was the first preacher who established Methodism in this island. And perhaps no preacher in the Connexion was better calculated for such a work; and his biographer no way exaggerates when he calls him 'the Apostle of the Isle of Man'. He established good order in all the Societies; and had everything among them as regular as clockwork. However he set up one rule, which in my opinion has been, and still is, a great evil. I mean his giving so much power into the hands of the Local Preachers. He began by meeting them regular every Quarter, but instead of giving it the simple and proper name of Local Preachers' Meeting he gave it the high sounding name of *Manks Conference*, and adopted most of the phraseology used in the Minutes of the English Conference. But the evil did not consist so much in the name, as in the nature of that meeting. For instead of attending to the simple business of a Local Preachers' Meeting, they also transacted the business of the Quarterly Meeting too, and I may say almost everything which belongs to the Leaders' Meeting. And at last [it] grew to such a h[e]ight of despotism, that no ma⟨n⟩, however well qualified, must be a Circuit Steward but a local preacher. The above particulars have been a source of much grief to many of the travelling preachers, and of much contention between them and the Local Preachers. Mr. Lumb[2] was the first who atacked their mixed system with any degree of success; for which daring attempt he brought on a paper war between himself and the Local Preachers, which was carried on with great spirit by both parties and ended in an appeal to the conference. Most of the

---

[1] John Crook (d. 1805, *aet.* 62), superintendent, Isle of Man circuit, 1778–1781, 1786–1788; Peel circuit 1798–1799. The Manx Conference published a hymn-book in the native tongue in 1799.

[2] Mathew Lumb (d. 1847, *aet.* 84), superintendent, Douglas circuit, 1805–1807.

preachers who followed Mr. Lumb have been doing a little towards pulling down this stronghold. So that through mercy we have so far succeeded as to get the Leaders' Meeting and the Quarterly Meeting raised up again as a separate concern from the Local Preachers' Meeting. And in Douglas Circuit [we] have prevailed so far as to get a man for one of the Circuit Stewards who is not a Local Preacher. And if the travelling preachers would be unanimous, and every one attend to his proper work, I have no doubt but this part of Methodism might be redeemed. Another part of discipline has also been wonderfully neglected. I allude to the manner of giving tickets to the country societies. About the year 1797 or 1898 [1798] there was a great revival through the whole island. Several hundreds joined the Society. And as the preachers never visited them but on the weekdays, and were accustomed to hold their meetings till twelve or one o'clock in the morning, there was no time to give tickets: consequently they were given to the Leaders to give to their respective classes. This laid the foundation of one of the greatest evils which ever happened to Methodism in the Isle of Man. For though the preachers one after another attempted to give tickets to the country Societies year after year, yet it was labour in vain, as not one in ten of them attended to receive them. And this was the case with many of the Leaders as well as the members. So that the preachers, not knowing what to do, added to the evil by giving tickets to the Leaders who were present for their absent members, and leaving tickets for those Leaders who were absent, without either seeing their class papers, or knowing the number of members in their classes. By these means I may safely say that every part of discipline, in the country societies, fell to the ground. This caused a separation between the preachers and the Societies, and hundreds of them knew not their prea⟨chers⟩ from other men, unless they happened to meet them on the road, and guessed that they were English preachers because they had saddle baggs under them. The weekly and quarterly collections were very little attended to, and hundreds looked on the travelling preachers as a burden because they were now and then asked for something to support them. Most of the preachers would complain of the existing evils; and if one now and then had resolution enough to attempt to reform them, he was sure to be opposed by some or other of those who ought to have come forward to his help. When I came to Douglas Circuit in 1813 I found things in this deplorable state. And though good Mr. Rawson[1] had been labouring among them with all his might for one year, and had done much good, yet a great deal more wanted to be done. We began

[1] John Rawson (d. 1850, *aet.* 73), superintendent, Douglas circuit, 1812–1814.

to give tickets to all that we could get to attend for them, and took good care to give tickets to none of the Leaders but such as brought their class-papers. By this means we cut off a great number of disorderly walkers. We also got a book for every Society and met the Leaders at every place. By this means we increased the weekly collections a little; and by pursuing these methods the three years which I stayed, several things were got into a better state. Myself and colleague pursued the same measures in Ramsey Circuit for the two first years. And in the course of last year we began to give tickets to none but to those who came for them, except in case of sickness, or some other unavoidable necessity. We still continue the same plan. And though we met with some opposition at first, the Societies are now pretty well satisfied, and many highly approve of it. Much good hath already been done, and if the preachers would only walk by the same rule and mind the same thing for years to come, Methodism would once more lift up its head, in point of discipline, in this highly favoured island. However I beg leave to make one remark in favour of the preachers who travelled here for the last twenty years. Though I believe a great deal more might have done, in point of discipline, than has been done, yet it was impossible for them to attend to it in all its branches while only four preachers were s[t]ationed on the whole island. Their Sunday labours were always confined to the towns, and they had no opportunity of visiting the country societies but on the weeknights. So that even the Love-feasts were given up to the Local Preachers. Since we got a fifth preacher we have done a little better. We are able to visit the principal Societies in the country on the Lord's Day once or twice a quarter. But still we want help. I do not believe there is a circuit in Great Britain which stands in more need of an aditional preacher than we do. I verily believe if Conference would appoint three preachers to Douglas Circuit, and three to Ramsey, that in a little time they would support six preachers with more ease than they now support five. And if you attend to what follows I believe you will be of the same opinion. In Douglas Circuit there are 34 preaching places, exclusive of Douglas and Castletown. Several of them have chapels and large Societies belonging to them. But how is it possible for two preachers and a half to supply them with a sufficiency of preaching? Seven of them they visit once a fortnight. Seventeen once a month only. And the rest are supplied by the local preachers. In Ramsey Circuit there are 35 preaching places exclusive of Ramsey and Peeltown. Thirteen of these have chapels and three more pretty large school houses. Some have upward of a hundred in society belonging to them. Nine of these have fortnight[ly] preaching, fifteen preaching once a month, and the rest are supplied by the Local Preachers. Now we find it hard to keep up discipline where we preach once a fortnight; and more so where we only preach once a month. And we find it utterly impossible to keep up discipline where we never preach at all. But by the help of another preacher we might visit the principal country chapels two or three times a quarter on the Lord's Day; several of the month places once a fortnight; and some of those places where we never come, might be benefited by our labours. This would have a good effect upon our financial affairs. For, notwithstanding the extreme poverty which prevails through the island, could we but have more access to the country societies they would soon give considerably more toward our support. And I think we might have an aditional preacher without adding one to the number, as I believe there are several circuits in England where the preachers have not more than half the labour which we have, and yet take plenty of deficiencies to Conference. Could we have one from such a circuit, it would neither increase the number nor the expence. I fear that the length of this inchoerent scrawl will exhaust your patience. However, I have so far eased my mind of a burden which has laid upon it for some length of time, I may say for many years. And were not my circumstances too much like the circuits in which I have travelled (that is very poor), I would collect a few particulars together and get them printed and send a copy to every preacher.

I shall be exceeding glad if you will favour me with a few lines as soon as you can make it convenient. Wishing you strength of body and mind to perform all the particulars of your arduous office. . . .

8. *From J. W. Cloake*[1]   Wednesbury, March 29, 1820

The situation in which you are placed, in the Methodist Connexion, commands the attention and respect of all your brethren, which consideration has induced me to present you with the following plain observations and questions: this is my only apology for writing to you.

1. Our connexion seems to be on the eve of certain changes which will produce a permanency of either good or bad effects. Of course every lover of God's cause among us will pray that the effects of those changes may be good, and nothing but good. But it is to be feared that the effects in some instances may be bad. I alude to the reducing the number of preachers and the circumstances which cause so much difference in the condition of the preachers. The great difference of the circumstances in the which the brethren are now placed, I fear,

[1] John W. Cloake (d. 1846, *aet.* 67, preacher, Wednesbury circuit, 1818–1820).

will operate to divide us in affection: and you well know, Sir, that this is our strong bond. A brother is placed in a poor circuit where he has no more allowed him than what some call the allowances of the connexion: half of this he cannot receive untill the end of the year; but, alas, he is not now sure that he shall be able to receive it then. He is necessarily led to the following reflexions: 'my Fathers and Brethren (many of them) in this District are very comfortably provided for; they regularly receive their good allowances at the Quarterly Meetings, and have nothing to trouble them respecting their accounts at the end of the year: their labours are not more abundant than mine: perhaps not more than two thirds of what I do throughout the year; now, if I am a brother and a son in this connexion, on what principle of justice and brotherly love can this difference of circumstances be justified?' The brother looks round, and gets himself informed respecting the strength of many of his fathers, brethren, and friends; and from the evidence he obtains, as the result of his enquiries, he cannot be reconciled to the principle, *i.e.* want of ability, on which certain proceedings are attempted to be justified. The evidence looks him in the face, and he cannot shut his eyes.

The reducing the number of preachers will be productive, I fear, of great evils in those places from which preachers may be taken. Different parts of our connexion are infested with preachers of a certain description who are anxiously waiting to enter upon the ground which we have stood on for a number of years: now it is realy vexatious that we should be under any kind of necessity to leave our feeble flocks to the hands of *such fellows*.[1] This is a term good enough for several of them that I know. I have also thought that there is another consideration of a weighty nature connected with subject of lessoning the number of preachers, and that is the circumstances of many of our affectionate and pious Trustees. There are many families in our connexion the younger branches of which are greatly disturbed on account that their fathers have brought such heavy burdens upon their shoulders by being Trustees for Methodist Chapels. These, Sir, are my simple thoughts on these subjects.

2. Could anything be done to make the concern of our book trade more productive? If it could be made more of a general concern, I have thought it would thereby be made more productive. Many of our preachers in the same circuit live at a considerable distance from each other—3, 4, 5, and 7, miles perhaps: now would it be practicable to allow those who live at such distances from the circuit town to correspond with the Book Steward and supply the places of their

[1] *I.e.*, Ranters.

residence and the neighbourhood with our publications? Many of the Superintendents are not so active in selling books as they ought. Perhaps it is from the false notion that it is not the duty of ministers to sell books; but certainly it has always been the duty of Methodist preachers to sell books. I have frequently been grieved to hear the complaints of the people respecting their not being supplied with the Magazine, etc. in a reasonable manner. The helpers, you know Sir, have nothing to stimulate them to sell books but the broad good principle of brotherly love; but such are the fews [i.e. views] of most men in our day that the[y] want something else to help them forward even in a goodwork. These observations, Sir, are not made out of ill nature nor disaffection, but with a view to the general good.

3. In our good new arrangement for our children there is one circumstance which I beg permission to suggest to you. According to the plan, as it now stands, there is ground to fear that some unpleasantness may arise from the following circumstances. If a circuit has more children, which will be a frequent case, than its proportionate share, and such circuit allows £8 per child I apprehend the allowance from the Children's fund will be but [£]6. 6. 0; here then will be difference of [£]1. 14. 0 per child. Now if the circuit cannot or will not pay that difference, shall one brother have this sum less for the support of his children, or shall the brethren share *alike*? And if in a case there are 8 children in a circuit and only 4 of them paid for by the circuit has the Superintendent an *exclusive* right, allowing that he has 4 children, to receive all the allowances for his children and his helper or helpers receive none till the end of the year? I understand what is expected to be done in sending the monies—but you know many circuits have nothing to send untill they receive it from the parish!

4. In our minutes, there are some places which stand for heads of circuits the names of which can't be found in any gazetteer; in consequence of this some friends of the brethren appointed to such places know not where to direct for them. To remedy this, is it practicable for the name of the county to be attached to the names of each separate circuit? . . .

5. Can the names and baptisms of children which were born and baptized previous to the institution of our General Register for Baptisms in London, with propriety, be registered in that Registry?[1]

---

[1] The Conference of 1818 requested 'the Committee of Privileges . . . to consider whether, in addition to the present General Methodist Register of Births and Baptisms now kept in London under their superintendence and sanction, it may not be practicable and expedient to adopt some method by which the local registers kept at our country chapels may be regularly copied into the books of our London

If you will have the goodness to answer this question, I will be very much obliged to you. . . .

9. *From Robert Pilter*   North Shields, July 5, 1820

[Will Bunting help them get McNicoll and Moss for the Circuit?] . . . Stevenson [*i.e.* Stephenson] and his radicals have done us hurt. A new chapel opened for Sunday evening service in the next street and occupied by an Independent youth said to equal the late Spence of Liverpool[1] seriously affects our congregations. So that we *must* have our pulpit well supported. The better part of our friends have stood their ground so well and have so loyally maintained the dignity and the decisions of Conference that they richly deserve help. . . . [It would also be invaluable if Bunting could find any financial help.]

10. *From John Riles*[2]   Chelsea, July 17, 1820

. . . I have by me a paper on the subject of *Ordination by the Imposition of Hands*, which I have had some thoughts to sending to the Conference, to bring the question before the brethren, for their consideration. I think if this *reasonable, scriptural* practice was introduced, and the young men ordained at the time of the Conference, it would be attended with a blessing, because it is God's ordinance. I believe the present state of Methodism, and the enlightened state of society requires this. An ordination *without* imposition of *hands*, is unscriptural.

I intended to have mentioned this to you, before you left, but had no opportunity. What do you think upon the business? Shall I send you my paper upon the subject? Whatever defect their may be in the reasoning, it would bring the question on. If you approve of it signify your wish.

---

office so as to be duly preserved and easily referred to'. *Minutes of Methodist Conferences*, iv, p. 456. The General Register, though promised for some years (*Life of Bunting*, ii, p. 78), seems not to have been begun till 1818; it was kept at 66 Paternoster Row, and was transferred to Somerset House after compulsory registration of births was established by statute in 1836.
    [1] Preachers appointed to North Shields circuit, 1820–1822, were Thomas Hill and Thomas Moss. 'The late Spence of Liverpool' was Thomas Spencer (1791–1811) who, appointed minister of the Newington Chapel in 1811, built up so vast a congregation that the Great George Street Congregational Chapel was built for him. He died in a bathing accident before it was finished.
    [2] John Riles (d. 1826), preacher, London (Great Queen Street) circuit, 1818–1820.

I hope a divine providence will superintend all the measures of Conference, and bless your purposes. . . .

[Enclosed]—To the President of the Methodist Conference assembled in Liverpool

As circumstances would not admit of my attending this year at Liverpool, I have taken the liberty of bringing before you and the brethren, a question of some importance, which I conceive demands the attention of so large a body of divines, professing to be sent of God to preach the everlasting Gospel, and to watch over so large a portion of Christ's flock.

The question is, 'Does the present mode of designating the young men to the ministerial office, after they have travelled their four years, agree with the established practice of the Apostles, the Primitive Church, and the usage of all Christian Churches?' Upon this question, there is no need to pause; it is too evident to admit of a doubt, that the mode of *ordaining* the young men (for ordination I must call it) is defective in one point, as it wants the *laying on of hands*, which is an ancient custom, and was used on various occasions: sometimes to implore a blessing upon a person,—to consecrate something to God in sacrifice, or designate to office. Thus Jacob gave his blessing to Ephraim and Manasseh, by *laying his hands on their heads*: Moses laid his hands upon the head of Joshua, as a *public official recognition* to his office; and when Jesus Christ blessed little children, he laid his hands upon their heads.

This custom was so well understood, and so generally practised amongst the Jews, and adapted to the state of the Church in all ages, that the propriety of using it was never called in question by any of the New Testament writers; and the Apostles and Elders had recourse to it as a ceremony which was in use upon all solemn occasions. I am ready to admit there is no express command for its use, yet there are precedents sufficiently numerous to give it authority. When Jesus Christ gave a commission to Peter and James with others to preach the gospel, it signified something high and important in its nature; but whether this authority was accompanied with the laying on of hands, it is difficult to determine, though I think it more than probable that it was. But when Barnabas and Saul were called to the ministry by the Holy Ghost, the elders after fasting and prayer, *laid their hands on them*. When Stephen, Philip and others were chosen as Deacons, the Apostles after prayer, *laid their hands on them*. It should be understood here, that in both cases no gifts were communicated in the act, and it was intended and fully understood, as a *public official recognition* of these holy men to the offices assigned them, Stephen etc. as Deacons, and Barnabas and Saul as *Itinerant Ministers*. It is unnecessary to multiply references as it was the uniform practice of the apostolic age and of the primitive church; and it appears unwise not to follow what received so high a sanction.

I admit, Sir, that the Methodist preachers are set apart to the ministry of the Word, and may found their right to preach the gospel upon what they conceive a clear call from God, and the approbation of their aged Brethren, after a close examination of their experience, orthodoxy, and qualifications. This method, though not exactly with the letter of the Apostolic Canon, yet is certainly consonant with its spirit, as it respects the fitness for the work and the approbation of those competent to judge; but it is defective as it wants the *imposition of hands*: and I would ask what good reason can be assigned, why the Conference should not add the outward and visible sign, as a *public act*. After going so far, why not go farther; as the present method of receiving preachers is an ordination, as rational and scriptural as any, with this single exception: the *laying of hands upon them*.

Some of my Brethren in the moment of alarm may say, 'Am I to be ordained after having laboured in the ministry for 30 or 40 years? Must I be placed beside a young man who has just entered upon his work?' I would reply, 'No, you have been ordained for these 20 or 30 years; your labours have been owned of God; you have been recognised by your Brethren and received by the Churches. But if you and your contemporaries have neglected to use a scriptural ceremony, what fair objection can you have to your junior Brethren being designated to the ministry in a way that is practised by all Protestant churches?'

As I shall not be present to meet objections to my proposition (and I am well aware it will have to encounter strong prejudice), I will anticipate an objection or two. It may be said, 'It would be a departure from the *Old Plan*, and that we are losing our simplicity by adding and altering.' To this I would reply with all deference to my Brethren, that the old plan, as it respects discipline, is a non-entity: it has no existence; it never had any. When our venerable father Mr. Wesley had taken his ground with respect to doctrines he maintained and defended them, and never departed from them. If this is the *Old Plan*, I hope the Conference will never concede a particle of it. But if by the Old Plan is meant what relates to discipline, Mr. Wesley never had any other plan but what arose from the exigencies of circumstances and the openings of Providence. He himself ordained by the imposition of hands for America and Scotland. Besides, has not the Conference from year to year since his death been

D

maturing our discipline by altering some of its parts, and making additions to others, as the Connexion has become more extended, and required new measures, and measures which so far from weakening the first principles of Methodistical discipline, have given solidity to the whole, and I believe have rendered it more efficient. It may be said, 'It would be a departure from the Church, and an open avowal of our Dissent.' But I would ask in what. The Conference certainly ordain[s]; and this part of the ceremony requires no *alteration* but the *addition* of the *imposition of hands*, to render the acct. [? action] more solemn and impressive, because it is scriptural. Why does the Conference allow its missionaries to be ordained by the *laying on of hands*, but to give them a degree of respectability, not amongst the negroes in the West Indies, but in the opinion of Europeans, and the civil governors there; and can any good reason be assigned why the brethren in England should not comply with an ordinance which can plead such precedents in its favour?

How the admission of this custom can lessen the usefulness of the preachers I am at a loss to conceive; as their usefulness depends upon their preaching the Gospel fully and faithfully, accompanied with a holy life, as required both by the scriptures and the rules of Methodism, and a step of this nature would not more identify them with the dissenters, than were they not to adopt it. Imposition of hands in ordination could not in the opinion of the unprejudiced so far alter the economy of Methodism to render their relation to the Church different from what it now is. . . .

11. *From Wm. Scholefield* [1]   Wolsingham, July 25, 1820

A charge having been brought to the Conference against the Wolsingham Circuit, by the Newcastle District Meeting, and which will come before you when the District Minutes are read, I hope that you will permit a friend, to say what he can, in truth, for the criminal in question, that when you have heard both sides of the business, you may be able to form your judgment and conclude accordingly. The number of members in this circuit is 405, half of whom I am informed are in debt, in consequence of the lead mines in this country not being very productive for some years past. From this statement, you will perceive that this is a necessitous circuit. And as you made provision for necessitous circuits at the last Annual Conference, on the ground of necessity, I put in my claim for relief at the Financial District Meeting, held at Newcastle. My claim was rejected, because

---

[1] William Scholefield (d. 1838, *aet.* 63), superintendent, Wolsingham circuit, 1819–1821.

I could not say that the members here gave one penny per week and one shilling per quarter. This is a most excellent law, but with all deference to your judgment, who understand the subject much better than I do, I think it ought to give way a little to very poor circuits. It is true that provision is made in the yearly Collection for poor members in poor circuits, who cannot comply with the rule, and when a claim is legally and Methodistically made it ought not to be rejected, as was the case at the Newcastle Financial District Meeting. It would be thought curious for the Parish officers, when poor persons apply for relief, to ask, 'Do you by your daly labour, earn as much as will keep you and your family? No Sirs? then you can have no relief.' I hope dear brethren, that our worthy Chairmen will never imitate the conduct of the Egyptian tax master's, by requiring the people to make brick without straw.

The Conference plan for supporting the children, is generally approved of in this circuit. Want of ability in our present circumstances alone prevented us from doing more than we have. In this circuit, we had two children and a quarter to provide for. The one upon the spot, has been provided for, consequently, there is a deficiency of one and a quarter, which amounts to [£]7.17.6. I sold the horse to save expence, and have walked the circuit, though upwards of 16 miles in length. I have the Conference allowance in every respect, Board, etc. etc. and no more, and, thank God, I want no more. I sent [£]6.0.0 for the Kingswood Collection [£]4.17.11 for the Chapel Collection [£]10.0.0 for the Yearly Collection. In making this, I told the people in every place, that we were [£]7.17.6 deficient with respect to the Children's Fund, according to the new arrangement, and that they must exert themselves, in order that we might more than cover that sum, they did so. I sent [£]18.7.6 for the missionary collection, in making which I left no stone unturned nor is there a single collector at present in the circuit. I have sent [£]3.10.0 for the July Collection.

And this being a new circuit,[1] we had a house to furnish. In addition to the [£]20.0.0 sent by Conference there was [£]42.0.0 more [£]30.0.0 of which, in the course of the year, have been rubbed off, and we have arranged matters for a general begging business, in order to get the debt entirely distroyed in the course of a few weeks. We have received no deficienc[i]es, neither ordinary nor extraordinary . . . Wolsingham Circuit has, in fact, more than cleared itself, and there are six circuits, in the District, which in fact are all defficient. And therefore why censure a poor circuit, for not conforming for

---

[1] Wolsingham was separated from the Barnard Castle and Weardale circuit in 1819.

want of ability, to the letter of the law, when it has fully conformed to the spirit of it.

Besides the charge from the District, this circuit has to contend with Bishops, Priests, Deacons and the Devil. The Bishop of Durham has built 7 School⟨s in the⟩ Dale all of which are endowed by his Lordship ⟨and other⟩ Gentlemen, so far so good. But the rules belonging to ⟨the⟩ schools are prohibitory, and almost damnatory. The Schoolmasters are all to be of the Church of England, and they are to go to Church, and nowhere else. By this means, three of our members have lost their schools, and there bread, in this Dale, two of whom are acceptable Local Preachers. The children, if not entered as Dissenters, are to go to Church, and nowhere else.

May the Lord help us, for the Members of old Mother Church, would swallow us up, root and branch.

Praying that the Lord may bless you abundantly, in all your consultations, and that you may have plenty of money to answer all your demands. . . .

12. *From James Nichols*[1]   London, July 29, 1820

. . . When any conversation about the *Christian Reporter* arises, I hope, dear sir, for my sake, you will notice the professions of our prospectus, which broadly stated that it was to be *a select work*, and not to consist of the mere every-day occurrences of high and low life, but that it was to induce a better taste, and a relish (especially among our own people) for literary and scientific topics. And though, to suit the demands of many of our purchasers, we have come down from that high ground of literature which we at first assumed, we have not relinquished *that select character*, which was a part of our early professions, and which still forms a strong ground of recommendation to pious families. On this ground I ⟨hope⟩ the preachers will be induced to recommend it in their several circuits.—As to its political principles, our prospectus stated them as of a moderate

---

[1] James Nichols (1785–1861), who had begun business as a printer and bookseller in Leeds, had recently been brought to London to launch the *Christian Reporter*, and printed the *Life* of Bunting's friend Edward Hare, the Methodist preacher and theologian. The *Christian Reporter*, with the assistance of Richard Watson and Jabez Bunting, was to support the policies of the Address of the Committee of Privileges (see n. 1, p. 25). When the ministry dropped the bill of pains and penalties against Queen Caroline late in 1820, Nichols felt some sympathy for her, but Bunting and Watson refused to write on the subject and the paper collapsed. Nichols subsequently printed much valuable work in the fields of theology, church history and literature, including his own translation of the works of Arminius.

cast, and it has been my study in the management of the paper to accommodate myself to those conditions; although, from the two rough-draughts of the first Prospectus which I furnished, it was evident that I wished rather more latitude to be allowed for the expression of political opinion, but this was inconsistent with the moderation which was prescribed to us as Christian Reporters. My attachments of a political kind are decidedly in favour of social order and good government, but I do not class myself under either of the two modern parties of Tories and Whigs, because it is easy to demonstrate that in many things both have changed places, and the French Revolution introduced a new aera into the history of these parties which is not yet terminated. Since I first formed an opinion about political matters, I have mentally placed myself under the auspices of those principles which were espoused and defended, at different periods, by Lord Somers and the first Earl of Chatham, both of whom are now called by way of distinction 'Whigs of the Old School'.—I think it necessary to state these things, because in many of the discontinuances which I have received and in some anonymous letters, I have been blamed for advocating despotic principles, which I can never be brought to do. But I am of opinion that I hav⟨e⟩ generally kept the golden mean,—for I have been told by one gentleman, and ⟨not only⟩ by him, that the principles of the *Christian Reporter* are not quite high enough. I am well aware that when the *Christian Reporter* begins to act the partizan in a sp⟨irited⟩ manner, it at once disclaims all title and right to the epithet of 'Chris⟨tian'⟩. It is of consequence, too, that a paper which, after all the endeavours of t⟨he⟩ proprietors to the contrary, is in the eyes of many persons clothed with a kind of semi-official characte⟨r⟩ should contain no political reflexions that could be perverted to party pur⟨poses⟩. With these views as a Christian and a Methodist, I have made my remarks on passing events very brief, and have at times felt great difficulty in introducing any mention of them in the way of comment. These are a few of the restraints to which I have been subjected in the course of my *recent political education*, and which I should not have experienced in an equal degree if the interests of piety had not been so intimately and appropriately conjoined in our paper with those minor ones of literature and politics.—These are only a very small portion of the desultory observations which have occurred to me in the course of rapidly penning this letter, and I offer them with all humility and deference. But before I conclude them, I must remark that I have been long of opinion that it would greatly serve the interests of the *Christian Reporter*, were it published on a Wednesday instead of a Monday. Ours is nearly the only respectable newspaper that is published on a

Monday, almost all the others being the shadows of Sunday p⟨rints.⟩ If any of those remain on hand with the newsmen, it is not at all unco⟨mmon⟩ for them to be substituted for one of ours, and sometimes even for a daily paper. All the newspapers published on Saturday in the midland counties contain very nearly as recent news as a London Monday paper, because there has been nothing fresh on the preceding day (Sunday);—while, on the contrary, worldly matters of all kinds on Wednesday have got into a train of *originating* (as a German would say) and an account of them on the Thursday or Friday morning will be acceptable to those in distant parts who take a Saturday's provincial paper. When our paper commenced, one of the greatest objections to Wednesday was its being the day on which the *Philanthropic* was published. But now there is no need to observe any such delicacy.—If there be any discourse among the brethren, you can ascertain with tolerable accuracy what their opinions are about Wednesday.

I congratulate you, dear sir, on the honour to which the Conference has elevated you this year, and by which it has at once honoured and profited itself. Mr. Benson[1] informed me of the election with great zest, and declared he was most heartily glad at the issue of it. He says he cannot think of coming down to Liver⟨po⟩ol as he feels he can do you no good. . . .

P.S. The Queen's business, it is positively stated, is still in a way of ⟨c⟩ompromise. I send you on this subject the leading article of the *True Briton* of Monday last. You will be surprized to learn that this new evening paper, supported as it is said to be by Mr. Canning, the Marquis Wellesley and other noblemen, has not yet risen to 300 copies daily. A very respectable young man who works at that office has informed us that they have not yet reached 250 daily. We manage far better than they do in this respect, and are capable with a little exertion and explanation of doing exceedingly well.

13. *From William Myles*[2]   Halifax, August 18, 1820

Without any flattery I can truly say, I greatly approved of your public conduct as President in Liverpool. The office now means something besides the mere name.

Since I came home I hastily read Mr. Bramwell's Life.[3] I think it

---

[1] Joseph Benson (1749–1821), Connexional Editor, 1804–1821. His huge Bible commentary (1818) was largely based on the work of Wesley and Thomas Coke.

[2] William Myles (d. 1828, *aet.* 70), superintendent, Halifax circuit 1819–1821.

[3] James Sigston, *A memoir of the life and ministry of Mr. W. Bramwell* (London, 1820), printed by James Nichols. Sigston was a Leeds schoolmaster who had led

is partially written. In my opinion it does not deserve the high encomiums passed upon it by some persons. When writing that part that treats of the division of circuits, he did not consider that we were nearly a married ministry. I hope if it is reviewed in our magazine it will be reviewed impartially. I have some doubts whether the author is a warm friend to our Body.

I have some fears respecting the Local Preachers. They well know we cannot do without them. Some of them appear to be jealous and envious of us. . . . . . I think we have at last hit, or rather was directed of the Lord, to the most equitable plan of supporting and increasing Methodism in Great Britain.[1] In all new regulations we must expect opposition. I fear it would not be good policy to get at present an exact number of our Chapels with the debts on each. It would give us to see how dependant we are on Local Preachers, and the whole of the debts would frighten us. Some of our Local Preachers are still urging the people to build chapels in country places where we cannot visit them on the Lord's day. . . .

14. *From Samuel Webb*[2]　　　　　Stafford, August 29, 1820

I am sorry that I am under the disagreeable necessity of informing you that the Killamites have lately taken possession of our preaching house at Stone in this Circuit. It appears, from information I have received since I came to the Circuit, that considerable disaffection has prevailed in the Society ever since it has been removed from Newcastle.[3] During the absence of Messrs. Dunn and Radcliffe;[4] at Conference, the two Leaders invited the Killamites to preach in our room; but in consequence of our preacher coming to the place sooner than was expected, their intention, for that time, was not

---

a secession of revivalists there in 1803, known as the Kirkgate Screamers. At the time Bramwell, who had aspirations to be a revivalist, had intended to link the Screamers with other revivalist separations in Manchester and Macclesfield, and resigned his ministry. Bramwell, however, was put under great pressure to withdraw, much to Bunting's disgust (M.C.A. MSS. J. Birchenall to L. Tyerman, December 22, 1870. Enclosed in Tyerman MSS, iii, fo. 1 : Jabez Bunting to Richard Reece, July 15, 1803) and the Screamers were received back into Society in 1807. Sigston, however, was a prominent leader of the Leeds Protestant Methodist secession in 1827.

[1] The Children's Fund (see n. 1, p. 30).

[2] Samuel Webb (1783–1847), newly arrived superintendent of Stafford circuit, 1820–1821.

[3] I.e. transferred from Newcastle-under-Lyme circuit to Stafford circuit.

[4] Moses Dunn (d. 1849, aet. 69), superintendent, Stafford circuit, 1819–1820. Charles Radcliffe (d. 1852, aet. 65), preacher, Stafford circuit, 1819–1821.

realized. Being in the neighbourhood just after my leaving Conference, I paid them a visit, for the purpose of softening them, and of
preventing a division; and was given to understand that they would,
at least for one Quarter, defer having any thing to do with them;
and a person was sent to countermand their coming. I visited them
again on the following Sunday, preached twice, and left them in
hopes that disaffection would end. Last Sunday, however, the Killamites occupied our pulpit; and our preacher was prevented from
preaching to our congregation. This room is rented of a person at
Stone, as a preaching house for the Methodists. The rent has been
obtained by public collections, and subscriptions; and has been paid
by the person who at the time has acted as our Steward. Mr. Chatter-
ton, Taylor and Draper, for some time past has acted as Steward;
and I believe the receipts from the landlord, since the commencement
of Mr. C.'s Stewardship, have been made in his name. Mr. Chatter-
ton considers himself the legal tenant, and at liberty to exclude us,
and admit the Killamites. Since the place has been in our hands we
have laid out on it upwards of £40, in plastering and washing the
walls, glazing, etc., etc. There are a few people left of our Society
who are sincerely attached to us, and who are looking up to me to
help them out of their difficulties. I confess I am at a loss how to
act; and shall be glad to receive your advice, and, if possible, your
assistance as soon as convenient. . . .

15. *From John Walton*[1]   Rothwell, September 1, 1820

I have long been waiting for your answer, and about a week ago, I
concluded that you did not intend to answer; but this day I have
found it at my brother's house, who lives at this place near Leeds. I
heard before I left Middleham that my letters had *offended Mr.*
Bunting, and the preachers in general, who have conversed with me
on the subject, view my present appointment as a punishment. For
several years, I have addressed the Methodist Conference with the

[1] John Walton was preacher at Middleham, 1819–1820. Before the end of 1820
Walton was married and again seeking a circuit; Bunting advised that he should
attend the next Conference to account for his contumacy (M.C.A. MSS. John
Walton to Jabez Bunting [post-marked December 13, 1820]). He received appointments down to 1826, but desisted travelling in 1827, was subsequently expelled and
began legal proceedings against the preachers' Annuitant Society in the hope of
recovering what he believed due to him towards superannuation (M.C.A. MSS.
Thomas Galland to Jabez Bunting, March 21, 1828: February 4, 1829: John
Walton to Jabez Bunting, May 7, 1830). The letter shows how resentment against
continuous service in poor circuits might occasion the exercise of discipline. The
following letters show why Hexham was regarded as one of the hardest circuits
in the connexion.

greatest *respect* and could not be noticed at all, which has distressed my mind exceedingly; this year, I acknowledge, I wrote in a different manner, because I was determined that the Conference should either serve me better, or dismiss me.

You seem to intimate, that it was a mere mistake that my name should stand the last; but I find in the corrected copy of the Stations, it stands the same—this has been noticed by others, as well as by myself. I know Alstone and Hexham very well, and am well assured I cannot do the work of those circuits. Bisides I was engaged to marry, and had urged the lady to consent, that the Conference might appoint me to a house. This was laid before you, and what a proof you have given me, that the brethren wish to serve me! I have written to Hexham and find there is no house, nor lodgings, nor is there any means in the circuit of providing for me. What woman of sense and descancy, would give up a more than comfortable home, to go to Alstone Moor, under such circumstances?

In my most cool moments, I consider myself used worse than a dog, since my wife died; and am determined that the Conference shall use me better, in future, or dismiss me. I am loseing my character, and if the Conference slight me a little longer, all the people will do the same; and it will be impossible to station me. I complained to you privately after the Bristol Conference, so that you could not be ignorant of the state of my mind; you are now the President, and I have a ten times worse appointment than ever: when I consider this, what am I to think? If the brethren do not consider me an honourable member of your body, I wish them to dismiss me, and not treat me as you have done for some years. At the two last Conferences, I requested to be removed from the North; and was this unreasonable? When I saw that I could not be served better, I requested to be sent to Skipton; and was this too much? I am obliged to you, for your promise in getting my name to stand the second; but I have a right to something more than this—I wish to have a circuit where I can do the work, the state of my health and strength will not suffer me to go to Alstone whatever may be the consequences—I wish to have some place where I shall be likely to make a wife comfortable; and as I have traveled 15 years, this is nothing more than common justice: and especially, when I consider what kind of circuits I have had of late years. As I did not expect you to answer my letter, my boxes have this morning reached Leeds, where I intend, please God, to have a lodging and remain, till you do something better for me. . . .

[*Endorsed*]: [*To John Walton*]
Answered September 6. No. 20 . . .

Nothing to do as an individual with his complaints against the *Conference*.

But as to his *Station*, I *have* a *duty* to fulfil. He says he intends to remain at Leeds, until something better can be done. I have no power to alter the deliberate decisions of the Conference. Unless he go forthwith to his circuit, he virtually withdraws himself from the Travelling Connexion—Beseech him to go at once and labour heartily till next Conference and then state his case.—If he do not, I shall on application be obliged to supply his place by another preacher.

Hexham etc. a pleasant and healthy Station. The two circuits now *united*;[1] and all the 3 Brethren will of course regularly travel through it.

It was fully expected that if he married the circuit would *then* provide accommodations, as its *numbers* in Society require, for a 3d. Preacher.

Exhortion not to be rash, and not to lean to his own understanding.

16. *To Thomas Kelk*[2] (Rochester)
London, September 19, 1820. [*Copy*]

John Walton appointed for Hexham peremptorily refuses to go to his circuit, I have written to him twice, but he seems obstinate, and the circuit can no longer be neglected, especially as Mr. Adshead the Superintendent[3] has been indisposed.

I have therefore determined to supply the vacancy by a preacher from the List of Reserve. There is one who has been on that list since 1817 to whom on that account some preference is due, besides a considerable number of 1818, 1819, and 1820.[4] But as the Conference gave me a discretion in such matters I am disposed to send

---

[1] According to the official records Hexham and Alston were separated in 1809, though at this time preachers moved in successive years from one to the other. Walton is recorded as having been appointed to Alston, 1821–1823.

[2] Thomas Kelk (d. 1836, *aet.* 68), superintendent, Rochester circuit, 1819–1821.

[3] Charles L. Adshead, superintendent Hexham circuit, 1820–1821. Supernumerary 1834, disappeared from ministry probably by death, between 1841 and 1847.

[4] The List of Reserve was filled by prospective preachers approved by Conference for whom no appointments had been found, and who might be stationed at the President's discretion to fill vacancies created by death or by preachers' desisting from travelling. The growth of the list owing to the restriction of ministerial recruiting under pressure of financial stringency in 1819, increased the practical ability of the President to deal with the candidates upon it, though he could not enlarge the number of appointments (cf. no. 18 *infra*).

your son William[1] to *Hexham provided* he can go thither *immediately*. This offer I am led to make by my respect for you, and by the favourable opinion which I entertain of the piety and talents of your son. Will you confer with him as I understand he is now with you, and acquaint me with the result *by return of Post* ? . . . There are 23 candidates for the home work on my list. May the Lord direct you and him in the decision on his proposal . . .

P.S. . . . Hexham is said to be a pleasant and very healthy Circuit.

17. *From Wm. Kelk*   Hexham, April 30, 1821

[His father suggested he should write] . . . in general I have been borne up with the assurance that in coming to this place I was not following so much my own will as what evidently appeared not only to myself but to all my friends the leadings of Divine Providence. Our circuit, which is situated in the three counties of Northumberland Cumberland and Durham, is between 40 and 50 miles in extent—it regularly takes us six weeks to go round it, during which we are always an entire month from Hexham, the principal town, travelling from one little place to another every day (and sometimes 20 miles in the day)—preaching *every night* in the week, and three times on the Sunday. In consequence of travelling so much and changing our lodgings so repeatedly, our opportunities for profitable study are very contracted, and those opportunities I find it absolutely necessary to devote almost entirely to direct preparation for the pulpit. I wish I could say that I had perceived much good resulting from my labours, but this has not been the case. Many indeed have professed themselves greatly profited under my ministry, and in some places a few new members have been added to the Society, but in general the work of conviction and conversion which I rejoice to hear is spreading so gloriously in different parts of the Kingdom makes but little progress in this circuit. The fault no doubt (in reference to myself at least) attaches considerably to the weakness and incompetency of the workman—though I fear the soil in which we work is not the most promising in the world. Throughout the Hexham part of the circuit the people are in general quite cold and worldly. I do not find among them that attachment to Methodism or its Preachers, or that willingness in the Local Preachers and Leaders and other principal members of the Society to co-operate with them which appears to be essentially necessary in order to their doing much or permanent good. And in the Alston part of the circuit, the people have been generally and are still to a great extent, quite disaffected

[1] William Kelk (1795–1866), Secretary of Chapel Committee, 1855–1860.

towards the preachers.[1] A few years ago a Local Preacher of some popularity, a religious radical, disseminated his principles through the Circuit, made a rent in the Society, and too extensively alienated the affections of the people from the preachers. This spirit still works, and is ever ready to manifest itself whenever an opportunity presents itself. This has been the case in n⟨o or⟩dinary degree during the last year. Irritated at the ⟨appointm⟩ent of Mr. Adshead to the circuit (an eminently peaceable and pious man, though in a few respects he may have been indiscreet) they witheld for some time their weekly and quarterly subscriptions, and when I came I met with murmuring and backbiting wherever I went. As I was determined not to make myself a party to their disputes, I closed my ears as far as possible against them—but still I found myself very disagreeably situated and often very sore tried. They have at length got into a little better temper, but their finances are very low. At our last Quarterly Meeting they gave me a very urgent invitation to remain with them another year—but on the above accounts as well as on several others I did not feel disposed to consent. I must confess indeed that I anticipate with some pleasure the approach of Conference, that I may be removed with its permission somewhat nearer my good friends in the South. For several months I enjoyed but indifferent health—the hard riding and continual preaching—the frequently getting wet through and the perpetual change of lodgings, to all of which I had been unaccustomed, induced such languor and weakness and want of appetite, as almost disqualified me for the work. Had not the winter been so unusually mild, I fear the immensely high fells over which we have habitually to pass, beyond description cold, barren, and rugged, would almost have mastered me. . . .

18. *From James Odgers*[2]   Barnstaple, October 16, 1820

[They urgently need a third preacher, and can just afford to pay one. Can one be sent from the list of reserve?]

[*Endorsed*] [*To James Odgers*] Answered November 4. President has no legal power, except to fill up vacancies occasioned by death or other failure of men actually stationed at Conference. The Conference itself can alone increase the number. This being the law I decline to go beyond it in this case, especially as though a 3d. single man might be kept, there is no provision for subsequent marriage

---

[1] The lead-miners of Alston, like the miners in many of the coal-field circuits, had a reputation for turbulence in church life.

[2] James Odgers (d. 1855, *aet.* 81), superintendent, Barnstaple circuit, 1820–1821.

and eventual demands on Contingent Fund, Children's Fund, Preacher's Fund etc.

19. *From George Douglas*[1]   Stamford, October 26, 1820

A few of our young friends in this Society wish much to send an address to the Queen. I told them I had not heard of any of our large Societies doing so and wished them to let it rest till I asked advice on the subject. Please favour me with your opinion—Will it be proper at present? . . .

[*Endorsed*] [*To George Douglas*] Heads of my *Answer dated* October 28 [1820]. Surprized and grieved at his information. If they mean to have an address in their *individual* character, to be signed by others with them, even then, it shews in *young* people a deficient sense of moral delicacy. More becoming to leave it to the calm decision of the Peers who will do substantial justice.

If they mean to address *as Methodists*; it is still more mischievous. I hope such an idea has entered into no heads but theirs. Exhort Mr. D[ouglas] and his colleagues to do all he can to prevent it. Unofficial and unauthorized individuals must not thus compromise the reputation and interests of the Body. If they must and will address, let them sign some General Address in the Town quietly, but not make themselves prominent and active or use the name and influence of Methodism in such folly or faction. Even if the Queen be *not* guilty of adultery, or if the *Bill* be *inexpedient*, still she *is proved* to have violated female decorum. This her own witnessess and advocates admit; and *they* try to palliate and justify it. But Methodists and Christians must not contribute to lower or demolish the barriers between virtue and vice. Perhaps she may not deserve *degradation*, that is a matter for different opinions. But at all events she does not deserve to be *addressed, caressed and applauded*.

Hope he will be able to quash the project. If not, it will be the Preachers' duty to let the public know that it is the unauthorized act of a few individuals, of which their ministers disapprove, and for which the Body is not responsible.

Beg him to keep my letter in his own hands, as, writing in haste I have no *copy*, and it may be necessary to prove that *I* did my duty.

[*Further endorsed*]
Mr. Douglas on the Stamford Folly.

---

[1] George Douglas (1764–1853), superintendent, Stamford circuit, 1820–1822.

20. *From Joseph Sutcliffe*[1]   Bristol, October 31, 1820

I feel much at home in Bristol. Primitive Methodism still exists here; and I hope ever will exist. The bands, both body and select, meet as well perhaps as in Mr. Wesley's time.[2] Mr. Pocock's party seem quiet,[3] or to me they seem so, as having no intercourse with them. Mr. Moore[4] thinks the preachers imprudent for bringing Pocock's case at all into the Leaders' meeting. Others lament that so many good men have left us, and think that things might have been better managed. Be that as it may, I feel grateful that my lot is cast among such a people; and to you for proposing me to this place, a circumstance which accidentally reached my ear. . . .

21. *From William Griffith*[5]   Hungerford, December 20, 1820

I am sorry to intrude upon your time which is so much occupied upon other matters, but shall esteem it a favour if you will *immediately* send me a few lines upon a point in which I fear I may err.

You are aware that Mr. Pocock is endeavouring to enlarge his borders and he has a party in Malborough which is a part of my circuit. They have already got one place from us, and I understand have procured premises in Malborough to have preaching there. And I find one young man an Exhorter and member of our Society has engaged to assist them once a month at Lockridge the place they have gotten from us, and another of our Local Preachers is disposed

---

[1] Joseph Sutcliffe (d. 1856, *aet.* 94), preacher, Bristol circuit, 1820–1822. Author of *A commentary on the Old and New Testament* (London, 1834–1835).

[2] The lack of mobility in Bristol Methodism as compared with the North, was a matter of comment. 'The people here seem rather of a dull heavy cast; and in the country in particular are ignorant, and stupid in a high degree, and seem to have very little religion, but if there are not as many flowing into the societies as in the North, there are not as many leaving.' (M.C.A. MSS. John Barber to George Marsden, October 22, 1814).

[3] George Pocock, a Bristol schoolmaster and local preacher, with the assistance of other local preachers, had begun missions over a wide area between South Wales and Berkshire in 1814, with an 'Itinerant Tabernacle' or tent. For a time he financed the whole venture, raised ten new societies and eight new chapels, but was expelled in 1820 for refusing to settle them on the Conference plan. Bunting's view of the Tent Methodists is given in no. 21. Pocock's view was that the preachers' 'only cry is Rule, Rule *Methodist* Rule, "Conformity or expulsion" '. See George Pocock, *A Statement of facts connected with the ejectment of certain ministers from the Society of Wesleyan Methodists in the city of Bristol* (Bristol, 1820); George Pocock, John, Pyer, Samuel Smith, *Facts Without a Veil* (Bristol 1820).

[4] Henry Moore (1751–1844), superintendent, Bristol circuit, 1820–1823. The assistant, travelling companion, amanuensis, literary executor and biographer of John Wesley, he was highly regarded in his earlier years as a theologian.

[5] William Griffith (1777–1860), superintendent, Hungerford circuit, 1820–1823.

to assist them. *I said I could not allow* of this. If they would preach for them, I could not let them be with us. Upon which one of them who is a Leader asked what *rule* was broken thereby. I answered if I did not recollect any rule for the moment, yet the usage of the Connection was so to act and I referred to our conduct at the time of Mr. Kilham's seperation. Now, Sir, while I would not willingly make strife or widen a breach which has taken place, neither am I disposed to neglect the exercise of discipline however painful to my feelings and hurtful to our feeble cause in this place. And therefore shall esteem it a favour if you will direct me how to act in this affair if the steps I have taken are not the best. I would rather expose my own ignorance by asking counsel than act at random and do mischief. We are in other respects doing pretty well and our congregations somewhat on the increase.

[*Endorsed*] [*Draft. To W. Griffith*]
Answered December 23, 1820.
His path of duty clear. If a Local Preacher persist after due and affectionate advice, admon[itio]n and expost[ulatio]n, to sanction a party avowedly opposed to us, which has in print calumniated us, and which is trying to divide our people, he offends against the whole spirit and substance of our Rules, against the scriptural authority of those who are over him in the Lord, and against many plain passages of Scripture, *e. g.* Follow peace. He should therefore be put away.

Even if no direct rule were broken by such conduct, still discipline is so violated in its essence, that it deserves the severest censure. There is no rule directly against wearing a fool's cap in our pulpits, but he who did so would be properly and legally excluded.

Men must not thus set up their individual will and judgment against those of their Brethren and Superintendent.

22. *From Joseph Griffith*[1]   Bury St. Edmunds, November 24, 1820

The object of this letter is to solicit advice in a concern which gives me and our friends here some concern. It is as follows. A few years ago a Benifit Club was established here and its meetings held in the Chapel because it was in a great measure made up of our members and friends. It was enrolled under the appellation of The Methodist Benifit Society. It for a time went on well. But a year or two since Cobbett's writings and radicalism took a strong hold of many of

---

[1] Joseph Griffith, superintendent, Bury St. Edmunds circuit, 1820–1822. Retired from ministry 1838.

their minds, which lead to much unpleasantness in our Society—One of the results was many of them separated from us. The Club have resolved to send a petition to his Majesty complaining of greviances and requesting the dismission of his Ministers etc. It goes as a petition from The Methodist Benifit Society. Many of our Leaders and friends object to this because they think it appears to make us as a Society as petitioners when we have in fact nothing to do with it as a Society; and that it may be prejudicial to us and our Connextion by leading the inhabitants, the country and the government to judge unfavourable of us by taking us to be what we are not. I have waited upon their leading man to request that the word Methodist might be left out that we might not appear to be implicated in a business with which we have nothing to do. I have intreated in vain, have placed before him the unwillingness of the Leaders and Society to have the appearance of connexion with the Petition to the King, or the Address to the Queen which they also send. Both the Petition and the Address will appear in our papers in a few days.—Our people wish something to appear in the following paper to explain it and counteract it, and to have the Club prohibited meeting in the Chapel. Mr. Crisp and I thought it would be best to state it to you and to request a line saying what will be best to do in the case.

If you will favour me with a line soon you will greatly oblige your affectionate Brother, and Servant in the Lord. . . .

[Endorsed] [To J. Griffith]
Answered November 25 and 27.
Advise him
   To publish a Protest against their using the term Methodist in their Petition and Address.
   To prohibit their further use of our Chapel for their Meetings on any occasion.
   To object to their any longer calling themselves a *Methodist* Benefit Society.
   To be as *short* in what they publish and as *temperate* as may consist with being firm, explicit, and decided.

23. *From William Bird*[1]   Burnley, November 30, 1820

Last week I was informed that several of the members of our Society in Burnley are also members of a Society denominated 'The Odd Fellows'. In the course of the last year, my predecessor,[2] with a

---

[1] William Bird (1781–1869), superintendent, Burnley circuit, 1820–1822.
[2] William Welborne (d. 1850), superintendent, Burnley circuit, 1818–1820.

majority of the Leaders, expelled a young man, because he had joined the company of 'Odd Fellows'. If the accused persons now belonging to us in this place are not also expelled, I cannot see how the consistency and impartiality of the Leaders' Meeting, can be preserved. As I wish to preserve *both*, and yet have no *rule* by which to act, *your advice* on the subject will be received as a peculiar favour. . . .

P.S. As the accused members declare the strict morality of their proceedings in their meetings, which from the secrecy of the thing I am not prepared to deny, I fear very unpleasant consequences on their exclusion from our society, which is my reason for troubling you with this letter.

24. *To William Bird* (Burnley)   London, December 12, 1820

I do not know much of the associations which are called 'The Odd Fellows';[1] but I own, from what I do know, I think it very 'odd' that any persons, professing serious religion, should wish to be members of such clubs; and all the Brethren here, whom I have had the opportunity of consulting agree with me in the opinion, that we ought by every prudent method to discountenance in our Societies the practice of joining combinations of that kind. I should even judge it better, if it came to that extremity, to sacrifice a *few* members than to run the risk of having *many* ensnared and contaminated, by sanctioning what has, at least, the 'appearance of evil', from which as Christians our Bibles require us to 'abstain'.

If these clubs have any *political* object or business, then, as *secret*, they are, I believe, unlawful, and certainly very dangerous. If, on the other hand, they are merely *convivial*, which I suppose to be the case, still it is *highly* improper and unscriptural that religious persons should join themselves with carnal and careless persons in such associations. This is not to 'come out from among them and be separate'. To frequent public-houses, without any call of business, necessity or duty, and voluntarily to choose for ourselves the company of the unawakened and ungodly, are practices which cannot be adopted without grieving the Holy Spirit, and endangering our peace and purity. On this ground I think you may fairly and firmly take your stand. Besides, if such clubs be in⟨no⟩cent, and have any good and beneficial effect, it is the duty of those members who belong to them, to *prove* those points to the satisfaction of their christian brethren, to whose good opinion they ought not to be indifferent,

[1] Bunting's pietistic view of the Oddfellows was not peculiar to him. Cf. M.C.A· MSS, J. Braithwaite to Barnard Slater, September 10, 1816.

E

and to the satisfaction, especially of their ministers and pastors, who are over them in the Lord, and watch for their souls. It is not for *you* to prove these clubs immoral; it is for *them* to *prove* (not merely to *assert*) that they are *good* and *beneficial*. On the face of the thing, it is wrong for *Christians* needlessly to associate in familiar intimacy with unbelievers. And unless they can and will demonstrate to you that they have weighty reasons which justify their venturing into temptation, you are authorized to put in force against them the Law of Christ and the Discipline of the Church, if haply they may be brought to a better mind, and others be made afraid to offend. In fact, if they have much of the christian temper, they will not long hesitate in such a case. They will make a sacrifice, if it be such, rather than grieve and offend their brethren in Christ. If these clubs be as innocent as they pretend, still they cannot plead *conscience*, or any *obligation* of absolute duty, for joining them. And if that which *we* think innocent and indifferent be found to offend *others*, and may be to *them* an occasion of stumbling, we are bound to forego it for their sakes.

It may perhaps be well for you to write to Mr. Welbourne before you proceed. He may give you valuable information as to the grounds of his conduct last year. Mr. Jacob Stanley,[1] of the Stourport Circuit, I am told, knows something on the subject of these clubs, and would doubtless be ready to afford you his advice.

25. *From John Kershaw*[2]   Derby, December 21, 1820

I think it my duty to acquaint you with the following circumstance and ask your advice in reference to it.

In a very populous part of the town of Derby, where the population also is rapidly increasing, a chapel was built A.D. 1816, by a denomination of dissenters. It is a very substantial building, without gallery, pewed throughout at the bottom, with burying ground behind. It stands where three roads or streets meet, in the midst of a population, some of which are respectable, some of the middling orders, and some poor. The inhabitants are numerous. This chapel is now on sale. Its original cost was £1100. It has a debt of £800 upon it or upward. Mr. Turner, one of our respectable friends, whom you know, and whose heart and soul is buried in Methodism, would purchase it at any reasonable sum. In fact it may be bought for £700.

---

[1] Jacob Stanley (1776–1850), superintendent, Stourport circuit, 1820–1822. President, 1845. A prominent Protestant politician.
[2] John Kershaw (1766–1855), superintendent, Derby circuit, 1819–1822; he obtained a London station as Book Steward, 1823–1827.

They ask that sum for it. It lies in a part of the town not much short of half a mile from our present chapel. Not 100 people, I am persuaded, from that part sit under our ministry. At this moment the *New Connexion* are moving earth and hell to get an interest in Derby. All is peace and quietness with us and we have considerable prosperity amongst us. That their hopes of success are very faint from that source. But they look toward this chapel. They preached in it last Sabbath evening (Sutton Junr. from Nottingham). If the proprietors would *rent* it, they would take it. Nothing however but *a sale* will be hearkened to. With my approbation and that of my colleague, enquiries will be set on foot perhaps today (though nothing determined till I hear from you) as to price and how far the Kilhamites have gone and are going etc. The quere is, 'Should it be bought?' You will ask what shall you do with it? How pay the interest etc.? I will answer the last question first—When some conversation took place amongst a few of our friends privately, upon this subject some time ago—one said, 'I will give five pounds per annum'. Another 'I will give two', a third two; another one guinea and a half, and so on till £15. 0. 0. was in a few minutes promised. Some rent from occupying it as a Sunday School and some from seat rents, was then looked to, independent of any more private subscriptions more of which were confidently looked for.

As to what we shall do with it? Though this question is not finally settled—the proposal is to give it from *us* one sermon every Lord's Day at 2 o'clock, eight or nine Sabbaths in 13, and one sermon every weeknight. From the Local Preachers a sermon every Sunday night—In the forenoon teach Sunday School in it. We have a very considerable one hear. I observe generally—more than one third of the population of Derby is within 5, 6, 7, 8, minutes walk of it, and we have no interest in that part of the town:—few come from there to our present chapel—Methodism would be increased by it—and—nothing will give the New Connexion a footing in Derby, like their occupation of it. As to money to purchase—a friend mentioned above, will find it all, and not charge more than 4 per cent. I think I have said everything to give you a correct view of the case, unless that I have ommitted to say the size. This I cannot speak to correctly. It seats, I conceive, 400 people—no gallery recollect—all pewed at bottom.

Now, my dear Sir, what advice do you give us in this case? I wait your early reply—or to give any further information which may be desired. I turn to another subject for a moment. Shall I be looking higher than I ought, and meddling with a subject which does not belong to me if I ask, suppose I move from hence at Conference, cannot I come to London? If I speak of right, of age, of standing, etc., have I not a claim equal who to some who are there, and who have been there? I shall not push this point, but I think I have a claim upon it, and will either ask to put it in force, or give it up as you may advise. . . .

N.B. If the chapel be purchased there is no other idea entertained than that of consolidating the two interests and making them entirely *one*. I conceive it due to the Building Committee as the authorized agents of Conference to acquaint them with the business after the receipt of yours. I apprehend they can give no legal sanction to it.

[*Endorsed*] [*To J. Kershaw*]
Answered December 30 [1820]
    The Brethren here think he should encourage the purchase if [it is] freehold property, and as the Old and New Trust are to be consolidated.
    But the Building Committee must officially determine. Danger of trusting too much to promises of annual subscriptions which may not be permanent.

26. *To James Wood*[1] (Manchester)   London, December 23, 1820[2]

. . . It is true that I fell, as I was going to Chapel, one dark night, and that I received a considerable injury in my throat, which for a time made speaking and deglutition very painful to me, but from which I am now nearly recovered. But I am not *sure* that I fell among thieves on that occasion, though from circumstances some have thought so. At all events I lost nothing. I have no suspicion of anything like political hostility in the affair.

    I greatly rejoice that Manchester has deserved so much honour on a recent occasion. Surely this madness of the people must subside ere long. I have the best private ⟨grounds for⟩ believing that it is the King, and not the Queen, who has most reason to complain of injustice and persecution.[3]

    I am afraid that neither I nor Mr. W.[4] are likely to find time for

---

[1] For James Wood, see Introduction, p. 13, n. 2.
[2] The holograph is in the U[nited] M[ethodist] C[hurch] A[rchives], Lake Junalaska, North Carolina].
[3] On December 9, 1820 the radical *Manchester Observer* reported that a Town's meeting held in Manchester to vote an address to the king had concluded by addressing the queen.
[4] Richard Watson (1781–1833), preacher, London (Great Queen Street) circuit, 1818–1821, with special responsibility for overseas missions. He was the principal Methodist theologian of his day, his *Theological Institutes* being published in six parts 1823–1829. Preacher in Methodist New Connexion, 1803–1807.

drawing up a paper on the advantage of the occasional use of a Liturgy in our chapels. If Mr Stephens or Mr. Jackson[1] would do it, in as compendious and pithy a form as possible, I think we could procure its insertion in our magazine, from which it might then be extracted and republished on a quarter-sheet. Its title might properly be, 'A Vindication of that part of the Methodist Discipline, contained in what is called The Plan of Pacification, which recommends the use of the Liturgy in the forenoon service of the Lord's Day'. I shall be anxious to know the particulars of what may occur at your meeting on the 28th. . . . I hope the opposition will not succeed in ousting my friend from his office. In this case it is not men, but measures and principles that are mainly concerned. . . .

27. *From John Stephens*   Manchester, February 1, 1821[2]

. . . I should be happy to give you an account of our affairs since the last Conference; but I have been so much personally concerned in them, that such a history from me would savour too much of egotism.

You will be pleased, however, perhaps, to excuse a few observations, without putting such a construction upon them; especially when I assure you, that, if no Superintendent was ever placed in a more trying situation, none was ever more cordially, steadily, or efficiently supported; and that if any plans have been adopted with wisdom and advantage the Connexion is more indebted to my excellent colleagues and to the sound part of this society than to your humble servant.

The objects we have kept in view are, 1st., to give the sound part of this society a decided ascendency. 2. So to put down the opposition as to disable them from doing mischief. 3. To cure those of them who are worth saving. 4. To take the rest one by one, and crush them when they notoriously commit themselves. The plan is likely to

---

[1] John Stephens (1772–1841), superintendent, and Thomas Jackson, preacher, Manchester circuit, 1819–1821. No article of this description has been traced. Thomas Jackson (1785–1873) was Connexional Editor, 1824–1843; Theological tutor, Richmond College 1842–1861; President, 1838, 1849.

[2] This letter relates to the outcome of Stephens's proceedings during the Peterloo crisis, when he had strenuously contended for order and loyalty in a sermon to the Stranger's Friend Society, and had used the machinery of Methodist discipline to expel large numbers of radicals from society membership, and to prevent political demonstrations by Methodist teachers in the undenominational Sunday schools. There were Methodists who thought him so 'intemperate with his loyalty' that he should be moved, but he became the first superintendent ever to be appointed to the Manchester circuit for a third year. M.C.A. MSS. John Hebblewhite to James Everett, March 15, 1820.

succeed. They are completely at our mercy. We have no long speeches; no moving and seconding wild and absurd resolutions; not a soul of them ventures to propose any thing without first consulting me and obtaining my consent. A few of the ring-leaders have taken the sulks, and seldom attend our meetings; but for this we are not sorry. We have peace; we meet and do our business; and part like men of God. They are down and we intend to keep them down. That they are not anihilated is rather for want of will than power; we wish to be careful in rooting up the tares, le⟨st⟩ we should root up the wheat also. [The] poor people are getting better wages. Provisions are cheap. Their leaders have deceived them in their promises of revolution. They are growing tired of radicalism, and as that dies religion will revive.

Our congregations are good. Methodism stands high among the respectable people. We have had some awakenings and conversions. Nearly every seat is let in the New Chapel.[1] The prayers are well attended. Much good is doing there, and I feel in the building of that Chapel, the introduction of the Liturgy, in our present success and future prospects in that part of the town, a reward for all I have suffered in Manchester.—We are determined to do all that men can do, to promote the work; and we hope our God will not withold his blessing. If we have gone forth weeping, we trust we have sown good seed; and if we are [not] to [be] permitted to reap the harvest, we hope our successors will; and that Manchester Methodism will rise higher than ever.

Mr. Jackson is too valuable a man to be buried in a little country circuit, in times like these. Should I go to London West next year, I should most earnestly wish to have him with me. Can you say a good word, or do a good thing, in that respect?

We have been very quiet here on the Queen's business. Though no men had stronger temptation, yet not one of us has lowered the dignity of the Christian pulpit by mixing up her name with the public Worship; and our numerous congregations prove that such cringing to a wicked faction was unnecessary anywhere. We feel justly offended at the conduct of some of our brethren in that respect. . . .

28. *From Thomas Jackson*   Manchester, March 26, 1821

. . . Our prospect in Manchester is at present very cheering. During the last Quarter we have had an increase in the town and country of fifty members; and have admitted n⟨ear⟩ twice that number on

---

[1] The Grosvenor Street Wesleyan Chapel, opened in 1820, soon attracted the wealthiest congregation in the connexion.

trial. The *radical* feeling has subsided very much among the lower classes in general. The *Observer*,[1] which has so long taught the people to blaspheme Christ, and to curse the King, is discontinued; and the stock and printing utensils of the publisher, were this day to be sold by auction. . . .

29. *From John Stephens*   Manchester, April 21, 1821

. . . Yesterday we had our Missionary Anniversary. The most glorious, they say, that ever was held in Manchester. To say nothing of the previous servises, our collection at the meeting amounted to near £200; including several sums I was privileged to lay on the table; one of which was in a Missionary Box set up in a factory, and which, I am happy to say, several manufacturers have since assured me they will imitate; and one of which amounted to £50!— This morning, we have received several donations; another of which amounts to £50!—The whole, in this district, amounts to several hundreds above any former year.

But what is much better, is, such a religious feeling has been excited, as, I trust, will produce *everlasting* good.

Can you pardon me, if I feel a little too much exillaration at such a result of a meeting, which I considered a sort of *popular* approval, or disapproval, of our moderate but firm, and steady conduct, in times the most trying, which Methodism has endured in Manchester, for, at least, a quarter of a century?—I write in breathless haste, from many engagements; and, perhaps, from feelings which will need the pardon of you and God! . . .

P.S. . . . Since writing the above, I have been obliged to spend hour after [hour] with Kilhamites and Ranters wanting to come to us for the sake of *order*, and *liberty*, and *protection*!—We have nearly all that was respectable among the former; and it seems likely we shall have all who are worth having among the latter. I seldom told you of my unexampled troubles; but I feel a (perhaps too) strong desire to tell you of my triumphs. To you I always think aloud—let this be my apology! Adieu.

30. *From Thomas Preston*[2]   Sowerby Bridge, February 2, 1821

There is a case in this circuit which I wish to state to you, and to

---

[1] The *Manchester Observer*, a radical paper much given to violent attacks on Methodist preachers and discipline, had commenced publication on January 3, 1818.

[2] Thomas Preston (1775–1834), superintendent, Sowerby Bridge circuit, 1820–1823.

request your advice with reference to it, at as early an opportunity as will suit your convenience.

We have a Leader belonging to the Society at Sowerby Bridge whom we cannot get to attend our Leaders' Meetings. He comes to the preaching on the nights the Leaders meet; and then goes away with the congregation. This practice I understand he has followed for several years; and he has been complained of by all the preachers who have travelled in this circuit. Since I came to this place, I have spent several hours at different times, in reasoning with him on this subject, and in endeavouring to impress his duty upon him; but all to no avail. The other Leaders are dissatisfied, and wish me to use means, either to bring him to the Leaders' Meetings, in a general way; or to discontinue him as a Leader. His conduct they say is hurtful to other Leaders who can only occasionally attend, and I am informed it is his practice to oppose almost whatever plans may be agreed upon in a Leaders' Meeting, with reference to financies, and other matters. My own opinion is in unison with that of the Leaders, for in addition to what I have named I have had information that his conduct sometimes is immoral, but I cannot get any clear proofs that this is the case, or the business would soon be ended. Now though I believe we should be better without him, unless he would act otherwise than he does, yet I was not certain whether I could in conjunction with the Leaders' Meeting, discontinue him as a Leader, unless some case of immorality was proved against him. When I have looked at the Rules of our Society, and notice[d], the duty of a Leader there expressed to be among other things, to meet the Preacher and Stewards etc., I have thought whether he might be dropped as a Leader, in the same way as we exclude members for non-attendance at their class. But as no similar case has occurred in my own observation, nor do I remember to have heard of one of the same kind, I thought before I took any further step in this matter, I would state the case to you and solicit the favour of your advice with reference to it. I might have added that the greater part of the members of his class are much dissatisfied with [h]is conduct in the same particular of which I complain. . . .

[Endorsed] *[To Thomas Preston]*
Answered February 8 1821.
Under the circumstances it seems right and expedient, as well as legal, to take measures of discipline against the non-attending Leader.

Give him written notice, that unless he come to the next Meeting and promise to attend as regularly as he can, he will be suspended:

and that, if after a month's suspension, he still persist in non-attendance, you will remove him from office for habitual breach of the Rule.

31. *From William Griffith*   Hungerford, February 9, 1821
I am under the necessity of troubling you once more, to beg an answer to the following questions.

How far is a person considered by law a trustee of a chapel who has not signed the deed but whose name is inserted. And is it not necessary to have our chapels enrolled, as well made over for our use, by the donor?

I wish for information upon these points. As scarcely a chapel in this circuit has more than one Trustee who has signed the deed. And as one of our chapels (nearly free from debt) and where we have the largest society, has not a single living Trustee who has accepted the trust, and one person who was named in the former deed, but not now a member of society is likely to be the legal heir to the property, I have proposed to have a new Deed, with fresh Trustees. Can any of the forenamed persons now sign the deed and then make it over to other persons? Or what is best to be done? With respect to enrolling the deed I have hitherto considered it needful *but our friends here say they have have legal advice and it is not necessary, though the Conference is not to be blamed by* so doing. And upon this principle they seem disposed to act in order to save expences: But I will endeavour by your direction to do what is right. Mr. Pocock has made a separation at Malborough but hitherto has done us no real injury, as but few of our people have left us, except the Local Preacher of whom I wrote before.

P.S. I see by the printed schedule sent me I am to insert the Class Money and Quarterage for Tickets. It is rather difficult to do it in this Circuit as each society brings a stated sum. So that the principal *friends* in each *Society* are obliged to make up the deficiency of each quarter, but the whole number average about 3/6 or rather more quarterly. They are willing to pay the dificiency; but not so willing to give more for class money weekly nor perhaps to give more at the renewing of their Tickets. Must I not state what is brought to the Quarter board by each Society to make it appear what is produced by the Circuit?

[*Endorsed*] [*To W. Griffith*]
Answered March 21, 1821.
I *think*:
1. A person is in law a Trustee, whose name is in the conveyance,

whether he sign the deed or not:— he has a legal interest in the property, though not compellable to fulfil the trusts.
2. Enrollment *in all cases* is necessary.
3. The persons to whom the property is conveyed by a Trust Deed legally executed and enrolled may *at any time* sign the Deed, and convey it to others, subject to the provisions, if any, contained in the deed itself on that point.
Better, before he act, to consult a Lawyer. —Recommend Mr. Sutcliffe.
Refer to the Chairman as to the Schedule.

32. *From John Williams II*[1]   Llandysil, February 5, 1821

I understand that our worthy Chairman has informed you that my wife keeps a little shop[2]—and also that he received your answer on that head, but I should suppose that you was not informed what my reason was in giving her consent to go on in that way which I shall endeavour to do. 1. Seeing other of our Welsh preachers wifes doing something towards making the two ends to meet, each doing what they are most capaple of. 2.—Thinking that the conference would not be against us, as Welsh preachers to do something in an honest way, as our cause in Wales is so very low and so far from keeping the few Welsh Preachers as there is, and although the conference do so much for us every year. 3. Judging that our case in Wales calls for it in a special manner, seeing no hopes that Wales will ever be able to support her own preachers and for that reason will never be able to have a greater number of preachers, and while they will have no greater number the cause can never prosper. 4. Because our present plan is a deal to[o] expensive for Wales, that may be seen in the first place if you was but to look unto Wales and see so many different sects and denominations which are numerous and respectable. 2 To see the poverty of our members and hearers in general, we have no able nor rich men in Wales, such as are in England, men that can give larg[e]ly not only quarterly and monthly but likewise

[1] John Williams II (d. 1834, *aet.* 45), superintendant, Cardigan circuit, 1818–1821.
[2] The accusation of the chairman of the District had been that Williams himself kept the shop, and was using every device to postpone meeting the remonstrances of his colleagues. Bunting had no option but to insist that shopkeeping was incompatible with a preacher's separation to the itinerant ministry. Bunting had reported in 1802 that 'the Welsh mission prospers amazingly' (M.C.A. MSS. Jabez Bunting to George Marsden, December 30, 1802), but it did not sustain its first promise, and in this letter Wesleyan Methodism can be seen taking its place as the smallest of the Welsh denominations.

weekly, but the poor and needy. 3. Because of the notion they have in Wales to support the cause; if some of them were to know that we get what we get they would withhold from us what they now give. 4. The great difficulty that still remains in Wales of about four to five hundred pounds every year after receiving largely from conference, and what would the difficiency be, if this help was to be taken from us. 5. Because we have too few preachers by one half in Wales, and on the present plan it is impossible for us to have more because more cannot be supported, and we have no strong circuits so that we might [send?] large families to, and if we had, we have no young men to send to the poor circuits. 6. And every one that knows the alphabet a little plainer than another go to England; they leave their own country and brethren after bringing them under a burden of near twenty two thousand pounds—that is of Chapel dept [debt]— 7. Seeing some of our Chapels sold, others shut up, and a great number of Societies gone to nothing, and if the Welsh preachers are still lessoned it might be as well for us all to leave Wales, yea and go further than England or else the disgrace will take hold of us. I believe that these reasons will be sufficient and shew that the present plan of Methodism is to[o] expensive for Wales—but if the conference which has bore so much owing to our poverty would allow us, or adopt some other method so that each Preacher might do something to maintain their families this at once would relieve our cause in the Principality and likewise in a great measure lessen the burden that now is so heavy on the conference. Viewing things in this light, I thought it no harm to give consent. I had not the least intention to leave off the ministry. After you consider our case— according to the above statement—and think it an exempt case, I should feel obliged if you would [let] that matter stand as it is till next conference, as I don't interfere with any thing but my circuit, and you may be assured that no part of my duty in the circuit is neglected. Be pleased to write me an answer as soon as you can as our chairman seems anxious to hear from me. . . .

33. *From George Cubitt*[1]   Boston, February 10, 1921

You will much oblige me by your opinion on a subject, arising out of a regulation made at the Conference in 1811 (see *Minutes* V. 3. p. 224) by which Superintendents are required, twice in the year to institute a strict enquiry into the moral character and official proceedings of the Classleaders. This enquiry is to be made in the

[1] George Cubitt (1791–1850), superintendent, Boston circuit, 1820–1822. Assistant Connexional Editor, 1836–1842: Editor, 1842–1850.

Leaders' Meeting. On the importance of a measure which so evidently tends to preserve in a state of at least comparative purity, a body of persons, whose spiritual welfare almost identifies itself with that of our Societies generally, I need not say anything—and if the expression 'Leaders' Meeting' had not been inserted in the Minute, I should not have felt any difficulty in carrying it into effect.

In *most* circuits, there will probably be two or three places in which Leaders' Meetings *can* be held,—with several in which the contrary will be the case and whilst in very many circuits, perhaps by far the greater number of places will have but one or two Leaders.

Could an effective Leaders' Meeting be held in every place the very letter of this important minute could be observed; even now perhaps it could thus be observed, by the preacher meeting the *one* Leader, and the two constituting a meeting; but it seems to me to be the spirit of the rule, that not merely an official enquiry should be made, but a public one; and this publicity of the investigation appears to be one of the most valuable parts of the minute.

I have thought, could the investigation be at a Quarterly Meeting, the proceeding would in its operation be powerfully and extensively beneficial. The Leaders would then expect a regularly returning examination, the same as the Local Preachers, and the expectation would I think be productive of much good.

I see that something of the kind is required as to Local Preachers— that in those circuits in which regular Local Preachers' Meetings cannot be held, candidates are to be proposed to the Quarterly Meeting.

Shall I do right, to instance in a particular case, if in this Circuit, in which we have between twenty and thirty Societies, and not more than two places (Boston and another) in which we can have an effective Leaders' Meeting, I have the required investigation at a regular Quarterly Meeting?

[Endorsed] [To George Cubitt]
Answered February 24, [1821]
I do not think it adviseable to have Leaders examined in Quarterly Meetings.

Where there are two Leaders, there may be a Leaders' Meeting and the Rule be *literally* observed.

Where but one Leader, the *Spirit* will be kept, if the Preacher do it in private.[1]

---

[1] This judgment should be compared with that in the Liverpool case, *infra.* no. 71.

34. *From Frederick Calder*[1]   Brighton, March 5, 1821

... The dissenters here are preparing petitions to oppose Mr. Brougham's Education Bill.[2] They invited me to a meeting on the business. I am apprehensive our people will take no active steps in the affair. I mean our committee for guarding our priviledges, but I should wish to know if it would be thought imprudent on my part if I gave my sanction to the petition or petitions. That I am opposed to the bill I candidly confess and though no enemy to the Church I am *opposed to a bill* which I judge will be a powerful instrument in the hands of a persecuting clergyman to annoy the consciences of (by bringing under his power to a certain extent) the lower classes of the people. Should you have a few moments to spare and give me your opinion on the above you will greatly oblige. . . .

35. *From James King and others, Stewards and Leaders of Carlisle.*
                    Carlisle, March 9, 1821

We have been sometime anxiously waiting for information from our Committee of Privileges respecting Mr. Brougham's Education Bill; being repeatedly solicited by the Dissenters to unite in preparing to oppose its probably not designed but evidently persecuting spirit. We feel our warm attachment to our parent Church, but know also that the Great Shepherd has sheep not of this fold, who are equally entitled to his protection and our love; and who must necessarily suffer if the Bill should pass. We believe general benefit is expected to be consequent upon it, but should every anticipated advantage be realized, the 'general benefit' must be limited to the Establishment as being the sole instrument of effecting it; and to the male children, no provision being made for the girls. And all this expected good must accrue from it at the expense of the Dissenters being compelled to support the instruction of other Creeds and Catechisms while their own is neglected.

The Bill is also very inaccurate in its statements of schools and scholars: in Carlisle and its vicinity we have ten times the number of schools and scholars than is therein asserted; Whitehaven and other neighbouring towns are similarly represented.

This is our knowledge we have of the Bill and lest we should err,

---

[1] Frederick Calder (d. 1851, *aet.* 65), superintendent, Brighton circuit, 1818–1821.

[2] Henry Brougham's proposals, which had to be dropped, provided for the building of parish schools at state expense, for the teachers to be members of the Church of England, and for the clergy to control the education, which should be based on the Bible, but should not include the catechism.

believing our Committee have some cause for their silence, we write for your counsel, that we may either give a reason for being dormant or awake with the universal alarm it has excited in our city. Waiting your kind advice and direction. . . .

[*Endorsed*]—Answered March 15, 1821. *Addressed to Mr.* [*Joseph*] *Womersley*.[1] Our Committee of Privileges does not view the Bill in so *alarming* a light. Party interests and petty considerations should not hinder so great an object. Particular clauses it is desirable to have omitted or modified; and to this the Committee will attend in due time. But as to opposing the Bill *in toto* and *limine*, this would *on our part* be unbecoming and improper. Dissenters are opposed to all *Religious Establishments* and of course to every form of National Instruction connected at all with an Establishment. But the Methodists as a Body have not adopted such views. What we ultimately may do must be done by ourselves and not in common with them.

36. *From Thomas Bersey, John Wevill, and W. O. Croggon*[2]

Liskeard, March 16, 1821

You will excuse the liberty we take on this occasion to address you for your advice relative to the line of conduct we should adopt concerning Mr. Brougham's bill for the education of the poor.

The dissenting minister in the town has just called to request our aid in getting petitions signed against the proposed measure. Though we are decidedly of opinion that Mr. Brougham's Bill will not answer the design intended and that there are clauses very objectional yet we are rather reluctant to exert ourselves in this matter, having no directions from the committee for guarding our religious privileges to get petitions. Next Friday is the day fixed for meeting on this business. If you would be pleased to signify (by return of post if convenient) the way we should act it will greatly oblige. . . .

[*Endorsed*] [*To Thomas Bersey and others*]

Answer to *this* letter [March 20, 1821]

Our Sub-Committee thought that under all circumstances we, as Methodists, ought not to unite with the systematic dissenters in opposition to the *principle* of Mr. Brougham's Bill; and that the

---

[1] Joseph Womersley (d. 1851, *aet.* 81), superintendent, Carlisle, circuit, 1819–1821.

[2] Thomas Bersey (d. 1857, *aet.* 78), superintendent, and John Wevill (d. 1874, *aet.* 74) and Walter Oke Croggon (d. 1854, *aet.* 62), preachers, Liskeard circuit, 1820–1822.

modification of its *clauses* will be better effected privately than by petitions to Parliament. The Committee will attend to that matter in proper time. In this opinion I concur. The rigid dissenters act consistently in this business; but we cannot as a body go to their length on any such questions, as we fundamentally differ on some points connected with the line of argument which they pursue. If we ultimately act it must be by our own committee and on our own neutral ground. The advantage of anything like a national education, connected with principles in religion sound in the main, is not to be sacrificed for minor considerations. This letter [is] private.[1]

37. *From Robert Melson*[2]   Pickering, April 4, 1821

I have been a Methodist Preacher almost 18 years, and have often had occasion to keep a horse for the use of the Circuit, but never was charged with Horse Tax before now.

This morning I have been called upon by the tax gatherers who have demanded £2. 17. 6. as Horse Duty and 10/- for an occasional groom. The horse we keep is the property of the Circuit and is kept of necessity for to carry us to distant places.

I have called upon the magistrate here, who is one of the Commissioners, by way of appealing against the duty, and *he* informed me that our case is *doubtful*, but he said we could state the case to the 12 judges and get their opinion for 40 *shillings*. But, Sir, I thought it best to state the case to you as one of the members of our Committee of Privileges, and you would have the goodness to informe me whether we can claim our exemption or no.

Our circuit is poor, and we have not £3. 7.6. to spare, and therefore we are not disposed to pay it unless the law demands it. . . .

[*Endorsed*]—[*To Robert Melson*]
Answered April 9.
Not a question for the Committee who guard our *Religious* privileges. Consult, if thought necessary, a legal gentleman, and act accordingly. From all I have heard, I think he is liable,—certainly so, if the horse be ever lent, or used for private convenience.

---

[1] In a similar reply to an enquiry from the superintendent of the Diss circuit, Bunting added, 'On the Catholic Bill, we may act individually as we think fit. But we should not meddle with that difficult *State*-measure, in our public or collective character.' (M.C.A. MSS. Wm. Hinson to Jabez Bunting, March 26, 1821: appended draft of Bunting's reply, March 28, 1821.)

[2] Robert Melson, superintendent, Pickering circuit, 1818–1821. Disappeared from ministry between 1847 and 1853.

38. *J. Sedgwick*[1]   Easingwold, April 10, 1921

A number of very ungodly persons, in this town and neighbourhood, entertaining the idea that we cannot keep our doors at our Love Feasts, apply for admittance without any note from the preacher, and if refused by the door keeper, they then enter by force. This greatly curtails our Christian liberty, for though when in the chapel they do not behave in such away as that we can take hold of them by Law, yea [yet] there are evident singnes of *contempt*; ten, fifteen, or twenty come in this way every quarter, and come, *I am sure*, with designe to show to others, that we cannot keep them out. Now, Sir, what must I do in this case; is it true that according to an act made in the Reigne of Queen Elizabeth, we cannot keep out persons who are not members of our society. . . .?

[Appended]—[To J. Sedgwick]
Answered May 10.

No *legal* remedy, as to Meetings for Worship. All the Toleration Acts require free access when demanded.

But you may either

1. When persons not members refuse after request to withdraw turn the Lovefeast immediately into a meeting for Prayer, reading the Scriptures, or Preaching—which might after a few times weary out and shame the troublers:

Or 2. Make no stir at all, but quietly admit the few obstinate for a season hoping that prayer and patience will subdue them.

The former plan seems necessary, if the evil be not merely temporary.

39. *From John Furness*[2]   Sleaford, April 21, 1821

[Has had a sort of stroke on his rounds and much other illness—additional assistance is really necessary] . . . No town is in a more *critical* situation than Sleaford. We have the high *Church party:* the high Huntingtonian party;[3] my Lady Huntington's and the Particular Baptists, all are striving to undermine our cause. We have the Ranters [who] are also taking the advantage on my absence on account of my affliction—and to add to my troubles one of the best Local

---

[1] John Sedgwick (d. 1852, *aet.* 73), superintendent of Easingwold circuit, 1818–1821. His letter concludes with a reference to the Toleration Act of 1689, mistakenly attributed to the reign of Elizabeth.

[2] John Furness (1760–1830), superintendent, Sleaford circuit, 1819–1822.

[3] Followers of William Huntington (1745–1813), coal-heaver and high Calvinist itinerant preacher, who subscribed himself S.S. (*i.e.* Sinner Saved).

Preachers ... has now turned Ranter and his lifting up his heel against us. ...

[*Endorsed*]—Answered April 23.

Will call out a regular preacher if necessary, but recommend that he should hire Spink, if the Superintendent approve, or Tatham.[1]

40. *From William Beal*[2]   Exeter, May 3, 1821

I do not desire to force myself unnecessarily on your notice, nor to add to the variety of business that comes before you. But I do most respectfully beg your attention to the following case; and as from the highest authority, I ask you, what is, and what is not, our constitution.

In a circuit in the West two preachers have lived, and do live together in peace. The one wished to remove, the other to remain. At the Quarterly Meeting it was resolved by a large majority (only *four* lifted up their hands against it) that it was desirable that the one who wished to remain should remove.

Suppose it should be said by him—this is not the will of the people; that, as the people contribute to the support of their preachers, so their opinion ought to be taken by all the Leaders of classes; that no Leader should vote at a Quarterly Meeting untill this is done; and that, when it is done, he should vote not according to his own judgment, if it should be in opposition to the majority of his class; but according to theirs! Is this *Wesleyan* Methodism? The question is not, whether, when a Leader cannot easily make up his mind on a given subject and has in his class aged, and judicious persons, it would be prudent (in secret) to take their opinion and advice theron, and to make any discretional use therof. Nor whether all our members have the most free access to our Quarterly meetings, and there, liberty to express their opinion on the business of the meeting. But whether the government of Methodism as far as the people are concerned, is in their expressed opinion whether at their class—or other meetings—by which the Leaders and Stewards *must be* directed—or in the deliberative judgment of the official persons in the Leaders' and Quarterly Meetings.

The former has been stated to be just and right and the privilege of the people,—and many members in consequence therof, have

---

[1] Bunting himself became increasingly loath to permit the engagement of 'hired local preachers', a practice compromising to the status of the ministry in the eyes of the flock. Cf. M.C.A. MSS. Endorsement to W. Clough to Jabez Bunting, October 21, 1844.

[2] William Beal (1785–1872), superintendent, Exeter circuit, 1819–1821.

F

attempted at the conclusion of their class meetings, to turn them into deliberative and legislative assemblies with a view no doubt directly to oppose the decisions of the Quarterly Meeting, and have refused to pay their yearly collections, and class monies untill this is done. A Leaders' Meeting has been held on the subject, where all were unanimously of opinion, that the matter must be prudently yet firmly opposed. A deputation was to wait on the person on other matters, who had made this assertion, but this was introduced.

He still retains his opinion: the language of the deputation is, we must know speedily, and from undoubted authority, what is the truth [on] this subject. You, Sir, can furnish ⟨th⟩at undoubted and unquestionable authority; and not to slight the worthy chairman of the District, whom none respects more than I do, but to obtain a decision from the very highest authority, an appeal is made to you, that peace may be preserved; will you favor me with a speedy reply? The matter it is true appears quite plain to me—the advice I have given has been acted on—but I will not dispute with the persons immediately concerned where there is no umpire to decide—lest it should lead to the disgraceful issue of quarrels among those who teach others to live in peace, and to love each other. . . .

[*Endorsed*]—[*To William Beal*]
Answered May 10.
Quarterly Meeting may express its opinions and wishes; and the Conference will give to such representations what weight they deserve. Further than this our constitution knows not. The more quietly such matters are managed in the Circuits, the less the Preachers say *out of Conference*, in general the better.

As to taking the *sense of the people* in classes or otherwise except in Quarterly Meetings, it is unmethodistical, absurd, and mischievous. Our system is not democracy. The interests of the people it substantially provides for, but not by a plan of universal suffrage, than which nothing could be more fatal to real liberty, whether in church or state. The Leader who allows such discussions in his class, forgets one of his prime duties.

Advise all parties under present circumstances to agree in leaving the Station altogether to Conference for this year. A preacher lessens himself who *wishes* to stay against the wishes of any considerable portion of the Society—or allows himself to be made the occasion of faction or disquiet.[1]

---

[1] William Beal and his assistant preacher, Joseph Sanders, were both removed from the Exeter circuit by the Conference of 1821, Sanders after only one year's service there.

41. *From Thomas Heywood*[1]   Littleport near Ely, June 7, 1821

According to the request of last Conference (see *Minutes*, page 69) on Saterday the 2nd instant, (it being a pleasure fair day) I took my stand in order to preach the gospel on a large stone in the publick street, at the woolpack corner, about 100 yards from the market place in the City of Ely. A considerable number of people were soon collected together, who from first to last were very serious and attentive. But while I was praying the first time, Mr. Bacon the Constable, came and interrupted me, and commanded me to leave off. I asked him what authority he had to interrupt me. He showed me his staff. I told him as I wished him well, I would advise him not to interrupt me without a warrant from a magistrate, for if he did he would bring himself into trouble. He then left me. When I had almost finished my sermon he came again, saying he had orders to take me. I wished him to wait till I had finished my discourse, and with (appearant) reluctance he did. He wished me to go with him. I said I would not go without a warrant, unless he took me by force. He laid hold of my coat and draged me with such violence, I thought he would have torn it to pieces. Indeed I believe he did tear it, for I found it torn afterwards, and I do not know it was torn before. I said to the people 'you are all witnesses that he is taking me by force.' They said 'We are witnesses'. He brought me before the magistrate (Sir Henry Bate Dudley a Prebendary of the Ely Cathedral), who asked me by what authority I had been acting as I had. I said by the authority of the Methodist Conference. That I was a Methodist itinerant preacher, and the Conference requested me to preach in the open air occationally, and Joseph Butterworth Esq.[2] and a number of gentlemen in London had formed themselves into a committee, and would protect me in the same. 'I do not care', said he, 'what there is in London, but you shall not come here to cause a tumult, especially on such a day as this.' I said, 'I have not caused any tumult, nor has there been any tumult, nor did I design to cause any; but I see sinners go on in sin, and'—'What', said he, 'are you to be a judge?' 'Well,' said I, 'I see

---

[1] Thomas Heywood, second preacher, Ely circuit, 1820–1821; superintendent, 1821–1822. Excluded from ministry 1826.

[2] Joseph Butterworth (1770–1826), founder of the famous law publishing firm, pressed Conference to found the Committee of Privileges in 1803, and was one of its first members (*Life of Bunting*, i, 230). A stout defender of the Protestant constitution, he was independent M.P. for Coventry, 1812–1818, and for Dover, 1820–1826. Thomas Allan, the connexional solicitor, canvassed actively for him at Dover (M.C.A. Thos. Allan's MSS. Thos. Allan to Joseph W. Allan, February 20, 1820). Butterworth's political and legal advice was much in demand by the Committee of Privileges, and he was closely connected with influential evangelical philanthropic circles.

sinners go on in sin and I feel for them, and wish to be instrumental in doing them some good'. He said, 'you shall not do them good that way. Where do you live?' I replied, 'I live at Chatteris'. 'Well I will give you your choice, you shall either go to prison or leave Ely immediately'. I said, 'I am appointed to preach in the Methodist Chapel tomorrow morning, I shall leave Ely after I have preached.' 'I have nothing to do with the Methodist Chapel,' said he, 'I suppose it is licensed according to law. Will you not go to yonder place again to cause a tumult?' I said, 'I am now going to a friend's house, and after I have preached in the Methodist Chapel tomorrow morning I shall leave Ely'. 'Well,' said he, 'if you cause any more tumults, I will put you in prison'. He then let me go, but told the Constable to take care I caused no more tumults. As far as I can learn, the constable interrupted me the first time without being ordered, then went and informed the magistrate, who gave him orders to apprehend me. When he apprehended me, he said he had orders from a magistrate to do so; and when he brought me before the magistrate, he said 'This is the man that has been collecting the people together.' Some of our principal friends have particularly requested me to write to you immediately, to know if a constable can according to law, at the request of a magistrate without a warrant make me his prisoner, for preaching the gospel in the publick street and if he cannot, whether the committee that is appointed to guard our privileges, will suffer it to pass by unnoticed. Please to write soon. . . .

[*Endorsed*]—[*To T. Heywood*]
Answered by Mr. Blanshard, June 9, 1821.
Commends his zeal. Advises him to desist at Ely, since not *allowed* there—but to try elsewhere, where no opposition may be made—to take no notice of the Constable, etc. Not to mention Mr. Butterworth or the Committee, etc.

42. *From John Davis*[1]   Macclesfield, June 21, 1821
[Will Bunting preach their Sunday School sermon during or after Conference?]

I need not say to you that our school here is properly a *Methodist* Sunday School, and at present it promises fair to be a blessing to our society—nor need I tell you what our friends have still to contend with—The Macclesfield Sunday School—[2] for which every effort is

---

[1] John Davis [or Davies] senior (1780–1852), preacher, Macclesfield circuit, 1819–1820, superintendent, 1820–1821.

[2] The Macclesfield Sunday School was founded on an undenominational basis in 1796, under the leadership of a Methodist, John Whitaker. When funds were

still made to keep it going—besides our friends are considerably in arrears in consequence of building—and under all circumstances your kind compliance with our request, will, I am persuaded, materially serve the cause of Methodism in Macclesfield.

Through mercy we have had a peaceable prosperous good year— our congregations very good, and our Societies have been regularly increasing. . . .

Mr. Lane and his party have still an existence, but they are so lost in their own obscurity that we seldom hear a word about them. They still have their regular preaching, and now call themselves 'Protesting Methodists'[1] . . . .

43. *From P. C. Turner*[2]   Hereford, June 30, 1821

I gladly avail myself of the permission you have kindly granted me by Mr. Tayler to lay before you a more particular account of the state of Herefordshire. It is gratifying to me to know that you approve of the plan of my labouring here, as it forms the height of my wishes to have the approbation of God and of my respected fathers in the ministry.

You have heard, I expect, Sir, that I came into these parts by the kind interferance of Mr. Irving and some other friends, who pitied the state of this county, and thought I might be made useful. I have laboured in conjunction with my friend Mr. Adams, and have taken the appointments of the circuit regularly with him—adding to our list such places as circumstances would allow; this appeared to be the most eligible plan for several reasons for permanent good, and it has been pursued with advantage. Although the tone of religious feeling has been considerably raised in some parts of the county, yet it still presents to the pious mind cause for mourning—the minds of the inhabitants forming a sad contrast to the richness of its scenery and the fertility of its soil; they are generally behind other parts of England in *mental cultivation* and evidence a stupid indifference to almost everything *like religion*. Methodism is little known and *much despised*. The Baptists and Independents have their missionaries

---

raised to build the 'large school' which was opened in 1813, there were disputes over the continuance of Sabbath writing lessons, as a result of which Anglicans and Wesleyans withdrew their support, and opened rival schools. Whitaker left the Methodists, continued the writing lessons, and made the school one of the great English Sunday schools, even obtaining royal patronage.

[1] Probably the successors of the revivalists who separated from the Wesleyan society early in the century, and published their rules as Christian Revivalists in 1803.

[2] Philip C. Turner, became preacher 1821. Governor of the Theological Institution, 1841–1846. Ceased to be recognized, 1846, after proceedings upon an immorality charge.

in several villages, and some pious persons in the Church are zealous in the establishment of Sunday Schools and other good works. Much, *very* much, remains to be done, many important stations are yet unoccupied and present to the laborious minister a stimulus to exertion and a prospect of success. Calvanism generally prevails among professors, who generally appear to view our doctrines as *dangerous* and stand at a distance from us.

We have now on our plan 20 places regularly visited, so that by preaching almost every night in the week (Saturday excepted) we each of us see most of the places once a month, and one or two of them have preaching *weekly*, we have on the evenings we have no appointment gone to places not yet entered on the plan. We have preached at several promising places and could at many more if we had time. Leominster,[1] a large and populous market town containing it is thought 4000 souls, might be advantageously occupied as its neighbourhood is generally without the gospel and several villages are at a convenient distance from it: we visit it regularly, but our stay is so short, the house in which we preach so small, etc., etc., that it does not appear that very extensive good can be effected till a minister can devote a great part of his time to it and the vicinity; several parties of dissenters are there but *none* of them are doing much good, indeed they are all sinking. We have about 15 members. The town of Bromyard about 14 miles from Hereford and about the same distance from Leominster, has never been regularly supplied with preachers; I know of no means for the religious benefit of the people but a dissenting place of worship, where there is a resident minister. Weobly, about 11 miles from H. and 10 from Leominster, a small market town with perhaps 800 or more inhabitants has no means of religious instruction but from an Independent Missionary who has lately gone there under the patronage of Lady Southampton;[2] this is perhaps one of the most *unlikely* to be successful, as nearly all the houses belong to a nobleman, who from political motives receives no rent, or a very trifle, and who is I understand an opposer of the Gospel. Many villages are yet without any public means of Grace save the mere moral lessons heard from the preachers in the churches, and these are very *badly attended*. I am frequently distrest when I look around at the inefficiency of the means for the benefit of the people. I labour and am willing to do as much as I can for their good; some success I am thankful to have observed, but this is comparatively very small; thousands are perishing, and 'no man cares their souls to save'. It

---

[1] Leominster did not become head of a Wesleyan circuit till 1873.
[2] Francis Isabella (d. 1838, *aet*. 60), 2nd da. of Lord Robert Seymour; widow of George Ferdinand, 2nd Baron Southampton.

would perhaps be unseemly in me to point out to you, Sir, the plan that might be advantageously adopted; suffice to say that there is plenty of work, with prospects of success for 2 or 3 zealous men of God. . . .

44. *From John Hustus Adams*[1]   Hereford, July 4, 1821

Feeling deeply interested myself in the moral and spiritual cultivation of this county, I rejoice that it has not been unnoticed by *you*, while contemplating the state of this country at large, in order to the evangelization of all its parts that as a whole it may be the Kingdom of our God. This country (as you know full well) is nearly half a century behind some others in mental, moral and spiritual cultivation. This City imbraces many teachers but few spiritual ones. The Establishment can boast of the Rev. H. Gipps,[2] a rich, pious, and zealous man of moderate talent, but whose preaching is strongly shaded with the sombre hue of Calvinism. ⟨His church?⟩ is well attended, and many of his hearers feelingly exclaim, 'Oh wretched man that I am,' etc., which they think the summit of Christian experience. Lady Huntingdon's cause is rather on the decline. The Independent cause appears to have remained *in statu quo* for many years. No Baptists, and only a few Quakers. Methodism was so low three years ago that 20 or 30 formed a Sunday evening's congregation; we have now about 50 in society and a respectable congregation. But as it is now *in its infancy* much will depend upon the zeal, piety and prudence of the preacher who is stationed here next year. Leominster and Bromyard are important places, the former 13 miles from Hereford and 10 from Ludlow, the latter 14 from Ledbury and 14 from H. In Leominster we preach once a fortnight in the week evenings and either ourselves or our local Brethren visit every Sunday. I have not been able to find any man in Bromyard at all friendly to us. If a young man of talent, piety and zeal were placed at Leominster and a very judicious man at Hereford as Superintendent, under the blessing of God much good might be done. The present success of Methodism in this Circuit is viewed with jealousy, A preacher a few miles from Hereford has endeavoured to dissuade some from joining us, by declaring '*Class Meeting[s] to be of the Devil*' and that it was a shame for us to receive so much money from the poor. But calling upon him last week, he acknowledged he had acted improperly. Lady Southampton lives near Hereford, has preaching in her own house,

[1] John Hustus Adams (1788–1846), sole preacher in Hereford circuit, 1818–1821.
[2] Henry Gipps, Vicar of SS. Peter and Owen, Hereford, from 1824 till his death in 1832.

and when able reads a sermon herself, and often blends with it some remarks of her own. I have had several interviews with her Ladyship: I think her deeply pious, but strongly tinctured with the pecularitis of Calvin. She and Mr. Gipps unite their influence to disseminate the seeds of Calvinism. So that Methodism here has to contend with the profane, who openly attack us, and with Calvinism, which aided by title and wealth secretly opposes us. But if Mr. Turner who has favour in the eyes of the circuit, be stationed here, with a *judicious Superintendent* I then trust Methodism will hold the same prominancy of station in this county that it holds in others.

On Thursday week three persons will appear before the Sessions charged with disturbing us when engaged in religious worship on April 25th. If we could have some help from London we should be very thankful as we expect a strong influence against us, both from Clergy and Magistrates. I have written 3 letters to Mr. Blanshard on the subject, but as yet he has left us to our own resources. I confess my feelings at the present moment with regard to this business are not enviable; much of the weight of this affair rests upon my shoulders. If we fail, our feelings will be accutely mortifying. I did expect help from the Committee of Privileges, but hitherto I have been most compleatly disappointed. . . .

45. *From E. B. Lloyd*[1]   Cambridge, July 13, 1821

[His opinions as to the next preacher for Cambridge]

1st. I think he should be a *respectable man*, rather than a good *preacher*. If he would assist the funds of Methodism he must have occasional intercourse with some very respectable Dissenting and Church families, as well as University men.

2nd. He must have a small family, as there are only two small chambers in the house.

3rd. He must be healthy and able to walk 5 or 7 miles after preaching occasionally, winter or summer. This is very unpleasant but necessary.

4thly. If he have been in but *middling* circuits, so much the better, he will then feel less inconveniencies of this *poor* circuit; for it is certainly a *very poor* circuit, and would not be suitable for a man who has enjoyed many of the comforts of life.

And 5th. one that can turn financier, for unless there be some contrivance the resources will prove deficient and I know not a person in the Society that can advance a loan of £5. You will smile at my

[1] Edward B. Lloyd (d. 1823, *aet.* 32), sole preacher, Cambridge circuit, 1819–1821.

enumeration of particulars, but I am convinced the nearer you can come to them the better . . . .[1]

46. *From Thomas Roberts*[2] Raithby Hall, near Spilsby, July 16, 1821

Though I hope, by divine permission, to be at Manchester at the commencement of the Conference, I feel it my duty to trouble you thus early, soliciting your attention to a subject which will be best served by the Stationing Committee. I allude to the state of Methodism in Lincolnshire. Having been a few weeks in these parts, I have had many opportunities for observing the interest which our cause universally obtains. The Missionary Meetings, as you may hear from Mr. Watson and Mr. Marsden, were not only well attended, but zealously supported, and the pecuniary exertions through the year have been equal to those of any District in the Connection. Such a field for Methodism cannot be found in England—this extensive county is open to us, with scarcely any sect preoccupying town or village. Nothing seems to be wanting under the blessing of God, to make our conquest universal and complete,[3] but such instruments as are qualified to effect a consummation so devoutly to be wished; and surely, if the Brethren will but candidly turn their attention to this great object, I do think the importance of this District, in its present most favourable and inviting circumstances, will induce them to make every possible effort to appoint such preachers as will, in all probability, raise, establish and extend the interests of Methodism.

I take the liberty of offering this suggestion, being presented by the pleasing appearances around me, without adverting to this country as giving birth to our venerable Founder,[4] or being the scene of the long, zealous and successful labors of that late, most pious and blessed friend and patron of Methodism, Mr. Brackenbury,[5] whose memory will ever be dear to all in these parts. . . .

---

[1] Conference found to succeed Lloyd not a single paragon, but (for the first time) two preachers.

[2] Thomas Roberts (d. 1832, *aet.* 66), former preacher, for many years supernumerary at Bath.

[3] Lincolnshire became one of the strongest Methodist areas, despite persistent friction between Methodists and Ranters who reaped a second, and smaller, harvest from the Wesleyan mission field.

[4] John Wesley, b. Epworth Rectory, 1703.

[5] Robert Carr Brackenbury (1752–1818), one of Wesley's assistant preachers 1784, and occasionally his travelling companion. A county magistrate and a large Lincolnshire landlord. Raithby Hall, Spilsby, was his residence.

47. *From James Gill*[1]   Tunbridge Wells, July 25, 1821

From the conversation I had with you in London on the dissemination of religious tracts, the encouragement you gave me to write my thoughts on the subject and the immediate insertion of my observations in the *Magazine*, convince me that your heart is in the great and good work of distributing, extensively, these silent preachers of salvation. I shall feel obliged by your communicating the following observations to the Conference, and supporting them with your influence and arguments if you consider them worth attention,[2] which I trust will be the means of the Conference taking up the subject ardently, reviewing their former minutes on the distribution of tracts, and of inducing them to establish a Tract Society in every circuit on a systematical and permanent basis, that would by the blessing of the Almighty be beneficial to thousands of immortal souls. It is an observation of our venerable founder that the preacher must have a hand in everything connected with the welfare of Methodism, and without the preacher nothing can be permanent, or prosper. If the preachers generally take up the subject of distributing religious tracts systematically, they will be widely disseminated. And I know my fathers and Brethren are ready to every good work, and that their hearts burn with zeal to extend the Redeemer's kingdom in the world. The pecuniary embarrassments of our Connexion the last few years, the glorious object of sending missionaries to the heathen, and various other things have occupied our attention, and caused us partly to overlook the design of former Conferences to cover the land with our tracts. I say partly, because the distribution of tracts has never been abandoned. It has only slept a little through the mind being occupied by other great objects.

Tract Societies formed in every Circuit connecting the country places with the circuit town might, according to my views, by the Divine blessing, prove a powerful auxiliary to the ministry of the gospel, a mighty engine in checking and destroying infidelity, and a means of increasing morality, sobriety, piety and good order in the land. There seems no way of reaching that class of people, who attend no place of worship but by the distribution of Tracts on a systematical plan, agreeably to the observations you inserted in the *Magazine* for May last.[3]

[1] James Gill (d. 1844, *aet.* 74), sole preacher, Maidstone circuit, 1820–1823.

[2] At this Conference Bunting became Connexional Editor, a place he held till 1824. In the recent years of business difficulty, the Book Room (the connexional publishing house) had very often failed to produce the profits for general connexional use on which Conference had built great expectations.

[3] James Gill, 'On the utility of disseminating religious tracts . . .' *Methodist Magazine*, n.s. xviii (1821), pp. 364–368.

Of this plan, I have now sufficient proof, both of its practicability, and utility. It works well, and has been the means of removing prejudice, of considerably enlarging our congregations in town and country, and of increasing our Societies. I observe: 1. If the plan be acted upon universally, it is likely to ensure extensive benefit to mankind. We divide the towns and parishes into districts, lend the tracts, renew them weekly, have upwards of 50 distributers who visit each house in their districts, and issue weekly 2500 tracts. Supposing three persons to each family, then 7500 read our tracts weekly. A valuable correspondent in Manchester observes, I think, that the Manchester and Salford Tract Societies issued 40,000 tracts in a year, but on this plan our small circuit issues 130,000 annually. When we formed our Tract Society, our number of members in the circuit was about 300, but that the calculation may not be too high, we will say 400. The number of members in the Methodist Societies in Great Britain the last Conference was 191,217, this number divided by 400, the number of members specified for Maidstone, leaves a quotient of 478. If we multiply 2500, the number of tracts weekly issued in this Circuit by 478, the result will be 1,195,000 tracts weekly issued in Great Britain, by the number of members stated in the minutes of the last Conference. And supposing three in each family, 3,585,000 persons would read them weekly. Annually 62,140,000 tracts would be distributed. So great a number of tracts issued and read must be beneficial. But great as the advantage is likely to be in circulating so prodigeous a number of tracts, this is not the only one resulting from this plan. Our zealous warm-hearted distributers would have access to more than a million families, to impart religious instruction, and communicate to them a knowledge of that salvation, which they themselves have received from the Lord. And many induced to attend the ministry of the word would feel it to be the power of God to their salvation.

2. It would be the means of considerably enlarging our congregations and of increasing our Societies. Supposing only ten persons were brought to God annually by the distribution of 2500 tracts weekly, and were to join our societies (and this is a small number to suppose), this would be an increase of 4780 annually, an object worth our attention and exertion, if one soul be worth more than the material world. We have *many* steady members in consequence of the distribution who were brought under impression by reading the tracts, or induced to attend the ministry of the word and there were convinced. At our last monthly meeting, we were informed of one joining, another on the point of joining, a sabbath-breaker reclaimed, a deist shaken, another wicked man under impressions, in consequence

of the tracts. To keep the business alive, I pray in the congregations for prosperity to the institution, and for the distributers.

3. It appears calculated to augment our pecuniary resources— 1. The Book Room would be benefitted. Our expenditure for tracts is £30 annually. This sum multiplied into 478 amounts to £14,340 for the annual sale of tracts. At only 10 per cent profit this would be £1434. In addition to the above, the new members, and those persons induced to attend the ministry of the word, would purchase hymn books, magazines, and other works, which would increase the profits of the Book Room, and advantage the Connexion. To meet the demand of tracts, the preachers might turn their attention to the subject and write a multitude calculated for general usefulness.

2. The finances of each Circuit would be improved, by an increase of hearers and members, by letting the seats, by publick collections, class monies, etc.

3. The Missionary cause would be benefitted. ⟨The⟩ issuing tracts would prepare the way ⟨for the⟩ Missionary collectors, and induce many ⟨to su⟩bscribe weekly or otherwise towards ⟨the⟩ support of the Mission fund. We are about attempting to enlarge our plan of collecting for Missions, by appointing collectors to canvass the districts where tracts are distributed, not by tract distributers but by other persons.

It may perhaps be objected that annual subscriptions for tracts to the above amount may injure other funds of the Connexion. To this I reply: Many of our people now subscribe for tracts, but it would be more effectually applied by a systematic plan of distribution. Many of our hearers would be glad to contribute to an Institution like this. Some of the people who receive the tracts wish to subscribe, and others who have no connexion with us, convinced of the utility of the plan, would give donations. A great object calculated to benefit mankind will call forth resources without injuring other funds. It was supposed by some persons that Missionary exertions would materially injure other funds of the Connexion. But what funds have been injured by the Mission cause? None. Nor would this injure any, but in my opinion increase them. I have not known a single halfpenny less subscribed to any fund in consequence of the Tract Society.

From the above observations I conclude that, if this system were carried into effect, it would be conducive to the glory of God, the salvation of multitudes of souls, the extension of the cause of Methodism, and the increase of our finances. . . .

48. *From James Gill*   Maidstone, July 29, 1821

A few days ago I wrote to you on the distribution of religious tracts, trusting you will recommend it to the notice of the Conference; at present I wish to introduce to your consideration the County of Kent as an important country for home missionary exertion, if the finances of the Connexion should be in a condition to engage in so good a work.

In 1811 the population of Kent was 373,095, and agreeably to the increase of population in several places, already published from the late Census, and the ratio of increase of population from the year 1801, which was then 307,624, at present the population of Kent must be upwards of 400,000.

Last Conference, the number in our Societies in Kent, including the Deptford Circuit was 5149, and the number of members among all the Dissenters, does not amount I think to above 10,000. On this point I asked Mr. Slatery[1] of Chatham, who supposed they could not exceed this number. So that Methodists have only, according to this statement, last year about 16,000 in a population of 400,000. This year I suppose our increase in Kent will be 1000, which will make 17,000.

Evangelical ministers in this county are but few. Infidelity abounds. The people generally speaking are astonishingly ignorant of Divine things. Multitudes in the country places cannot read, such appears to be [the] deplorable state of this county.

There is a small town about six miles from Maidstone called Town Malling; population 1,200, and from this place as a centre are 32 parishes within nine miles where there are no Methodists, scarcely any dissenters—and few evangelical ministers in the Church. On this ground I think are three towns, and many villages, some large. At Town Malling the two ministers in the Church I understand are pious. From a friend I have the names of the places and distances from Malling, both towns and villages—I sent my paper to another friend to mark the situations of the towns and villages, and to give me the population of the parishes but it is not yet returned. There is sufficient room to form two circuits between Maidstone and London, if it were practicable.

Town Malling would be a good centre but as there are two pious ministers in the Church, Wrotham would probably be a more eligible station for a missionary, which is a town 10 miles from Maidstone on the London road. Here is an ample field of labour for a zealous

---

[1] Rev. Mr. Slaterie, an Independent Minister at Chatham. He had been one of the individuals unsuccessfully assisted by the Protestant Society in resistance to the assessment of meeting-houses to the poor-rate. *Evangelical Magazine*, xxvii (1819), p. 749.

enterprising man. Farningham is another market town 17 miles from Maidstone on the London road.

The ground we occupy in this circuit is sufficient for two preachers, but our finances have been so deranged that it is impracticable at present. The Circuit was nearly £100 in debt the first quarter day after I came, but we have made private subscriptions, collections in the classes, and publick collections and our finances are improving, so that in another year if it please God to continue to bless the Circuit it may have an additional preacher, but at present as we are not out of debt, it would be impracticable. Our people wish to be out of debt, before they have another preacher. . . .

49. *From Aquila Barber*[1]   Lynn, February 9, 1822

[The circumstances of his being called from the list of reserve]

. . . The Circuit absolutely needed an Itinerant Preacher long before I came, for being supplied wholly by Local Preachers, they had become extremely negligent, the congregations much fallen off, the country chapels shut up during the week, the Quarterly Tickets in a great measure neglected, the Quarterly Meeting put off till January was far advanced, the Ranters attacking our Society, and carrying off our Members, and the Circuit complaining to the President that no help was sent them. . . .

50. *To William Dalby*[2] (Newark)   N. pl., February 12, 1822

On my return from a long journey this morning, I found your letter.

I wish you had written to the President. He is the proper person to give advice on such matters of public business as affect the interests of the Connexion of which he is by office the constituted guardian. Several of the points referred to require more legal knowledge than I possess, or have now the opportunity of acquiring by consultation, before one can give an opinion with any confidence. I think, however, I am certainly correct in stating, that no alteration whatever, be it good or bad, can possibly be made in a Chapel-Deed, once legally executed. None but the Lord Chancellor himself can subsequently interfere with its provisions. If all the Trustees were unanimous in favour of an addition or omission, that would make no difference. All that your Trustees have to do is to fill up the vacant places, and convey a joint-share in the premises to the persons elected on precisely the same trusts under which they themselves are bound. This

---

[1] Aquila Barber (1797–1870), preacher appointed to Lynn from President's List of Reserve, December 1821.

[2] William Dalby (1783–1860), preacher, Newark circuit, 1820–1822.

they are compellable to do by law at the time specified in the deed. But among honest and godly men such legal compulsion cannot be necessary. A Trustee may *wish* he had more power than the Deed gives him; but since he cannot have it legally, he will not attempt to steal it, or take it by force, if he be a man of conscience. As to triennial stations, Mr. Wesley's Deed of Declaration, to which all local deeds refer as our Methodistical Charter, *allows* them. I doubt whether any local deed can consistently prohibit them. At all events no *new* clause can be introduced for that purpose into an *existing* deed. Nor have Trustees *as such*, and acting *by themselves*, any business with that matter. It concerns not *one Society*, but the *whole Circuit;* and the Quarterly Meeting, not ⟨the⟩ Trustees of one Chapel in it, is the official organ of the circuit for such matters. Such Trustees as belong to the Quarterly Meeting can *there* oppose any request for a triennial Station, and my judgment is, that if such requests be not unanimous, or nearly so, the Conference ought in all ordinary cases to decline compliance.[1] Thus every object of such a clause as you mention will be practically secured by our admirable system of well-adjusted checks and balances of power (so similar to what the constitution of our country exhibits in civil affairs) without incurring the evil which would result, if Trustees could despotically controul the wishes of the whole Circuit. You will consider this letter as strictly private and confidential. If I were President, I would not hesitate to give a public opinion, when required: but I am not bound to take on me the responsibilities which belong only to office. You may use my arguments but not my name. I write in great hurry. . . .

51. *To John Wilks junr*[2]   London, February 28, 1822

My engagements are so numerous, and so completely occupy my whole time, that I cannot undertake any additional service, of any kind, which will require much personal attention.

---

[1] The Conference of 1818 required a formal case for a third year appointment to be stated in Conference before such an appointment could be confirmed. The convention was that preachers would not be stationed in a circuit for a third year, unless, at the end of the second, the circuit was in the middle of a revival or a building scheme which made their reappointment desirable. In practice third year appointments, though not frequent, were somewhat commoner than this. John Wesley's Deed of Declaration forbade the appointment of a preacher to the same station for more than three years, and a Conference minute of 1807 required 'that no Preacher shall return to a Circuit where he had been stationed till he has been absent from it eight years'. A system of rapid circulation made both preachers and circuits more tolerant of disappointed expectations.

[2] John Wilks, junr., founder of the Protestant Society, which defended the liberties of evangelical dissent, but sought to avoid Catholic Emancipation.

I have, however, for a considerable period, deeply lamented the alarming increase of open profanations of the Lord's Day; and am convinced that, even if nothing else can be done, religious people ought, if they wish to be 'held guiltless', at least to bear their bold, public, and, if possible, *united* testimony against the evil. I therefore rejoice to learn that something is likely to be attempted in that way; and, though I fear that I cannot take any very active or useful part, I will, if possible, gladly attend the proposed meeting on the subject. . . .

52. *From Zachariah Taft*[1]   Pickering, May [18], 1822

There are two things which I have felt on my mind to mention to you, as improvements if adopted, one of which may be easily done. . . . [The first is to bring forward the dates when the Addresses on the Yearly and July collections are sent out].

The *second* thing I wished you to recommend is the providing an *Iron Chest*, for the more effectually securing and preserving our Chapel Deeds.[2] Let an iron chest be deposited in the vestry, or chapel, or chapel house in every circuit town, and let all the deeds of our chapels in that Circuit be lodged there; for want of this some deeds have been lost, and others have got into hands where we have not access to them. I have succeeded partially in recommending and adopting this plan in several Circuits, and in making enquiry and search for deeds, for this purpose, I have reason to believe that a few have been lost or destroyed. *If you think with me, that what is suggested above, would be any improvement, you would oblige me much, by using the best means for their adoption.* If you think otherwise, you will I trust pardon the freedom I have taken in suggesting them. We are making a little improvement in this circuit, both in number, and piety, but not much if any in our *finances*. This place and neighbourhood is but thinly inhabited, hence our congregations are small, and as the whole population depend upon agriculture, the people are poor, and this increases. I have taken considerable pains to perswade Mr. Sergeant[3] and the friends in the Scarborough Circuit, to consent to the reunion of the two Circuits. But I cannot at present succeed. This circuit with 530 members cannot support more

---

[1] Zachariah Taft (d. 1848, *aet.* 75), superintendent, Pickering circuit, 1821–1823. Husband of Mary Taft, noted woman preacher.

[2] Not till 1866 did Conference require that 'suitable provision shall be made in every circuit for the safe custody of trust deeds' (*Minutes of Methodist Conferences*, xvi, p. 568).

[3] George Sargent, superintendent, Scarborough circuit, 1821–1823. Died 1823 in a coach crash on the way to Conference.

than one family and 3 children at Conference allowance—with the quarterage for both preachers—indeed more money used to be allowed to it when a single man was appointed than is now allowed to support two families. As we have full work for two preachers, to make it a circuit with one preacher, would oblige us to give up many places, since we have small societies (however this might please the *Ranters* who preach in every place in this circuit): it would be exceedingly painful to those pious few who are united with us, and what am I persuaded the Conference would never concent to. We have taken a *house* for my colleague and we have begged a good deal of money and furniture, so that it will be pretty comfortable when we get the £20 allowed by the Conference. We were under the necessity of doing this to save expence and to promote the comfort of the second family; no preacher would stop two years in the hired furnished lodgings we had. . . .

53. *From Adam Clarke*[1]   Dublin, June 27, [1823]

I have duly received your letter and t⟨he⟩ minutes of the two special Missionary Committee meetings, held on the concerns of Ireland, and read them all *publicly* this morning in the Conference. They were referred to a Committee and that Committee has reported to the Conference as follows.

'We unanimously agree to the general plan of the Missionary Committee—in some minor matters we may suggest perhaps, some improvements, but we see the Plan, taken *in the whole*, as the very best that has yet been proposed on the subject; and believe under God, that it is most likely to serve the interests of the cause of God in this Kingdom: and desire to return our unanimous and most cordial thanks to the English Brethren and the Missionary Committee for this additional proof of their concern for the interests of this most distracted and nearly ruined country; in which every means are now in active operation to destroy totally the Protestant Religion.' This, with a blessed feeling of encouragement, to which, we were till then,

---

[1] Adam Clarke (1762–1832), President of Irish Methodist Conference, 1823. (The President of the Irish Conference was always deputed from England by the English Conference.) The foremost Methodist scholar of his, or perhaps any, generation. Widely versed in oriental and classical languages, he was also employed by the Record Commission in editing Rymer's *Foedera*. He produced a valuable 8-volume scripture commentary, but his orthodoxy was always suspect to Bunting and his friends, on account of his denial of the eternal sonship of Christ, and his affection for John Taylor's *Key* (1745) to the apostolic writings in which an anti-Calvinist view of original sin and atonement was developed. President of the English Conference, 1801, 1814 and 1822.

G

strangers, was carried unanimously by the Conference. ⟨When th⟩ese letters came, I had almost given ⟨up⟩ *all hopes of Ireland*—I have travelled ⟨th⟩rough the nation from the remotest North ⟨to⟩ the South, preaching to the uttermost of my strength: travelling both in Scotland and Ireland, at the rate, on an average, of 40 miles per diem, ho[l]ding meetings and preaching in various places. From the time I entered Ireland, I trod on *hostile ground*. I had got only a *few hours* out of Maghera, when it was attacked by the *Ribbonmen*, all the Protestants were driven out of it; the few military over-powered, their officer badly wounded, and the Tavern taken and retaken with the loss of 10 killed, and about 70 or 80 wounded. I had left Magera-felt only a *few hours*, when four men were killed there. When I got to Dublin I found the principal part of the South from within 12 miles of Dublin onward, by *Proclamation* put under the *Insurrection Act*. I had been pledged for Cork and Bandon: but at a meeting of the Preachers and several friends was earnestly intreated *not to go*. In a short time an account came that 10,000 of the rebels had repossest Vinegar Hill: and then my friends earnestly intreated me to take the Packet, and set off without delay for Eng⟨land. For?⟩ a moment I was humbled; and then occur⟨ed the thought, shall⟩ *such a man as I flee*? I took the Mail, set off ⟨for⟩ Cork in the evening, that I might pass through the *disturbed* districts in the *Night*, that by morning I ⟨might⟩ *see* my danger. It was formidable to see the road traversed by armed horse and foot—at different distances—while all was silence and terror. I got through mercy, safely to Cork—held a Missionary Meeting there, and preached twice; and then went to Bandon, and preached for the missions—Sabbath evening a report was spread in Cork, that many stand of arms and ammunition were secreted ⟨in o⟩ne of the Mills—the Magistrates went with *some of our principal people* and spent from 5 p.m. to 3 a.m. in ransacking and tearing up the mill, to come at these concealments—none was however found when I came away. I took the mail, set off on Tuesday morning from Cork, got in company with the *Limerick Mail, doubly guarded*, and travelled together all night, to six the next morning. The appearance of the country was alarming, hundreds of people in the *streets, by the way sides, etc., etc.*, all in *sullen silence*, neither *eating, drinking*, or *sporting*, but apparently meditating deep designs. In this state, through such squads, we arrived safely in Dublin, having scarcely seen a man in this long journey, who was not an *enemy*. The Papists were insultingly bold, and, if strong measures are not resorted to by government, I have no doubt that a general massacre of the Protestants is at the door. It was only ⟨the support o?⟩f the *missionary resolutions* that gave me any ⟨strength? . . . . ⟩;

indeed these Resolutions have had a wonderful ⟨effect? o⟩n all the preachers—no man seems to consider ⟨the world?⟩ dear to him and they are now preparing to go afresh ⟨on⟩ward in his strength who can bruise down Satan ⟨un⟩der their feet. Whoever was the agent, I believe God has ⟨bless⟩ed your Missionary Meeting and led you to the plan you have ⟨pr⟩oposed. All are quite willing to work double tides ⟨and⟩ hasten the Conference, that they might get back to their flocks, and to their desolate families, left as lambs among wolves . . .

54. *To George Marsden* (Leeds)   London, September 17, 1823

. . . Experience has taught me, that while I am Editor,[1] I cannot be absent for more than one or two days from my post in Town, without *real* and *very serious* injury to the concern. The office business by every absence of mine is thrown into confusion; the compositors and pressmen complain that I injure them and their families; matters are postponed or neglected which ought to receive prompt attention; and I have to work double tides (usually *all night*) both before I leave, and after my return, in order to keep even our periodical works going, by which my health suffers, and, as even that will not fully meet the case, I am rendered̦ habitually and thoroughly uncomfortable in my work, when I am at home, by the consciousness that there are such accumulated arrears of unfulfilled official duties. . . .

55. *From Joseph Taylor*[2]   77 Hatton Garden, [London], October 31, 1823

The subjects on which it is in my opinion of much importance to dwell in missionary meetings are

1st. The present state of our missions—as it respects conversions—their influence and hold on the rising generation—the extent to which they have recommended themselves among persons of influence and authority—the disposition which they have created among heathens far beyond the limits of our present mission stations.

2nd. The present state of the world as viewed with reference to missionary labours—as it respects—*openings* and *calls* for the spread of the Gospel—*In Africa—In the West Indies*, where *in Jamaica alone* we have a call for *four additional men*, and must send them or

---

[1] As Connexional Editor, 1821–1824, Bunting was responsible for producing the *Magazine* and other regular commercial publications; and as the preachers were supposed to publish exclusively through the Book Room, he had editorial oversight of the literary output of the whole ministry.

[2] Joseph Taylor, jun. (1779–1845), missionary, 1803–1811; secretary for foreign missions, 1818–1824; assisted by Bunting and Richard Watson, 1821–1824. President, 1834.

leave some of the most populous parts of that populous island without help, where the *masters desire it* and *the negroes are pleading for it—In India*, where the opening is all but unlimited. As it respects the *access* to almost every part of the world. 3rd. The views and feelings of the Christian church generally. All who have taken part in missions consider themselves as pledged to their *perpetuity* and *extent*. Those who are not yet engaged, in most instances need only to be respectfully and persevering[ly] asked. In the small town of Bawtry, near Doncaster, where the population is about *one thousand* and the influence of the friends of missions not equal to what it is in many places, while other institutions prosper, the collectors of the Wesleyan Missionary Society obtain to the amount of nearly ten pence per head per annum on the whole population. . . .

56. *From Edmund Grindrod*[1]   Green Street, Calton, Glasgow,
January 12, 1824

. . . At the next Conference I hope your office as Editor will be no bar to ⟨your⟩ election to the Secretaryship. I have ⟨som⟩e apprehension that an effort will be made by certain brethren to get Mr. Isaac into that office, in order to diminish the influence of aristocratical and monarchical principles, and to advance the influence of democracy and republicanism. Should that attempt be made, I think it will not be wise to meet it by putting Mr. Waddy in competition. Unless I see reason to alter my opinion, I am disposed, not only from personal respect to you, but from regard to good principles, to be one amongst the active promoters of your election at the next Conference. . . .[2]

[1] Edmund Grindrod, superintendent, Glasgow circuit, 1823–1825.
[2] In 1824 Bunting retired from the office of Connexional Editor (for other comments on this see no. 57 *infra*. and M.C.A. MSS. D. Watson to Jabez Bunting, October 14, 1824) to become Secretary to Conference, an office he held until he became President for the second time in 1828. He was succeeded as editor by Thomas Jackson, one of the most scholarly and also most politically conservative of the younger preachers. Daniel Isaac (1778–1834) had achieved early distinction by attacking in pulpit and press Wm. Vidler's doctrines of Universal Restoration (*The doctrine of universal restoration examined and refuted* (London, 1819)), but in 1815 the Book Committee refused to publish his *Ecclesiastical Claims*, and was supported by a Conference minute which led to an acrimonious exchange between Isaac and Bunting, the former sending a circular to superintendents of circuits ascribing his difficulties to the Book Committee's suspicion 'that it might give offence to Government'. For many years Isaac was regarded by the dominant leadership in the connexion as a prospective leader of political and theological opposition (cf. no. 100). In 1830 and 1831 he gave it out that he would not accept the Presidency if elected (M.C.A. MSS. R. Wood to Jabez Bunting, January 21, 1831). On Isaac generally, see J. Everett, *The polemic divine* (2nd ed. Manchester, 1851). Richard Waddy became preacher 1793: d. 1853.

57. *From John Riles*   Salford, January 21, 1824

. . . My coming to this Circuit was extreamly unpleasant, as it was the first time (after having travelled five and thirty years) I had been openly opposed. However, as the Conference had thought it good to appoint me, I was determined to look the *people* in the face, and I feel thankful, I have now no opposers, and even those, who were the most violent are now my friends. Mr. Newton's[1] conduct has been the most *manly, Christian,* and *Brotherly,* in the whole affair. We are labouring together in perfect union, and see some fruit of our labours. Praise the Lord for this.

In the interval between one Conference and another, one naturally look[s] with more coolness at what has been done, than in the bustle of Conference.—The address of the Conference[2] was not done well: it is a very *megar insipid* thing, and does no credit to such a body of pious sensible men, who in their annual meeting should always be careful of committing themselves in the opinion of the public. . . . In such a Connexion as ours, there is always sufficient matter for general remarks. For instance the causes of a declention in religion, arising from connections formed with irreligious men, in the way of partnerships, or marriage:—The defects of domestic worship—Some of the causes, why so few of the children of our opulent people join our Society, or are even willing to acknowledge they are indebted to Methodism for all they enjoy, except their *ingratitude*. . . . But this ought not to be left to the spur of the moment.—The Conference ought to appoint two or more individual[s] to prepare, each an an Address, and to choose that which in its wisdom is thought the best . . .

Do you intend to give up the Editorship at Conference? I hope you do; for I think your labours are wanted in a different part of the vineyard, and in different employment. The *Magazine* has claims, but they are of a subordinate nature, when compared with preaching the Gospel, and caring for the *internal* state of the church. I hope you will excuse my freedom, and attribute my mistake, if it is one, to the best of motives. You have done much for the *Magazine,* and we all feel indebted to you for it; now leave the drudgery to others. I suppose by this time, the Book Committee, have been turning their attention to a successor—Mr. Edmondson, would fill that post in many respects, at least, as far as I can judge. But is his taste sufficent to keep up the tone of the *Magazine,* with its spirit? Is his literary

---

[1] Robert Newton (1780–1854), superintendent, Manchester (Irwell Street) circuit, 1823–1826. President, 1824, 1832, 1840, 1848.

[2] The annual address of the Conference to the Methodist people.

knowledge of that description calculated to maintain the popularity of a periodical work? Has he any Classical knowledge? No one would guard our doctrines with more faithfulness, or study the interest of Methodism, than Mr. Edmondson.—What do you think of Mr. Townley?[1] He has some Classical knowledge, and his style of composing is above middling; though, I confess, my knowledge perhaps is not sufficiently extensive, as to warrant me to give a correct opinion. But perhaps you have already fixed upon the man the Book Committee intends to recommend to the Conference.

When I came into this neighbourhood, I was very much surprised to find that the plain Lancashire folks had no Methodist Sunday School, avowedly as such, though such under the title of *Union Schools*; but in which the Preachers had no part, or voice, except in begging annually for them, while the Church have schools, and the Ministers have some influence; the Roman Catholics have schools; the different denominations of Dissenters have schools, recognised publickly as such.[2] Though I feel it a delicate subject to meddle with, yet I have thought it my duty, to tell some of the most zealouse advocates for Sunday School Unions, that it is my opinion that upon the present plan, they are doing more *evil* than *good*. The children are trained up without any regard to God's public worship; and reverence for the sanctity of the Sabbath, or any respect for the Ministers of the Gospel. Every thing associates itself with the School-room, their Teacher, and the visitor. No respect is paid to God's House, because they have only gone their occasionally, and then it has been, perhaps to be *shown*. Ask nineteen, out of every twenty, of the boys and girls, you find running about in the streets of a Sunday-evening, in this populous town, whether they did not belong to some Sunday School, and they would answer, 'Yes', and perhaps the major part of them, to the *Union Schools*!! Is not this a serious evil? . . .

---

[1] James Townley (d. 1833), educated by Rev. David Simpson, the evangelical incumbent of Macclesfield. One of secretaries to Missionary Society, 1827–1832. President, 1829.

[2] Founded in 1784, the 'Sunday school for the children of all denominations' in Manchester had originally been supported by all the churches, including dissenting and Roman Catholic. In the political upheavals of the later 1790's, however, dissenting schools began to be opened outside the town's system, and in 1800, when parliamentary legislation restricting Sunday schools was expected, the Anglican clergy separated from the town's committee, and taking part of the joint property, established on organization under their own control. Much the strongest party amongst the remnant, the Wesleyans gradually assumed authority over the rest of the town's system, but did not move for formal control till 1826 (cf. no. 85, *infra*.) and even then retained the name 'A school for children of all denominations'.

58. *To James Wood*   London, February 17, 1824[1]

[Embarrassments in the Stationing Committee make it impossible for him to allow himself to be invited by the Manchester Quarterly Meeting]

... Now, as to the subject of your late kind letter, for which I most affectionately thank you. When division [of the Manchester circuit] was talked of, it never appeared to me that any plan of division would be proper at *present* which did not provide for remedying the great mischiefs which resulted from the injudicious and unmethodistical mode of the Salford division.[2] If Manchester and Salford, as they now stand, could be formed into *three* good circuits, in which there should be a *strictly territorial* division of the whole ground, on fair principles, so as to prevent the present system of interference, and consequent animosity, I should think *that* a great public object, to which almost every minor view should be gladly sacrificed. But your present project of division leaves that great object quite untouched. Nay it even goes to retard, if not to prevent, its accomplishment at any *future* period, and thus to perpetuate the existing evils, which, while they last, will always tend to injure brotherly love, and interfere with proper Methodist discipline. This alone, is to me, an insurmountable objection to your plan. I think it also very undesirable that the proposed South Circuit should have *two* preachers, after being accustomed so long to so much variety. It seems to me that, even if Salford must be left out of any new arrangement, Manchester is not ripe for another division, until each of the new circuits is likely to be strong enough to support three preachers. This the Grosvenor Street Circuit could not do at present, unless Altringham and perhaps some places from Stockport Circuit could be joined with it; which is an arrangement that cannot be *now* made. The Oldham St. preachers would have to pass *through* the heart of the other circuit, in order to get at Altringham; and thus the *territorial* or *geographical* principle which should be observed in

---

[1] The holograph is in the U.M.C.A.

[2] A Salford circuit, carved from the Manchester circuit in 1813, was transformed in 1826 into the Manchester (Irwell Street) circuit. In 1824 the Grosvenor Street chapel became the head of another circuit carved from the original Manchester (Oldham Street) circuit, and despite his disclaimers in this letter, Bunting became its first superintendent, 1824–1827. A further division led to the creation of the Great Bridgwater Street circuit in 1827. Circuit division in Manchester, though accompanied by a great increase in membership occasioned and continued to occasion much complaint (M.C.A. MSS. MS. Resolutions of Manchester preachers and Quarterly Meeting representatives, January 26, 1827: J. Entwisle to Wm. Lord, November 16, 1829: R. Wood to Jabez Bunting, June 28, 1830: *Life of Bunting*, ii, p. 84 n.)

all divisions, and for want of which the Salford division has done harm rather than good, would, on your project, be continually infringed. I must doubt whether such a project *ought* to pass either your Quarterly or District Meeting. The Conference I am persuaded, with the example of Salford in its recollection, would hesitate to agree to it. Perhaps there may be reasons for pressing it which I do not see; but it could not be carried, either in your Quarterly Meeting or in the Conference, without contention and difficulty. And, after eleven years of absolutely *public* life, in which all my private studies and comforts, and in some degree my domestic duties also, have been suspended or given up, I really must have rest and quiet; and nothing but the regular work of an established circuit, in order that I may refit my bark, after the wear and tear to which it has been exposed. My mind and body alike require this. Any plan, or any place, which involves difficulty and opposition and struggle, is quite unfit for me *just now*. With repeated and most cordial thanks therefore to you, to Mr. Marsden, and to any other of my much-esteemed friends, who have had a part in this business with an ultimate view to the nomination of *me* in your March meeting, I must wholly decline to be nominated at present. On the plan of a division of your circuit, I could not comfortably come to it this year. And if there be no division, I had rather come at a future time, if regularly asked by the proper meeting, than now:- 1st. Because a much smaller *charge* than that of 3000 souls will better meet my wishes and circumstances, till I have been in *port* for a while, and have so renewed my mental and moral energies: 2dly. Because my long friendship with Mr. George Marsden,[1] and with his family connexions will not allow me to think for a moment of standing in the way of *his* appointment. . . . But I feel that I am *public* property; and I conscientiously think that I can better serve the cause by taking charge of a smaller circuit elsewhere, for two or three years, than by going as second preacher to Manchester. Considering my standing in the work, I may without arrogance express this opinion to you, and through you to Mr. John Marsden (to whom I beg you to shew this letter) though of course, as it is open to a misconstruction, I should not wish it to go much further.

There is one other view of your project of division which I ought just to notice before I conclude. I see no *public object* whatever, of any material importance, that would be answered by any *immediate* division of *Manchester alone*. *Difficulties* there would be, *many*; but *advantages* I cannot discover. It would therefore be said, that

---

[1] George Marsden, superintendent, Manchester (Oldham Street) circuit, 1824–1827. John Marsden was a lay member of his family.

the division was a contrivance of my friends, to accommodate me; and *that* I really could not bear, and, as a public man, to whom high character for *principle* and *disinterestedness*, is everything, I *ought* not to be party to it.

On the whole I feel it right cheerfully to submit to the indications of Divine Providence by taking another circuit, rather than agree to anything which would look like *forcing* myself to the place of my personal inclinations. I have declined a pressing request of the official persons at Leeds, to allow them to nominate me in their meeting; because I decidedly feel that the charge of 5000 souls is too onerous for me to undertake with innocence. *Probably*, Bath may be my station for 2 or 3 years to come, if I am spared. . . .

59. *From George Cubitt*[1]   Oxford, March 24, 1824

Will you allow me respectfully to *suggest* the following remarks, on the subject of the Sunday Lessons, to which you alluded in the last *Magazine*.[2]

I think with you that a chapter in our evening service would be very useful. I think with you too, that so far as is practical, the reading of Scripture should be regular. But it has sometimes occurred to my mind, that, owing to our peculiar circumstances, a Table of Lessons published by the Conference, and conforming as nearly as possible to the order of the Church on the subject, would be very beneficial.

1. The Sunday lessons of the Church are arranged, not without reference to the arrangement for the *daily* lessons. These latter, we have not.

2. It sometimes happens that one of the forenoon lessons is *scarcely calculated* for public reading. I have heard you make considerable omissions in reading the chapter. I usually, when such a portion comes in course, take one of the *afternoon* lessons. Mr. Wesley, in his omission of certain Psalms, and the Church in the omission of certain parts of some chapters, both admit the principle of omission and act upon it.

---

[1] George Cubitt, superintendent, Oxford circuit, 1822–1825.

[2] This article on the 'Public Reading of the Scriptures' (*Wesleyan Methodist Magazine*, 3rd ser., iii (1824), pp. 191–2) held that while the reading of scripture had always formed part of public worship at town chapels 'it ought equally to form a part of the constant plan and system of our Sabbath-worship in our numerous village-congregations'. It could no longer be presumed that 'the great mass of those who attend the Sunday-evening services of the Methodists were in the habit of attending also the Church-service or some other place where the Scriptures were largely read in the earlier parts of the day'.

3. In those cases where we have not the liturgy[1]—as in many of our Circuit Towns, and in those villages only visited by Local Preachers, the reading of the Psalms is not provided for by the Church Order.

Now, *all* things considered, would it be proper to have an arrangement for the regular public reading of Scripture in our chapels, adapted, with immediate reference to our own peculiar circumstances.

I know there are objections against this, and, very likely, objections that may be far stronger than the reasons to be advanced in its favour, but still, as the subject is of importance, and has evidently occupied your attention, a few hints will I know be not unfavourably received by you. . . .

60. *From Robert Johnson, John Doncaster, David McNicoll, John Lancaster and William Entwisle*[2]   Hull, February 19, 1824

We are induced, from our opinion of your judgment and experience, in regard to the discipline of Methodism, to solicit the favour of your friendly observations and counsel on the following case.

A person at Beverley in this Circuit, who is a Leader, Local Preacher, and Trustee has lately written a letter to another official member of our Connexion,[3] from which we here present you with an extract.

'It has long appeared to me, and several respectable friends who are members of our Society, that there is a rapid dissent effecting in the country from the Established Church by the Methodists, who seem determined to set up a rival Church, as is intimated by morning service, administering the sacrament, burying the dead, erecting organs, employing vergers with their uniforms and wands. We think also that there is a growing love of power in the preachers, which is shewn in the enactments of Conference, which will tend to increase the power of the travelling preachers, and to lessen that of the local preachers. We also think it a singular thing, that Government will not allow of a convention of the clergy which, by the way, was sometimes called a Conference, and yet our preachers have the assurance to hold one without any of the people being present every

---

[1] The use of the liturgy in Methodism, even where ministerial services were available, seems to have been gradually reduced to very small proportions by public distaste. M.C.A. MSS. Thomas Butler to Jabez Bunting, July 4, 1843.

[2] Robert Johnson (d. 1829, *aet.* 66), John Doncaster (d. 1828), David McNicoll (d. 1836, *aet.* 54), John Lancaster (d. 1829, *aet.* 47), William Entwisle (d. 1831) the superintendent and staff respectively of the Hull circuit, 1823–1824.

[3] cf. Mark Robinson, *Observations on the system of Weslyan Methodism: in a letter addressed to the Rev. R. Johnson, superintendent of the Hull circuit* (London, 1824).

year. And even when the clergy did meet in convention, the laws made by them were subject to the control of a Committe consisting of 18 laymen and 18 clergymen. But since William III^d they have only been allowed to meet when Parliament is summoned, but have not for the last 70 years been allowed to proceed to business.'

'You are perhaps aware, that thousands of our friends in Ireland have refused to take the sacrament at the hands of our preachers, and are now carrying on the original plan of itinerancy in unison with the established Church.[1] With this Society we have opened a correspondence, and have it in contemplation to apply to our own Conference to return to simple primitive Methodism, and that, if the Conference will not listen to it, to apply to the Irish Methodists to send over some efficient preachers to make the attempt. This plan has been laid before a meeting of the pious clergy, who have most heartily entered into our views, and will give us every assistance consistent with their office. Should you . . . think it a plan worthy of support, we shall be glad to include you as a member of our correspondence. At any rate be pleased to write by return of post, if possible, and give me your real sentiments and views on the subject. In the meantime you will please not to name this to any one till you receive our permission. Do you know any person in Scarborough Whitby or any of the neighbouring places who are likely to unite with us? I remain, etc.'

This letter with the signature cut off, was communicated to Mr. Johnson, the Chairman of this District. He immediately consulted some of our most respectable friends on the subject, who were of opinion with us, that though no fear could possibly arise as to the ultimate success of its projects, yet an obstinate and persevering attempt of this kind, might operate most painfully in disturbing the minds of our people. The letter was read and condemned at the last Quarterly Meeting. Suspicion fell upon the writer who was taxed with, and confessed it. He refuses, however, to express the *least regret* for his conduct. On the contrary he still warmly *defends* and propagates his sentiments.

We respectfully solicit your opinion on the following points:—

I. Can the local preachers' meeting, consistently with our discipline, refuse to continue this Brother on their plan, supposing they deem his conduct in this instance to merit this refusal. Or, does the rule, *Minutes*, vol. 1, p. 325, 8th on Discipline, imply that they *cannot*? Please also to refer to vol. 1, p. 375, 2d. on the removal of local preachers.

---

[1] The Irish Primitive Methodist Connexion, formed by a secession from the main body 1818, insisting that the sacrament be received from the Anglican ministry, not from Methodist preachers.

II. Is not the Rule, vol. I, p. 300, 2d. concerning Trustees, the *only* proper Rule under which he may be arraigned?

III. Or, are we to infer from what is said in the Rule first referred to above that the *Quarterly Meeting* may try the writer of the letter? We ask this question because the Quarterly Meeting represents *the society so disturbed* as expressed by the Rule, the disturbance in this case having extended beyond Beverley, and throughout the Circuit.

IV. As the writer of this letter, and his party, seem resolved to demand, and that soon, the public discussion, at the Quarterly Meeting, or elsewhere, of the matters contained in the letter, are we, as preachers, at liberty to admit the introduction of *such disputes at all*? Is not this expressly prohibited by the Rule, vol. II. p. 347, Q. 21?

V. As we have reason to believe that the subject of *lay delegates* is the darling one of the party; and as the agitation of this subject at present has convinced us that considerable numbers in this circuit, and most probably in other places, are friendly to the measure, we should be happy to learn your opinion as to the steps we ought to take in quashing the thing entirely; or as to the arguments to be used in confutation of the scheme.

We have already had two private meetings with the party in order to conciliate affairs, and bring about peace, but without effect. This opposition has been nobly met by many of our best official men, and private members, especially by our valuable and worthy friend Mr. Thompson.[1] Still, it has unhappily received some very respectable patronage, which operates as a powerful obstacle in our way. How far this disturbance may extend, through the restless dissatisfaction of the writer of the letter, we know not. He asserts that he is a thousand strong. That he has poisoned the minds of numbers of our pious friends in this Circuit, we are well assured, and lament. Before we proceed to adopt any decisive measures, we are anxious to obtain the counsel of two or three of our respectable Brethren, more experienced in the Discipline of Methodism and most capable, we presume, of affording us advice. Of these our excellent President of course is one; and we hope you will have kindness to think the matter over, and favour us with an *early* reply. . . .

61. *From Humphrey Sandwith*[2]   Bridlington, November 10, 1824

The Pamphlet, which Mr. Mark Robinson wrote on the system of Methodism, has made a strong impression on the Clergy in this

---

[1] Thomas Thompson (1754–1828) of Cottingham, M.P. for Midhurst 1807–1818, a member of Wilberforce's parliamentary group. Local preacher and the first lay treasurer of Methodist missions.

[2] Humphrey Sandwith, surgeon at Bridlington, and from 1842 one of the leading

neighbourhood. And he has contrived to give greater effect to the performance by personally visiting numbers both of Clergymen and Magistrates, and corresponding with the Poet Laureate and other persons of influence on the present aspect and position of Methodism in relation to the Establishment. From long acquaintance and an intimate knowledge of his character, I feel convinced that he is intent on some great scheme, and that with the inflexibility of a Thomas à Becket, nothing will bend him from his purpose. It strikes me, either that he is obtaining all the clerical influence he can muster to co-operate with him in bringing Methodism into a closer connexion with the Church, or he intends laying the foundation of a rival system by importing Church Methodism from Ireland. Early last year he addressed a letter to me, developing his dissatisfaction with Methodism partly on account of the want of a representation in Conference, and partly on the departure of the Society from its primitive and more cordial relations to the national Church. As I disapproved, however, of the part he had taken, which I considered to be rather that of an enemy than a friend, a revolutionist than a reformer, I wrote him a reply, which disconcerted him and offended him so much, that from that period our intercourse has been suspended.

My acquaintance with several of the Clergy has placed me in rather an awkward predicament for the following reason. Mr. Robinson has shewn my letter to several of them and amongst others to Archdeacon Wrangham of Hunmanby.[1] As I did not anticipate this, I was somewhat unguarded in my strictures on the Church, although attached on the whole to its venerable institutions. Mr. Wrangham has just mentioned to me an interview he had with Mr. Robinson but a few days ago; and I could gather from his remarks that the conversation had hinged on the practicability of effecting a return to Methodism towards the bosom of the Church. That the Clergy should be desirous of establishing more friendly relations with Methodism, cannot be matter of surprise; indeed Mr. Wrangham candidly confessed to me that such are his wishes. And he anticipates great advantage to Methodism from the union, particularly

---

physicians at Hull. Brought up with Mark Robinson at Beverley, where his brother T. Sandwith was also a doctor. Published a major unsigned essay on 'Methodism in its relations to the Church and the nation' in the *Wesleyan Methodist Magazine* for 1829 (M.C.A. MSS. H. Sandwith to Thomas Jackson, October 1832). Editor of the *Watchman* (the Buntingite newspaper) from its beginning in 1835 to 1842.

[1] Francis Wrangham (1769–1842), rector of Hunmanby, 1795–1842, archdeacon of Cleveland 1820–1828, and of the East Riding, 1828–1840.

the advancement of our Preachers in learning and respectability. As he expressed a strong wish soon to have a formal interview with me for the sake of an extended discussion of the subject, it is principally that I may be prepared for the encounter that I have thrown myself on your anticipated aid, respectfully soliciting you to favour me with a luminous statement of the present and future probable bearings of Methodism and the designs of its leading men. . . .

62. *From Robert Johnson*   Hull, December 4, 1824

I believe you have the purity, respectability and welfare of Methodism at heart. I therefore communicate my thoughts to you the more freely, on a subject which gives me no small concern; and yet it is of so delicate a nature as it regards certain individuals that the man who openly sets his face against it, will by some, most probably, be branded as invidious and unfeeling.

The evil to which I allude is the frequent occurrence of a few friends in sundry places, and even certain preachers themselves, sending something like circulars, begging money of generous individuals in *other* circuits, than *their own*, and some for objects, of which our friends entirely disapprove.[1]

Some friends are alarmed, and begin to fear that a selfish mercenary spirit is becoming more prevalent amongst the preachers than the spirit of oeconomy, self denial and retrenchment in themselves and families.

If something is not done speedily, with prudence and firmness, to discountenance and stop this growing evil, the consequences will be most injurious to our people to the cause of God, and to our regular funds. I do not know how it is in your part of the connexion, but in this circuit the evil is becoming alarming, and I am persuaded, that next to gross immorality, nothing has a more direct tendency to destroy our influence and usefulness among our people.

The regular calls which we are imperatively requested to make on our friends, for specified objects, are many. The local benevolent charities, which they support among themselves, are also various and numerous; that these applications coming in besides make me almost ashamed to apply to them for authorised contributions. Several of them are dissatisfied, they mention their dissatisfaction with such extra applications, to each other: this gets abroad, among our small friends at Beverley, as well as here, and also amongst the *Ranters*;

---

[1] Conference had set its face against one kind of itinerant begging, for the relief of distressed chapel trusts, in establishing the connexional Chapel Fund in 1818.

which furnishes them with texts and matter, which they do not fail to make use of, to the injury of our characters as preachers, and the destruction of the pious influence of our ministry. The consequences in this neighbourhood begin to be alarming.

I am aware that *we cannot*, and *should not* do anything to prevent the kind efforts of our liberal friends in the Circuit where a distressed Brother or family actually resides from helping them to the utmost of their ability. But for them to proceed beyond their own Circuit to shear other flocks in behalf of an individual or a few individuals, seems unfair, and I think ought if possible to be prevented, or at least discountenanced.

Unless death make great riddance of preachers and their wives, in the course of a very few, say 6, years the supernumeraries will be numerous, and the Funds will groan, being burthened. We ought not to suffer individual cases of necessity to block up the *way* to our kind and generous friends, least when general extremity arrives, we find *it* inaccessable.

The dissatisfaction produced by M[ark] R[obinson] of Beverley is coming to a crisis: it is developing itself more and more daily. I hope we shall very soon know the extent of it. Three Local Preachers have left at Beverley, and only two as yet have left here.

I understand two Irishmen are daily expected at Beverley. M.R. has got his Tickets printed. It is the exact size of ours. The following is the inscription, viz,

Church Methodist Society
⟨Establi⟩shed by the Rev. Jno. Wesley 1739
Quarterly Ticket for Decr. 1824
* "If some quit the church, others will adhere to
it; and then there will be dissenting Methodists
and Church Methodists"   J. Wesley.

63. *From Humphrey Sandwith*   Bridlington, January 31, 1825

Your polite refusal to communicate your views on the subject, to which I invited your attention in my last, I cheerfully acquiesced in, believing you might have reasons for so doing outweighing every other consideration. I subsequently dined with Mr. Wrangham and we had the subject talked over, and I found him very friendly to Mr. Robinson's scheme. I do not at all think however he has any wish to injure Wesleyan Methodism, but he is anxious to connect so powerful a rival with the Establishment. I have just heard, that Mr. Robinson has been dining with him the other day, and that the Archdeacon purposes to introduce him to the Archbishop! When I last wrote, I had no design whatever to reply to Mr. Robinson's first pamphlet. But being on a visit soon after at my Brother's in Beverley, my spirit was moved within me to observe what a mischievous rent my old friend has made in the society there, and how correct his opinions are with many of the Gentry and Clergy. These observations, coupled with the importunity of some of my friends, determined me to encounter him in honourable controversy. I immediately set to, and perused Wesley's *Journals*, the *Minutes of Conference* and every other book in my reach that would throw any light on the questions to be discussed, and excepting one point of any importance, I have finished my *Reply or Apology for the System of Wesleyan Methodism*.[1] To that single point I now take the liberty of calling your attention. It is the elucidation of the following clause, in the VIIth of those Articles, made by Conference in 1797. 'Nevertheless, the Quarterly Meeting rejecting a new rule, shall not by publications, public meetings, or otherwise, make that rule a cause of contention, but shall strive by every means to preserve the peace of the connexion.' Now I own I am not sure I understand this. Mr. Robinson has made it the basis of his 4th objection and has some remarks on it which are plausible to general readers. My only fear is lest the rule invade religious toleration or the liberty of the press and be on that account difficult to be defended. But does the prohibition apply to the interim between the objecting to any new rule by a Quarterly Meeting and the confirmation of that rule by the second conference, or to the period after its confirmation? In the next place is the prohibition levelled against the Quarterly Meeting in its corporate capacity alone, or does it extend to any individual, who might wish to write a pamphlet on a new rule? Thirdly can it be interpreted so as to mean a prohibition not of publications and public meetings as such, but of contention merely by their means? On this only point, which is so cardinal an one, that I should be sorry in any way to commit myself, do I feel embarrassed; and as you can in five minutes relieve me from my anxieties, I really hope you will kindly come forward to my help. Mr. Shelmerdine[2] is aware of my proceedings; indeed I have read him the whole of the performance, with which he expresses himself well satisfied and is anxious the pamphlet should

---

[1] H. Sandwith, *An apology for the system of Weslyan Methodism, being a reply to Mr. Mark Robinson's Observations on the same subject* (London, 1825).

[2] William Shelmerdine (1759–1849), superintendent, Bridlington circuit, 1823–1825.

make its appearance. I have no fear that the cause will be discredited by the production, although the matter might doubtless have been taken up by abler heads. Having now however been at much pains, and my friends in this neighbourhood being in expectation of the speedy appearance of the reply, I hope you will not inflict on my mind the pain of a disappointment, which I own I should feel severly. May I also hope that you will favor me with an answer as *soon* as will suit your various engagements. . . .

64. *To Humphrey Sandwith*   Manchester, February 10, 1825

I am sorry that your last letter has not been sooner acknowledged. It reached me just as I was on the point of setting out on a journey; and since that time, the 'five minutes' of leisure, which you specify as necessary for my reply to its questions, have not until now been afforded to me. My opinion, as far as I am able to form one (on so hasty a view of a subject which is altogether *theoretical*, having as far as I know, never once occurred in *practice*) is as follows:

1. The prohibition in the Rule of 1797 applies, I think, to the interim between the objection of the Quarterly Meeting to any new regulation, and its confirmation by the succeeding Conference. It was obviously intended to guard the peace and piety of the Connexion against the evils which recent experience had proved to be the result of a spirit of faction and debate.

2. The prohibition applies, I think, to a Quarterly Meeting, in its corporate character; though, doubtless, any individual who *publishes* his opinions is responsible for the matter, tone, and spirit of what he publishes to the body of which he is a member.

3. I am not sure that publications so drawn up, if that be found practicable, as to be manifestly free from the mischievous tendency of exciting contention, or of disturbing the peace and *unity* of the Connexion, could fairly be brought, whatever might be thought of their *inexpediency*, within the scope of *this* Rule. As to *public* meetings, on such subjects, and under such circumstances, these appear to me to be essentially *contentious* proceedings; because the Quarterly Meeting of official persons is a constitutional organ, already provided and recognized, and can peaceably express its opinions or wishes, without the risk of inflaming popular feeling, and diverting the attention of the *Societies at large* from 'things which most concern them'.

After all, it ought to be remembered that in matters of this kind, whether they refer to civil states, or to christian churches, a wise man will look more at the practice than at the mere *theory*. Probably

H

our Constitution, as it stands on paper, may, like that of England, appear to the speculators to have some defects, and even some blemishes; and for the same reason, for neither the one nor the other was settled by professed Constitution-makers in their closets, arranging before-hand a complete and finished system, but both have arisen out of providential circumstances. Various additions have been made to each at different times, which may possibly somewhat injure the outward form, but are yet, all things considered, helpful rather than injurious to the interior conveniance and practical utility of the whole. Our machine, on the whole, works well; it perhaps never worked *so well* as at present; it would therefore be rash to pull it to pieces, for the sake of reconstructing it on principles more critically nice, in some men's estimation, and that with the certainty of doing immense mischief, during the operation, by opening the door to endless disputation about unessential things, and without any reasonable hope of satisfying all parties when we have done our best.

You will not, I am sure, omit to observe, that the 'New Rules' referred to in the article on which Mr. R[obinson] grounds his attack, can only be such as do not at all interfere with any of the rights and liberties secured to our people by the *other* Articles of the same Code, and by various Regulations made in *subsequent* years, several of which contain the most important concessions and provisions, in favour of public freedom. These 'New Rules', which may by possibility be finally confirmed, notwithstanding the objections of a *few* Quarterly Meetings, can only relate to affairs directly *spiritual*, to matters which belong exclusively to men invested with the responsibilities of the *Pastoral* Office, or, at most, to *very minor* regulations of any other class. It is really a monstrous unfairness, that Mr. R. should have taken up 'Article VII' *by itself*, and descanted upon it as if it stood alone, unconnected with other parts of the same plan, which do undeniably secure to the Leaders' Meetings and Quarterly Meetings no small influence and moral control over the proceedings of our executive government. Mr. R's strange assertion that this article gives to the Preachers 'the sole power of making *whatever* laws they please', is contrary to all the rules of common-sense interpretation, and to all practice.

Christian Societies ought not, in points of doctrine, to be 'ever learning and never coming to the knowledge of the truth', nor yet, in matters of discipline and order, to be ever disputing and never finally agreeing upon any settled plan of government. Eternal controversies about 'modes of government' may suit a few speculators, and please many who like to be employed about anything but the best things;

but they would not contribute to 'godly edifying'. As ours is only a voluntary society, those who, having joined us in ignorance, find our *fundamental principles* to be such as they cannot acquiesce in, ought at once to leave us, and go elsewhere. It is too much to ask, that we should *frequently* be forced to expend that time and effort in *defending* our system against a few dissatisfied individuals, which ought rather to be employed in *applying* the system to the experimental and practical benefit of those who have long ago made up their minds to be trained up for heaven under its teaching and discipline. Every Church owes more to the mass of its own humble and contented members than to the few who complain of those rules which it has, after mutual consultation, adopted as its basis. Those who really cannot in conscience build with us on that basis, ought not to hinder us in our work, but go at once to the erection of some new structure, more to their minds.

The idea of Methodism ever 'becoming the Established Religion of the Country with the power of demanding temporal supplies' never surely entered any brain but that of Mr. R. Methodism is an invaluable auxiliary to the National Establishment; but it has no pretentions whatever to be itself established. No 'Preacher', I am certain, ever uttered any such sentiment, 'in Conference' or elsewhere. Mr. R. ought, in honesty, to have had better authority than his favourite *on dit*, before he fathered such an absurdity on any but himself.

It is a gross untruth to say that 'the oldest member of Society is not allowed to enter any meeting of the preachers, except as a Circuit Steward he attend at the District Meeting to pay in his money'. For 1. The Circuit Stewards are authorized and invited to attend the District Meetings during the transaction of *all temporal affairs*, and have, on those affairs, an equal right to speak and vote. 2. The Circuit Stewards do not *pay in* the money raised for the Yearly Collection; but assist in *distributing* it, after the Preachers have *begged* it. 3. The 'old and respectable members', if qualified by office, do all regularly meet with the Preachers in Leaders' Meetings, and Quarterly Meetings; and there, in their proper place, have very important and influential privileges, which in point of fact they do habitually exercise. That the Preachers have *some* private meetings, of which mere members in Society do not form any constituent part, is not strange; for surely they have, as Pastors, some business which is *exclusively pastoral*. This must be allowed by all who think that Christ has instituted a distinct order of men in his Church, to be its *Pastors* and executive Rulers, as well as its teachers. If Mr. R. do not allow thus much, let him be honest and say so. But then what becomes of his

Churchmanship? What will his pretended friends the clergy say to a denial on his part of any *jus divinum* of that kind? The notorious fact is that our people have their official representatives in *all* our meetings, where *their own temporal affairs* are transacted, or *their own local officers* whether temporal or spiritual, are appointed. No Leader, no Steward, no Local Preacher can be appointed as such, without the direct and formal concurrence of their representatives in their own proper meetings. Even at the Conferences, the temporal part of the business is conducted in Committees, of which respectable laymen are always some of the most active members.

What can Mr. R. mean, in his pamphlet, by 'the attempt to introduce *Episcopal* ordination into the Conference?' If this apply to anything at all modern, it is one of the many dreams into which he has been led by his zeal to degrade the Conference, and to draw some of the uninformed clergy into a ridiculous and inconsistent sanction of his schismatic and democratical system. We already have among us, and had before Mr. R. was born, what is substantially a good and valid *presbyterian* ordination of our ministers, which every preacher receives when admitted into full connexion. And some of our wisest and oldest men, both Preachers and laymen, have thought, that the ordination, good as to its *essentials*, would become still more exactly scriptural in its *mode* and *circumstantials*, by adding to our present edifying ceremonial the ancient and expressive custom of the 'laying on of the hands of the *Presbytery*' (not of the *Episcopacy*, to which *in Mr. R's* sense of the term we neither do make, nor wish to make, any pretension) on the part of such ministers as the Body may from time to time appoint to officiate on these solemn occasions. This would not be *Episcopal* Ordination. It would only be *Presbyterian* Ordination still, though *with* imposition, instead of our present presbyterian ordination *without* that imposition of hands. Mr. R. can talk upon occasion of the 'sanction' of the 'Church of England', the 'Church of Scotland' etc. Does he not know that the imposition of hands in ordination has had from time immemorial the sanction of nearly all Churches? At all events, this is a question of *ecclesiastical* propriety and decency, and the decision of it belongs to Pastors only, not to the people or their representatives. 'The appointment of pr⟨eachers⟩ to hold missionary meetings' did not originate at all with the Conference; but was adopted on the earnest recommendation of a Committee at Sheffield, many of whom were laymen, who advised and pressed that measure, as one which all other missionary societies had adopted, because their Secretaries could not personally meet the numerous applications for deputations from the parent-institutions to the country auxiliaries. Yet this is one of Mr. Robinson's proofs that Methodism is despotism, and wants a revolution! *Ex uno, disce omnes.* You will see that I have written these remarks *currente calamo*, and without time to classify or revise them properly. If you can make any good use of them without any allusion to me, do so. If not, excuse the lengthened proof I have given that I duly appreciate your zeal in behalf of our abused and calumniated system. I only request, that when you have done with these sheets, you will take some opportunity of returning them; as they may on some future occasion refresh my memory with a hint. . . .[1]

65. *From Humphrey Sandwith*   Bridlington, March 5, 1825

By the same post, which conveys this, you will receive an invitation from our Missionary Committee to attend our Anniversary. . . . And I doubt not the Beverley friends would rejoice to have you there. . . . Should such a route be practicable to you and eventually realized, I am sure, my brother[2] though no Methodist, would feel honored by making you his visitor and give you an introduction to some of the well-informed Clergy there. You would thus plunge into the heart of *our* controversy. For, I do assure you, all classes in Beverley are deeply interested in this affair. In a letter from my brother yesterday he says, 'The strongest anxiety is evinced by all classes for the appearance of your Reply. Poor Joseph Coltman[3] (the author of the sermon I once sent you. H.S.) will be amazed. He thinks it impossible you should disprove Mark's assertion, that Conference has all the power. He trusts too that your friendship with Mr. Robinson will not be destroyed. But this I think inevitable. He has had too high an opinion of Mark's honesty and judgment. I am told, many of the Clergy at a distance bought up Mark's pamphlet by the score for distribution. He is the Dr. Sachaverel of the party. You will have the applause of all good men, honest men, and able men, I feel most confident, and the sneers of witlings, blockheads, and clergymen. I am most curious to see what Mark and his ideot disciples will do. If they do not unmask themselves, call me noodle. Already they talk

---

[1] To this letter Sandwith replied that his pamphlet had already gone to press, but he felt confirmed in his views by Bunting's statement. 'Your long silence, however unavoidable, induced a feeling of despair in my mind that you would not write,' he added; for Richard Watson had not replied to a request that he should revise the pamphlet, and Adam Clarke had replied to an inquiry too late to be of assistance. M.C.A. MSS. H. Sandwith to Jabez Bunting, February 12, 1825.

[2] Dr. T. Sandwith.

[3] Joseph Coltman (*c.* 1775–1837), Rector of Hanmeringham with Scrafield, Lincs. 1801–1837; Rector of Beverley, 1803–1813.

of answering you, I am told; and MacAfee, the Irish Preacher,[1] promises to shew us what Methodism is made of. This of course is *sous la rose*. And I may tell you as a little secret, that Mark's MSS was submitted to Mr. Coltman and Mr. Wm. Gilby,[2] both great friends of mine and both clergymen and magistrates, for their revision and correction. Of course his discomfiture will be less agreeable to them, than if they had not in any way implicated themselves in the affair. But his sophistry is so imposing he has cheated many of the Beverley gentry into a recognition of his plans. Young Mackenzie Beverley for example is one of his most fervid disciples and champions, having written a two-penny Pamphlet entitled *Reflections on the system of Methodism*.[3] This beardless boy pushed himself into notice on the platform when the last County Reform Meeting was held at York. His father is one of the Beverley aristocrats and the son has returned recently from college. He is doubtless an excellent scholar, and has the reputation of first-rate talents. This however does not appear from his pamphlet, which is little better than a school-boy's theme. I have not noticed it at all, thinking it below contempt. Nor do I wish to provoke his vengeance.

Poor Mark, I pity him from my soul. We are relatives and I am religiously indebted to him for having imbibed my first seriousness under God, from his conversations. We were for years too bosom-friends. But our friendship has been in no state of activity for some years. Our characters are flatly opposed in almost every point; and besides several private incidents occurred to cool down our mutual esteem. The public in Beverley know our friendship, but nothing of its abatement. So that I stand on delicate ground in coming forward as his opponent. I trust however I have not used greater harshness than the occasion will justify, even taking our early history into the account. I have mentioned these circumstances with a view to solicit your attention to the *Spirit* of my pamphlet. And do tell me frankly (for I love the plain truth as much, I think, as Mr. Wesley himself) if I have at all committed myself in this pirticuler. If I have, Mark will be sure to take advantage of it. For he is indebted to his constitution for a moderation in his language, which is an equally rare and valuable accomplishment in a controversial writer. There is doubtless

---

[1] Daniel M'Affee (d. 1873), the Irish Primitive Methodist brought by Mark Robinson to minister in his chapel at Beverley. He was received into the old Irish connexion in 1827.

[2] William Robinson Gilby (*c*. 1777–1848), vicar of St. Mary's, Beverley, 1823–1833.

[3] *Reflections on the present system of Methodism* (Hull, 1824). This appears to be the only reference to the authorship of this pamphlet.

a radical injustice, and the *appearance* even of a settled malignity in Mark's statements. Still I honestly believe he has not sinned against the present convictions of his mind. It strikes me he has fallen into his errors by habitually indulging a disposition to find out every flaw, and thus dwelling on the defects of Methodism, to the utter exclusion of every consideration of its excellencies.—Your admirable letter was quite in time to enable my Brother, to whom I entrusted the correction of the press, to send for the MSS from the Printer and incorporate most of it in my composition. And I do indeed feel deeply grateful to you for so many valuable suggestions, which so powerfully strengthen and enrich my reasonings. It is in the meantime highly gratifying to my mind to perceive that I had taken substantially the same view of Mr. Robinson's book as yourself. I fancy too my views on our modified dissent from the Establishment agree exactly with yours. I may justly feel proud in such a coincidence, being indebted solely to my own resources and independant researches for the view which I have exhibited of that important subject. The review of Moore's Life in the *Magazine* for this month I take to be yours;[1] and, if I mistake not, your remarks where you contrast John and Charles Wesley exactly harmonize with my own. In the review of the same book for February, which I guess to have issued from the pen of the author of 'Goodwin's Life',[2] from the *laboured* style here and there, there are some remarks on this subject, with which mine do not agree. The writer labours to shew that Wesley did not *innovate* from the Church. I have stated the contrary, and I think no candid mind can avoid the conclusion that he did.

I hope to startle Watson by my production, whose incivility in never answering my letter[3] I can attribute to no other motive than a contempt of my pretensions. If I err in this, I beg him ten thousand pardons. But I cannot divine a plausible apology for such manifest rudeness. This feeling however is merely ephemeral in my bosom, and I hope I shall obtain his better opinion in future!

If you see the Hull Papers, you will perceive another reply to Mark announced from the pen of Mr. Charles Welsh.[4] I am not

---

[1] 'A review of Rev. H. Moore's *Life of Rev. J. Wesley* [Vol. ii (London, 1825)], 3rd ser., *Wesleyan Methodist Magazine*', (1825), pp. 179–186. On pp. 183–184 there is a discussion of ordination in Methodism in Wesley's time and since, in terms very similar to those of no. 64, *supra*.

[2] The concluding part of a review of the first volume of Moore's *Life of Wesley* appeared in the *Wesleyan Methodist Magazine*, 3rd ser., iv (1825), pp. 106–112. The author of the *Life of John Goodwin* (London, 1822) was Thomas Jackson.

[3] Cf. n. 1, p. 109.

[4] Charles Welch, *An investigation of Mr. Mark Robinson's 'Observations on the system of Wesleyan Methodism'* (London, 1825).

acquainted with the writer. Mr. McNicoll, the Hull Preacher, speaks highly of it, having heard read or seen the MSS. In truth I suspect he has assisted Welsh at least by his advice and perhaps by his pen also. Mark, I think, will find himself awkwardly hemmed in, being exposed to two fires. From Mr. Welsh's announcement, I guess we are pursued a totally different course. His production will I think be a more artificial exposition of our Constitution, in all its branches. Mine is rather a natural and direct reply to my opponent's charges. I attack him and dislodge him at the point of the bayonet from every position which he successively occupies, giving him no quarter till the whole field is my own. I am most curious to see Mr. Welsh's production, which I expect will get the start of me and perhaps reach Bridlington today, Saturday. Mine, I confidently expect, will appear next Saturday. I shall send you a copy, with your letter, by one of the carriers, which will be a cheap mode of conveyance.

May I finally request your assistance at Conference in the appointment of our Preachers. We really retrograde sadly in public opinion here by having such, on the whole, miserable appointments. We are quite below par. Could we once have piety and ability united, we might hope to revive a little, raise our preachers' allowance and go on better in future. I beseech you, do us a service so all-important to our interests in this place. . . .

66. *From Thomas Galland*[1]   Beverley, June 30, 1825

[They have had a successful missionary meeting. Without regretting his choice of religious position, he often feels ill at ease at the lack of cultivated and literary society to which he is used, and has wondered whether he would not be more useful to the Society as a supernumerary.]

. . . when I take into account also our *destitution* of local preachers in this town and neighbourhood, and that there is every indication that Mark Robinson's party (being already engaged in the erection of a *splendid and spacious chapel* in this town, and contemplating others) mean to make *a life or death effort* in this neighbourhood during the ensuing year—I say all these considerations induce me strongly to solicit *two young men* to be appointed with me on this Circuit: one of whom I request may be *Joseph R. Stephens*,[2] and the other if he be

---

[1] Thomas Galland M.A. (d. 1843, *aet.* 48), first superintendent of the Beverley circuit, 1824–1827. A man of local property, he was reputed the most wealthy and most Whiggish of the Wesleyan preachers of his generation.

[2] Joseph Rayner Stephens (1805–1879), preacher, Beverley circuit, 1825–1826. The son of John Stephens (q.v.), he became a schoolmaster at Cottingham near

not previously engaged, Mr. *William Bunting*:[1] . . . I should be glad to read Greek and Hebrew with these young men, for my own improvement and theirs. Mr. Stephens who has been with me since the commencement of the year is a truly valuable young man, and likely to prove both as regards depth of piety, superior abilities and assiduity in their cultivation, a very efficient servant of the Connexion.

I suppose every District will urge its claims in the *Stationing Committee*, but I will assure you that this neighbourhood claims especial care, *things are low at Hull*, and *very much out of order in Holderness* (*Patrington Circuit*). Driffield and Bustington too, are only *so so* as the saying is. Bustington especially seems to have *very respectable capabilities* as a *Methodist station*, and past appointments seem to have been not well suited . . . even [to] its *continuance in statu quo*. . .

67. *From Humphrey Sandwith*   Bridlington, July 20, 1825

I avail myself of Mr. Shelmerdine's polite offer, to convey to you the high gratification I have derived from *your* able defence of Methodism.[2] In assuming that point, I cannot possibly discredit you should the conjecture be erroneous. Yours or Mr. Watson's the article is most undoubtedly, but I think the style is yours. The Connexion must feel itself under lasting obligations to the author of so powerful a composition. I put it into the hands of Archdeacon Wrangham, who acknowledges its ability. I observe with pleasure the promise of a further exposition and defence of our system in its political relations. This is much needed, alike from the *radicalism* which prevails no little in our own society, and from the view which many intelligent men in the nation entertain of the power of Conference. You have doubtless heard, that Mr. Robinson's pamphlet has even prejudiced the Revd. Robt. Hall[3] against us.

Hull in 1823 and now received his first circuit appointment. After leaving the Wesleyan ministry in 1834, he achieved national fame as a violent popular agitator in the Ten Hours, anti-Poor Law, and Chartist agitations.

[1] William Maclardie Bunting, (1805–1866), eldest s. of Jabez Bunting by his first wife, Sarah Maclardie. Became preacher in 1824, receiving an appointment to Salford, 1824–1827. A prominent Protestant politician, he was very active in the Evangelical Alliance from its inception, and succeeded his father as honorary secretary 1858. *Memorials of the late William M. Bunting*, ed. G. Stringer Rowe (London, 1870), pp. 25, 160.

[2] An unsigned 'Review of pamphlets on Methodism' dealing with the publications evoked by Mark Robinson's case appeared in two parts in the *Wesleyan Methodist Magazine*, 3rd ser., iv (1825), pp. 459–468, 530–538. It was in fact written by Richard Watson.

[3] Robert Hall (1764–1831), celebrated Baptist divine, at this time minister of Harvey Lane, Leicester.

I am happy to learn, that my efforts have given you satisfaction. *Valeant quantum valere queant.* . . .

68. From James Bate[1]   Wisbeach, April 8, 1825

As you were so kind as to give me the information contained in yours of March 11th I judge it my duty to say in return—I did not know of any steps like those stated in the letter to Mr. Stocks.[2] Last week we had our Q[uarterl]y Meeting, and nothing on that subject was brought forward. When I received yours, I judged it proper to let no one know of the information I had received. Seemingly to know nothing but what came under my own observation. The matter was designed to be kept from my knowledge. But it came out that something would be agitated at the Q[uarterly] Meeting and [it] was also said that it would be opposed. I made very little reply to my informer. But my intention was if any motion was made, to observe that I am a Methodist Preacher from conscience and my determination is not to *mind*, but to *keep* our rules—and had it been urged, to break up the Meeting. But I feel thankful to God he ordered it otherwise. Our meeting was as it has always been, begun and ended in peace and love. And I feel a hope that the *secret ferment* will *subside*. I trust Mr. Stocks's answer and a little more thought have changed Mr. W.['s] views, or at least moderated them.

The newspapers had stated that all the Local Preachers in Beverley had withdrawn in consequence of the ill treatment sustained by one of their brethren from the Superintendent. The Local Preachers in several circuits felt uneasy; and were very desirous to see Robinson's phamphlets. And you can judge of the effect, where there was any previous tendancy to *reform*, etc., etc., especially where the subject was only partially known. I understand that some one has undertaken to answer Mr. R. My opinion is, the subject would die of itself, if they let it alone.

As the work Mr. Waller spoke of, I heard nothing of it lately, and fully believe it will never see the light. Mr. Waller is an upright man, and one of fair abilities, but he often forms opinions hastily, and is

---

[1] James Bate (1784–1855), superintendent, Wisbeach circuit, 1822–1825.

[2] This letter gives the first hint of the further repercussions of Mark Robinson's agitation, which are more fully dealt with in nos. 77 and 78 *infra*. The pamphlet literature referred to in the letter has not been traced. Samuel Stocks, a prosperous Manchester merchant and former Methodist circuit steward was the principal supporter of the Ancoats Tent Mission, and the communication opened with him by the Wisbeach men exemplifies the common tendency of opponents of the connexional management to combine. On Edmund Waller, see nos. 77 and 78.

equally free in speaking his thoughts. Yet I have often found that time and a little more acquaintance, have moderated his views. Mr. W. is a Trustee for some of our chapels, and has sometimes been brought into difficulties on that accoun[t]. He has also indulged in the idea that due attention has not been paid to thier complaints. This Circuit has 12 chapels and only two can meet the intrest, without extra exertion. We are obliged also to make quarterly collections to aid the Circuit, beside those for the cause generally. So that we can scarsely go round the circuit, without having something to introduce of money matters. And though we endeavour to do all in the spirit of the Gospel, the preachers are viewed by some as mercenary. As the Conference has made provision against building chapels improperly, and dividing circuits, where the number is already insufficient to support themselves I trust the above difficulties are got to the height. Yet if I may be allowed to give an opinion—no circuit should be divided unless that circuit can already maintain itself. I speak thus because I have often gone to newly formed circuits, and frequently witnessed the inconveniences which have followed.

But to return to Wisbeach. Our prospects are better and though I lament, we have had no increase in our numbers, I hope to leave things better than I found them. And my successor will have less difficulties to encounter. When I was appointed to the Circuit, some of the Brethren advised me to object [to] comeing, from what they knew. Their statements led me to forbode unpleasant things. But the Lord has been better than my fears. I may say if Wisbeach Circuit cannott do like many of their neighbours, I have always felt satisfied, they have done what they could. . . .

69. *From J. Roadhouse*[1]   Ely, April 29, 1825

You will I believe excuse the liberty I take in writing to you when you have read the contents of my letter and learn that my wish in writing to you is for you to bring forward at the ensuing Conference two or three subjects which I have for a length of time thought would be of real use to our connexion and bring glory to God.

The first subject I would name is the examination of persons who are brought forward at our Local Preachers meeting to be received on trial as Local Preachers. I have often thought it would be well if the Conference would publish directions or say what questions shall be asked them. How long they should be kept on trial, and how they should be examined before they are received on the Plan as regular Local Preachers? Would it not be well for them to undergo an examination

---

[1] John Roadhouse (1783–1872), superintendent, Ely circuit, 1823–1825.

when received as regular Local Preachers before either the Quarterly Meeting, or in the Chapel either before the Society or Congregation? And either in the Society, or congregation, be received as persons proper to be put on the Plan in a regular way. I am apprehensive that most if not all who are taken on to the Plan have various questions put to them conserning experience, doctrines, and decipline, and very properly, but I have heard it asked have we Rules to direct, or authorize us to ask such and such questions? I think that many are not continued on trial a sufficient length of time, especially in some of the smaller Circuits. Was the Conference to say what time they should be kept on trial etc. it would prevent much unnecessary conversation on the subject.

The second subject I wish you to take up relates to our Sunday Schools. I have often thought was the Conference too appoint three or four senior Preachers, and the same number of friends who are not Preachers, but who are well acquainted with Sunday Schools, and direct them to draw up Rules for the conducting of Sunday Schools amongst us many of our schools would be put on a better Plan and be more usefull:[1]

1st. Rules for appointing, and the direction of Committees for Sunday Schools, when appointed or formed.

2nd. Rules for appointing, and directing teachers for Sunday Schools, and who engage in them.

3rd. Rules for the instruction and government of the children, I here refer to what they should be taught when they attend the school and advice might be given as to what correction ought to be given—how they might, and ought to be catechized and attend the worship of God, etc., etc.

I think it would be well were Preachers and friends to draw up the best Rules they could, for those Rules to be recommended by our Conference for all our Sunday Schools to be conducted according to the said Rules. Had this Plan been adopted several years back I think it would have prevented several of our friends from intraduceing writeing into our Schools on the Lord's day—and I feel confident it would have prevented much unnecessary conversation in Sunday School Committee meetings, and in Teachers' meetings; whilest it would have been of great use in the establishment of ⟨Sun⟩day Schools. The Rules recommended by the ⟨Sunda⟩y School Union

---

[1] A Conference committee on Sunday schools in which Bunting was the moving spirit was appointed in 1826, and produced 'General principles and rules to be observed in the management of Methodist Sunday Schools', approved by Conference in 1827 (*Minutes of the Methodist Conferences*, vi, pp. 284–291). For one of the by-products of this committee's work, see *infra* no. 85.

are good—but some hav⟨e as⟩ked are these Rules most suitable for
Methodist Sunday Schools? and various answers ⟨have⟩ been given.
I think it would be possible for better Rules to be drawn up than
some of these are, at least for the use of our Schools. Would it not be
well for all the School Books proper to be used in our Sunday Schools
for teaching and rewards, etc., to be printed at our office and published by our Book Steward? This would be a means of keeping out
Calvanism and all other isms we think unscriptural. My dear Sir, I
hope you will turn your attention to this subject for I think [the]
sooner something of this sort is done the better.

A *third* subject I will take the liberty of naming relates to the
settlement of our Chapels. I am afraid that sufficient care has not been
taken by many Country Attorneys to assertain wether or not the
Title has been good before they have drawn up the deeds—and I
have thought it would be well for our Conference to employ a
Counsellor to examine abstracts of Titles before the Chapel is built
or deeds drawn out. Would it not be well and be a saving to our
Connexion was the Conference to allow a proper Conveyancer, who
belongs to the Temple, some thing annually to draw up all our deeds.
There is a Mr. Matthews from near Cambridge who is a Local
Preacher studying for a Counsellor, a cleaver young Man—is
qualified to act as a conveyancer, who would do his best for us if
employed I have not any doubt.

In a Circuit where I laboured a few years back a Chapel was built
just before I went; by the desire of the Trustees I called upon the
Attorney who drew up the Deed to pay him for it. When he had got
the money and I the deed—he gravely told me he would not give us
sixpence for the title but that it was as good a one has he could make
out.

Excuse me and I will name a fourth subject. I think we want
amongst us Notes on the Old Testament and Mr. Wesley's on the
New[1] to be published in Quarto and sold in numbers and parts—
the whole not to cost more than [£]3.0.0 in Boards. Many, very, many
of our members and hearers are taking Brown's[2] and others which
have sentiments in them opposed to ours. A cheap short commentary
on the Scriptures or Notes would sell well amongst us if not above
three Pounds and would tend greatly to the spiritual improvement
of our hearers—I do think could yourself be engaged by the Conference or were you to publish such a work yourself did you include

---

[1] John Wesley, *Explanatory notes upon the Old Testament* (London, 1765–7)
and *Explanatory notes upon the New Testament* (London, 1755).

[2] Probably the *Self-interpreting Bible* by John Brown of Haddington, first
published London, 1778, which went through numerous editions.

in it Mr. Wesley's Notes it would be of great use, and [the] sooner it is announced and published the better for our Connexion.

We have not anything very particular going forward in this part of the Kingdom. I am sorry to say there is not much union in the Cambridge Circuit betwixt the Travelling and Local Preachers. . . .

70. *From William Morley*   Doncaster, July 14, 1825

. . . I am wondering wether Conference will express any decided opinion and give any advice in their Yearly adress respecting the Anti-Slavery Society;[1] wether the hands of his Majesty Government would be strengthened . . . or wether it would be desirable for the whole of our Society to petition the Legislature . . . to abstain wholly if possible . . . from West India Produce (Sugar) . . . or in what way we could render assistance to ameliorate the condition of the West India slave . . . so as to hasten that period when he shall enjoy the rights and priviledges of a Man and a Brother . . . The Friends, or Quakers, in their Yearly Epistle tutch on this great Subject. . . .

71. *From William Myles*   Liverpool, July 13, 1825

It is a fact that a spirit of uneasiness prevails in this Society,[2] and whether I should say any thing concerning it, has been a matter of thought to me. If you think I should say nothing concerning it, burn this letter; on the other hand if you think my giving you my opinion will not be obtrusive you are very welcome to consider its contents.

The 1st thing that I observed that caused uneasiness was Mr. Wood's[3] mention of the wish of the last Conference respecting the division of the Circuit. He did it in the most inoffensive manner, would have no discussion at that time, but gave them a month to

[1] In 1825 Conference condemned certain Methodist missionaries in Jamaica who had compromised on the principle of slavery, and reflected on the character of the anti-slavery agitators in England. In November 1825, the *Wesleyan Methodist Magazine*, 3rd ser., iv, pp. 766–770 carried extensive extracts from the report of the Anti-Slavery Society. In 1829 Conference exhorted Methodist Societies to join with other Christians in petitioning Parliament for the abolition of slavery, and in 1830 condemned the principle of colonial slavery at length.

[2] This letter from William Myles, supernumerary preacher in Liverpool (1824–1828), sketches the local unrest created by the division of the Circuit in 1826, which inflamed the delicate situation in Leeds, and united with Dr. Warren in open revolt in 1835. The hostility between the decaying town-centre societies, and the pretensions of prosperous suburban chapels recognized in the new circuit division was here as sharp as in Manchester and Leeds.

[3] Thomas Wood M.A. (d. 1826, *aet.* 60), superintendent, Liverpool circuit, 1823–1825.

consider on it; Mr. John Russell immediately got up and said, 'he hoped as soon as it would be mentioned it would be scouted out of the meeting'. Several cried out there was to be nothing said at present. When the month was elapsed Mr. Wood in a religious spirit introduced the subject. Prior to this those that were against it had a private meeting, so that when it was introduced into the Leaders' Meeting Messrs. John Russell, P. McClintock, D. Rowland, John Dean, with several of the Welch Leaders,[1] and some of the English Leaders spoke against it, so that the majority of the meeting was against the measure. Messrs. Kirkpatrick, Atherton, Bell[2] and your present correspondent were on the side of the Conference. Mr. Highfield I think was newter, and the Welch Preacher Mr. Jones[3] was I beleive against the division.

21y. Matters went on tolerably quiet till the March Quarterly-Meeting. Mr. Comer got up and said, he respected all the Preachers; but thought they had all better remove, except Mr. Bell. This was objected to by Mr. McClintock, they proceeded to vote, and Mr. Wood, Highfield and Kirkpatrick were to remove; and Mr. Atherton to remain a third year. The Stewards' letter proves this. Since then the uneasiness has increased. I will now tell you, what I think has led these Leaders astray.

1. They seem to act as if they were an independant church. The Leaders meeting sometimes act as a parliment, make Rules, have a secretary beside the Stewards, who writes down what they call their measures and orders, sometimes as a Court of Justice; and, when they wish to use harsh language towards the Preacher, as a Court of Inquisition, by telling the Preacher particularly Mr. Wood, 'I heard such a thing', and immediately begin to question and examine him. As far as I have seen Mr. Wood has acted in the most peaceable religious manner, and only wished to promote the religious union of the society; and to attend to the Rules of the connection. At one time when Mr. McClintock gave him very hard speeches, by way of

---

[1] John Russell, basket maker, later lost his sight, seceded to the Wesleyan Methodist Association 1835. David Rowland became leader of the Liverpool Methodist reformers; unstable in personality and insecure in career, he was successively ship-broker, tea-dealer, secretary to the Liverpool Pilots' Association, and book-keeper; seceded to the Wesleyan Methodist Association 1835, but subsequently left it. The 'Welch Leaders' were the Leaders of the Liverpool (Welsh) circuit, which had had a semi-independent existence since 1803.

[2] Cleland Kirkpatrick (1765–1834), William Atherton (d. 1850, *aet.* 74), President 1846, Alexander Bell (1788–1851), preachers, Liverpool circuit, the first two, 1823–5, the third, 1824–6.

[3] George Highfield (1761–1852), preacher, Liverpool circuit, 1823–1825. David Jones (2) (d. 1830, *aet.* 39), sole preacher, Liverpool (Welsh) circuit, 1824–1826.

salvo, he told him and the meeting, 'if it was the *King* sat there, he would speak to him in the same way, if he thought he did wrong'. And when Mr. John Russell used very hard words, his excuse was 'he would speak his mind let who would be pleased or, displeased'. I have heard a few of our respectable friends (I do not converse with many) admire the patience of Mr. Wood, Braike, and Mr. John Jones, Senr., considering the taunts and reflections they met with from these two men.

31y. I will now tell you what I think would make for the peace and prosperity of the Society; and I am satisfied I speak the sense of numbers of the Leaders and members. But the Conference is the best judge; and in their united wisdom I will chearfully confide. The Welch society should be wholly separate from the English society. They have a weekly Leaders-meeting of their own; they enter in their Books their Class-money, though they bring it in two days after to the Liverpool Stewards, who pays their preacher his weekly board and all his other expences. Not one of them subscribes a shilling annually to the Schools or to the Fund of mercy. They are one with the party here that are against the ⟨w⟩ish of the Conference, with regard to the division of the Circuit.

The Liverpool stewards wish them to pay their own Preacher and to be separate. But they will not, they come and vote for English Preachers, for, or against them, just as Messrs. McClintock and his friends wish them to do. Several of them signed this protest as it is called against Mr. Wood's conduct in this late affair respecting Mr. McClintock and Rolland. Their Preacher Mr. Jones it appears from his conduct must do, and say, as they do.

The Liverpool society should also be divided, it would answer many very valuable purposes. Numbers of the brethren assembled in Conference, know what would promote the welfare of the Society better than I do, and none better than the present President, Mr. Newton[1] and yourself. They no doubt will give their opinion.

Mr. Wood has committed himself and his conduct to your wisdom and judgment. Mr. McClintock and Rowland and their friends have done all in their power to prevent its going to Conference, they would do almost any thing if he would give that point up, he has stood firm and would lay it before you. What he has gone through has injured his health, in some degree. My prayer is that the Lord may direct you and the brethren to do what will be for the Glory of God, and the peace and harmony of this Society. . . .

[1] Robert Newton, President of Conference, 1824–1825.

72. *Report of Conference Committee on Liverpool disputes*, signed by
J. Entwisle,[1] President, John Gaulter,[2] and Jabez Bunting, Secretary
Liverpool, August 19, 1825

Report and resolutions of the deputation appointed by the Conference, at the request of certain persons in Liverpool, to examine the
matters in dispute there, and to take such measures as may seem to
them most likely to promote permanent peace and good order in
that Society.

The deputation who actually assembled at Liverpool were the
President and Secretary of the Conference, Mr. Gaulter, and Mr. G.
Marsden, Dr. Clarke[3] being prevented from attending by a mistake
as to the time appointed, and Mr. Newton by severe illness.

The deputation first met in private on Thursday morning, August
18, 1825, when they carefully read and examined all the documents
addressed to the Conference on the subjects which they were charged
to consider. They met, on the evening of the same day, a very large
number of the local preachers, Leaders, Stewards, and Trustees with
the Preachers last year stationed in Liverpool, in order to receive any
further information or evidence as to facts, which Mr. McC[l]intock
and his friends on the one hand, or Mr. Wood on the other hand,
might be desirous of communicating. They then retired into the
adjoining vestry for the purpose of deliberation; when they agreed
upon the following

Resolutions.

1. It is the unanimous opinion of the deputation that their
respected friend Mr. Thomas Wood, the Superintendent of the
Liverpool Circuit, has acted contrary to the Rules of the Connexion
in his manner of excluding Mr. McClintock from the Society; and
that, as the exclusion was illegal, Mr. McClintock should be now
considered as restored to his situation as a member, Leader, and
Local Preacher.

2. The deputation, however, wish it to be understood that if Mr.
Wood deem it right to bring any charges against Mr. McClintock,
whether for insulting language, or any other violation of his christian
or official duty, such charges may still be adduced and heard, according to Rule, before the proper meetings.

[1] Joseph Entwisle (1767–1841), President of Conference, 1812, 1825. Superintendent, Birmingham circuit, 1823–1826. Governor of Theological Institution,
1834–1838.

[2] John Gaulter (d. 1839, *aet.* 74), superintendent, London (East) circuit, 1824–
1827.

[3] Adam Clarke, now resident at Millbrook, near Liverpool.

I

3. The deputation also judge it necessary to state their conviction that Mr. Wood acted, in the case referred to, from error in judgment, and that he sincerely *designed* to promote the peace and prosperity of the Society. And they further declare it to be their conviction from what they have heard this night, that Mr. McClintock has been too much in the habit of using strong and unbecoming expressions in the various meetings and that even on his own shewing, he has not always manifested sufficient respect for the official character and decisions of those who are 'over him in the Lord'.

4. It appears to deputation, that much injury to the work of God must necessarily result from the largeness of the Leaders' Meeting at Liverpool; as it is absolutely impossible, while there is but one such meeting in so numerous a Society, that the Superintendent and his colleagues should sufficiently perform their duties in that Meeting as Christian Pastors, or that the *proper work* of a Leaders' Meeting, as defined by our Rules, should be duly accomplished. In conformity, therefore, to the original plan of Mr. Wesley, whose example in London we deem binding as a precedent in all similar cases,—and to the express direction of the Conference, whose judgment on this part of the subject was explicitly stated to the deputation,—we decidedly advise Mr. Riles and his colleagues to meet the Leaders hereafter in *separate* weekly meetings at the various chapels where their several classes are accustomed to assemble for the reception of their tickets: *viz.* one Leaders' Meeting should be held after preaching at Pitt Street; another at Mount Pleasant; another at Leeds Street, another at Brunswick; another at Benn's Gardens; and another at the Pottery.

This measure the deputation unanimously believe to be *indispensable* to the proper execution of Methodist discipline, and to the full spiritual prosperity of this extensive and important Society.

5. Considering that in London and Manchester it has pleased God so greatly to bless the division of our large Societies there into several Circuits; and that in Liverpool and its vicinity there are already such a multitude of persons gathered into our Society, who need the most minute and vigilant exercise of pastoral care, in order to their preservation and edification, as well as so many *tens of thousands* of ignorant or unconverted sinners, for whose sake we ought to aim at every possible enlargement of the work of God; *we strongly recommend to the Quarterly Meeting*, in the name and on behalf of the Conference, to agree upon some suitable division of the Liverpool Circuit, which may take place at the time of the next Conference, in August 1826. And our opinion is that the plan of division which will be found, on the whole, most conducive to general

peace and prosperity is *that* which would connect the Pitt Street, Leeds Street, Pottery, and Welsh Societies, with the country places on the banks of the Mersey and in Worral [Wirrall], and the preaching to sailors on the river, in one Circuit to be called *Liverpool West*, and the Mount Pleasant Brunswick, Prescot, and St. Helen's Societies, with the other country-places in that direction in another Circuit to be called *Liverpool East*.[1] The deputation believe that such a division would call forth, on each side, of the boundary that may be agreed upon, much additional zeal and exertion, in various departments which it would please God eventually to crown with success, in an increase of prayer-meetings, congregations, Societies, and chapels.

6. If it be a *fact*, that separate meetings of a part of the Leaders have in any case been held for the purpose of discussing subjects connected with the affairs of the Society, or of passing resolutions on such subjects, independently of their Brethren, and even without the sanction of the Superintendent; the deputation must strongly express their regret at such illegal proceedings, which are not only a direct breach of Rule, but naturally subversive of christian unity, and calculated to produce endless jealousies and animosities among those who ought to love as Brethren.

7. With respect to the proper business of Leaders' Meetings, and the best mode of conducting those meetings, the deputation will be happy to give their affectionate advice to the Brethren, in the meeting assembled this evening.

These resolutions on the return of the deputation to the Meeting, were diliberately read and explained. A conversation of considerable length followed, which was, on the whole, satisfactory to the deputation, and encouraged them to hope that peace, good order and prosperity will be forthwith restored. The meeting were pleased to express by an unanimous vote their satisfaction with the proceedings of the deputation.

Previously to their leaving Liverpool, the deputation again met each other, on Friday morning, August 19th, when it was further agreed,

1. That Mr. Gaulter, Mr. Marsden, and Mr. Bunting, who are going to Manchester, shall solicit an interview with Mr. Riles,[2] and fully explain to him the views and wishes of the deputation on the measures recommended in the preceeding resolutions.

[1] A division under the titles of Liverpool North and Liverpool South was in fact adopted.

[2] John Riles, superintendent, Liverpool circuit, 1825–1826.

2. That if Mr. Riles and his colleages find any unexpected difficulties in the immediate division of the Leaders' Meetings, as directed
by the Conference, those members of the deputation who are
stationed in Manchester and Salford be requested and authorized to
act for the whole deputation in giving such aid to the accomplishment of that indispensable measure as circumstances may seem to
them to require.

3. That the *principle* mentioned in the 4th of the resolutions
adopted last night, *viz.* that of the Leaders belonging in future to
the Society and Leaders' Meetings connected with the chapels at
which their classes meet for tickets,—is only to be understood as a
general rule; and must of course be modified in particular cases, at
the discretion of the Superintendent, as the convenience of individuals, and a supreme regard to the public good, may require. In
making out their next plan for the Quarterly Visitation of the
classes, these modifications will naturally occur.

4. The President is requested, if his convenience will permit, and
if circumstances at the time should appear to him, and to Mr.
Riles and his colleagues, to render it desirable, to attend at the
March Quarterly Meeting in Liverpool, or whenever the subject of
the recommended division of the Circuit may come on for decision.
Messrs, Marsden, Newton and Bunting are also included in this
request.

73. *From John Riles*   Liverpool, October 11, 1825

It is not at all unlikely, but various reports have travelled from
hence to Manchester, respecting what we have done, and how we
have done it. You shall have as short a history of the business, as is
consistent with facts. The afternoon I met with Mr. Gaulter, Mr.
Marsden,[1] with yourself at Chorlton Row. Mr. Gaulter said to me,
'Well no one needs fear going to Liverpool now, every thing is
favourable to peace.' I was happy to hear of the good effects produced by the visit of the deputation, but could not give my friend
Gaulter credit for the full extent of what his words might convey;
for I well knew of what sort of stuff the Lancashire materials were
composed off, when religious politicks were blended with radical
feelings. However, I knew the deputation had done much, and under
God we are indebted to their labour of love for our success so far.
On the first Friday night after our arrival we met the Leaders, as
usual, and there was a very full meeting. After I had taken my seat,

---

[1] Cf. final resolution no. 1, in no. 72, *supra*.

a young man on my right hand ascended to his seat, with an air of great self-importance; he mended his pens, and laid out his paper in due form to commence an opperation if necessary. I examined all the Class Books, which took up a full hour, and as there was no other business, I rose to sing a verse, when an old man tapped me upon the shoulder, with, 'Sir, I have something new to propose.' I answered, then we cannot hear it; and the meeting was concluded by 8¼ after o'Clock. So we proceeded the three following Friday evenings, when the *man at my right*, finding he had nothing to do, but mend his pens, and replenish his inkorn gave up his post, without observation, and we have not seen him since. By the time we had held our third Leaders' Meeting, various opinions were in circulation. 'It was a dead calm after a storm'—'They wondered what the Preachers intended to do'—Some thought the Preachers would give it up altogether—While others were busy in concerting measures to prevent the recommendation of the deputation from being carried into effect, which they (a part of the Leaders) had equivocally consented to. For they had no *idea whatever* of a division taking place, unless the question was fairly (as they termed it) debated in a full Leaders Meeting, and carried by a majority. To prevent this, several of the most active of the oposition, had been trying all their strength, and came to the meeting fully confident, they should successfully prevent the division. I was fully apprised of all their manoeuv[r]ing, and low cunning, and although I had the most perfect confidence in my Brethren, that they were good and true men, yet I had a thousand fears, least I should fail in accomplishing my object, by taking a step so noval in modern Methodism in this town. I felt for my own credit, least I should betray an important trust put into my hands by the Conference, and disappoint their expectation. For near a week, before the question was to be decided, I could not obtain five minutes sleep at one time, during the whole night. This was owing to my weak debilitated state, which has been much affected by the change, though I hope in the end will prove beneficial. On the Friday evening I was quit[e] exhausted, and had it been a subject upon any minor point, should have employed one of my Brethren. But, as matters stood, I was determined to risk every thing, and by looking up to *Him* for strength, who had always been 'Help at hand', I was enabled to go through the duties of the evening, at least to my own satisfaction. At 7 o'Clock the vestry was crowded with Leaders and Stewards, which made the place like a stove. I examined all the Class Books, and as they are all audited, it took up an hour and half. I then rose, and requested the attention of the meeting to what I was about to announce, *viz*. 'I stand hear as the accredited Pastor of the Liverpool

Methodist Society, by the appointment of the Conference, and as such, I divide the Friday evening's Leaders' Meeting held at Mount Pleasant Chapel Vestry into six divissions, to meet at Mount Pleasant, on the Tuesday evening; Brunswick, on Thursday evening; Leeds Street, Thursday evening; Pitt Street, Thursday evening; The Pottery on Monday evening; and Benns-Garden, on an evening in the week to be fixed upon.' As soon as I had concluded the sentance, a man from the other side of the room vociferated, with apparent bad feeling, 'What did we come here for, if we have no voice in the business?' To which I replied '*To hear what I have to say, and do what I bid you, as your Pastor.*' I then gave out a verse and concluded with prayer, and the meeting was dismissed by a few minutes after nine o'Clock. You will naturally suppose that in a meeting like that, where everything had been debated with noise and clamor, and authority trampled under foot by the majority, that such a step would create various feel[ing]s. I need not say that all the real friends of Methodism rejoiced; and the ungovernable were taken so much by surprise, that for the moment they were confounded. When they had recovered themselves, which they did not do, till they got in groups in the street, the first thing they could articulate, was, 'It is the most arbitrary, tyrannical step we ever knew or heard of.' We have reason to be thankful to the Great Head of the Church, that every thing appears to promise peace; for though there are a few rough spirits at Leeds Street, we hope 'ere long, either to kill or cure, by enforcing the Rules of Methodism, by firm but gentle measures. We have gained one important point, by having driven the factious from their *talking fort*, and we must ⟨no⟩w exercise them upon new ground (at least to some ⟨of⟩ them) where they will have *more to do*, and *less to say*.

Since the Friday evening's meetings, we have had our Local Preachers Meeting and Quarter-day, which concluded in peace; and last week we held an adjourned meeting of the Quarter day, to finish our arrangements for the classes belonging to each place; the local Society Stewards, and Poor Stewards; and appoint a Committee of Enquiry to build a new Chapel in that part of the Town called the Park.[1] This measure meets with almost universal approval; and we hope to have it opened before the next Conference. The intention of the friends is to go to the expence of £2500 including the

---

[1] Wesley Chapel, Stanhope Street, opened in Liverpool South Circuit, 1827, possessed of 'a powerful organ giving solemnity to its services', and 'a semi-religious light falling through an oval window of stained glass' which 'imparts a sacred shade to the communion table'. J. Betjeman, *First and last loves* (London, 1952), p. 102.

purchase of the land. This Chapel will belong to the Mount and Brunswick side in case of a division.

I remain very weak, but I have reason to believe my health is improving. . .

74. *From John Riles*   Liverpool, December 3, 1825

. . . I have very great pleasure in informing you that everything in our Societies and meetings begins to wear a Methodist appearance; and all our principle friends frequently express their satisfaction at the change which has taken place. I intend if spared till the Quarter Day to propose several of our principle friends as stewards at the several Chapels, which will add a considerable degree of useful influence into the Leaders'-Meetings. I have prevailed upon Mr. Comer to consent to be proposed as one of the Society Stewards at Leeds Street, where he is much respected for his attention to the Chapel and School their; and so of the rest. Brunswick congregation and Society are now in a better state than ever. Indeed we have great reason for thankfulness to the great head of the Church for our peace, and prospects. As I have began, I may as well go through the business stick by stick, till more is done. Already a few say I am the greatest tyrant that ever came to Liverpool. I intend to propose at the Quarter Day, that after the Christmas quarter the Welch shall maintain their own preacher, and defray all their own expences. They are upwards of 360 Members, which they gave in, in September, and how many more thay could have numbered, if they had been obliged to support themselves, I can only conjecture. They have been a very heavy burden upon the Liverpool Society for several years. I believe there will be no difficulty in carrying this point, as our Stewards are for the measure.

The Jordan Street School is properly secured for the use of the Methodist[s]. It cost near £5000, and [h]as but about £1000 debt upon it. You are aware that Mr. Comer was an active friend in promoting this day school. As he wished to be a Trustee, by a legal instrument he conveyed to me all right and tittle to it, and I went and took legal possession of it; and then by an instrument prepared, conveyed it to thirteen Trustees, all members of the Methodist Society. When the number of Trustees is reduced to seven, the survivers are to elect three, who are members of the Society, and the Quarter Day to appoint the other three. According to a clause in the Deed, if a Trustee ceases to be a member of the Society, he ceases to be a Trustee. Every thing has been done to secure this School to the Methodists that can be done. It appears to me that this day School is likely to prove a more efficient method of promoting our interest than the Sunday Schools. The whole proceeding does credit to both the head and heart of Mr. Comer. Then at the three School[s], wholly under our influence, who are in daily attendance 697 Boys, 382 Girls, and 345 Infants, making, with the Sunday School, 2,114. All these except the infants regularly and statedly attend God's public worship. What a prospect of a harvest!

You have no doubt heard of our intention to build another chapel in the Park. The building committee are in treaty with Mr. Foster, Lord Sefton's Steward, for a plot, or rather piece of ground at the top of Stanhope St. in the Park consisting of 20,000!!! square yards, at 7/– per yard. They are only waiting for his Lordship, when he comes into the town to confirm the proposal made by his Steward. They intend to build the chapel the size of Leeds St, and only to have a debt of £2,000, upon the chapel; with a burying ground of 1,000 square yards. Our friends are very sanguine in their expectations. The inhabitants in the Park come forward very generously, and it is expected to raise by subscriptions £2,000. If we succeed in the purchase of, which we know of no reason to doubt, we shall have it opened before the Conference. . . .

75. *From Hugh Carter*[1]   Coventry, October 5, [18]25

My circumstances compels me to write for your advice. I was secretly informed by one of our Local Preachers on the morning of our Quarter Day that another of our Local Preachers, a man of a very virulent temper whom Mr. Brooke[2] my predecessor had offended before he left by putting him out of a little office, had convened most of the local brethren in a private house where they were harangued on the utility of what he called 'standing by each other', and first not to tell anything in [the] Local Preachers meeting that they knew wrong in each other. 2ly. to object to make any collections but their own Quarterly collections. 3rdly. to refuse to preach at all unless they were allowed to preach in Coventry morning and evenings as well as afternoons. I thank God I was in no wise irritated—but when the meeting began, as a stranger who had not known them long, I charged them to act faithful towards each other as in the sight of God and of his Holy Angels—lest sin should be indulged among us, etc. And the countenances of some of them bespoke inward perturbation. I then proceeded to call the names in order to examine characters.

[1] Hugh Carter (1784–1855), superintendent, Coventry circuit, 1825–1826. For the sequel to this letter see no. 77 *infra*.

[2] James Brooke (1790–1881), superintendent, Coventry circuit, 1823–1825.

When I had named the first Local Preacher on the Plan, the person who had called the private meeting spoke, saying, 'Sir you are wrong you have not called the names of the Travelling Preachers.' I replied that is not according to our rules, they then demand the rule in print. I said that the general customs of the Connexion were rules to us and were considered so in the Apostolic Age. They said it was not their custom in Coventry and that they regard their custom as much as we did the customs of the Connexion and that they would not admit of an alteration. I said 'I am accountable to Conference for my attention or nonattention to our discipline and I dare not deviate from our rules'. They insisted that I should comply as all had complied before, 'When they were talked to in such a meeting as the present' for they would not submit to be examined by anyone whom they were not to try themselves in the same way. I told them we were subject to have charges prefered against us by them at the Quarterly Meetings and those charges might be sent to the Chairman of the district, but not at Local Preachers Meeting[s]. I observed that our characters were examined annually at the D[istrict] M[eeting] and that the members conserned were when necessary allowed to be present, to give their evidence. They replied that they would not be at that trouble; for if they were, they said they would meet with some rebuff or other as was the case with those who sent matter for the magazines which they said generally produced some unkind answer. I told them no editor was the whole Conference nor all that constituted a District Meeting; they said that if not, the *Magazine* was a fair specimen of the Connextion, they me[a]nt the answers to correspondents. But however that might be, they would maintain their right to examine and try the Travelling Preachers or they would not have anything to do with us. I observed to them that I did not object to their wishes from any fear of having my conduct investigated but from its irregularity, they observed that I had nothing to *fear*, but they would not allow me to violate their rights and customs. I then gave them to understand that I could not meet their wishes. Then they called for a vote that the sense of the meeting should be taken on the subject, but I did not feel myself at liberty to put such a subject to the vote, whether I was to attend to their customs or those of the connexion but I requested those who wished to follow our general mode of proceeding to stand up and am sorry to be under the necessity of saying *they all kept their seats.*

Then Brother Walker[1] in the hope of doing some good rose to say, 'I will be examined by you here'. Then they began to think or at least

---

[1] Thomas Walker (3) (d. 1829), preacher, Coventry circuit, 1825–1826.

to speak worse of me. I told them again that I could not comply because I considered it a deviation from Rule—I was not influenced, I observed, either by fear or *pride*, as they intimated in order to keep *upp* the distinction between us and them.

I said I am sent by Conference to serve you and to see that its discipline is attended to, and placed between you and the Conference having to do with both. They said as Mr. Walker had consented to comply with their views I ought and must. Thus we talked for about 2 hours. Some I think in expectation of creating a flame urged me to say I *will not*. I continued to say I *cannot*. They used a variety of methods to get me to submit. Some smooth and some much to the contrary. I was told that Mr. Simon Day[1] who had complied was older than me, that Mr. Fletcher desired first to be examined by those he was going to examined, that Mr. Mason[2] who is a Secretary in the Connextion had complied, etc. At one moment I was told that they revered me as much as the *President of the Conference* at another asked to quit the chair and room and let the local preacher who sat next me examine them as they could examine him, that they never would be priest-ridden. The Minutes of Conference were so foolish that they were ashamed of them. Magazines were bad. Conference the same and many of its preachers going [to] the Devil—these were the subjects that were introduced in their turns—and when they were weary of talking as they did and not gain any ground thereby the speechifying shoemaker said then let us separate and with the exception of one man they all walked out. I went after them and told them I would obtain the oppinion of leading men of the Connextion on the subject for them. And if it turned out that they were right they should as Local Preachers try me as soon as such information came to hand that it would be but us adjoining a meeting for a few days they said *No*. I then thought as there was not any printed rule on the subject and as the Superintendents differed in their modes of proceeding in that case that it possibly might be viewed as an act of arrogancy in me to let so many Local Preachers go away or give up their Plans for the case in dispute, without consulting with the leading characters in the Connextion. Therefore I said '*Then I will meet your wishes* for the time, come in'. We went in and I said, 'Is there any charge against Brother Carter,' and of course none. We then proceeded through the business without hearing any objections to making collections. Our Local Brother who gave me the secret information of their clandestine Quarterly Meeting, which is held a few evenings previous to our

---

[1] Simon Day (1745–1832), superintendent, Coventry circuit, 1811–1813.

[2] John Mason (d. 1864, *aet.* 82), jun., sole preacher, Coventry circuit, 1820–1823. Secretary for foreign missions 1824–1827. Book Steward 1827–1864.

Quarter Day, said that they had been lower in their clamour and claims than he expected. The first dispute cooled their ardour. They requested to be planed in Coventry morning and evenings sometimes as well as afternoons. I wa[i]ved this by saying that as the Trustees bore the burden of debt they ought to be consulted[1]—the congregations are wonderfully increased and these men wish to let fly at a goodly number. But if the request be granted it will find a *cure* without my interference.

I am apprehensive my conduct will be viewed in different lights. Some will think I was wrong in resisting for such a while, but my reason was because it was declared anti-Methodistical at our last District Meeting. My reason for complying was lest I should be [be]having unwarrantably to my own understanding without obtaining the opinion of the official characters in our Connexion and might thereby give occasion to the enemies of our prosperity as Methodists to triumph by acting precipitately.

Allow me to add we have not had any dispute since I came with the exception of the above and requesting this virulent man to produce chapter and verse for saying in the making of the Trustees of a small chapel now building, where he had no right to be present not being a Trustee, as he is a poor, though proud man, that if the deeds which he called Conference deeds were signed, that they might be sold up without being able to sell the chapel and that some had been sold up every stick and pennyworth—or forbear making the brethren uneasy where there is no cause.

How soon higher claims will be made I know not; but hitherto with the above exceptions we have had peace in our borders and thank God some prosperity. Nor am I apprehensive that anything of a painful nature will be in anywise general nor exist at all if we allow a few to reign without us. But in order to know how to act without buying peace to[o] dear is my reason for troubling you with this. And hope you will (if possible) oblige me with your advice by return of post. . . .

76. *From William Harrison*[2]   Bacup, November 7, 1825

In my last I said if any thing of vital importance took place I would step over to Manchester and consult you; however, thank God, we

---

[1] Trustees, in whom the chapel properties and debts were vested, commonly held that itinerant preachers attracted better congregations than local preachers, and thus increased the revenue from pew rents and collections.

[2] William Harrison, senior (d. 1835, *aet.* 63), sole preacher, Bacup circuit, 1825–1826.

had a very excellent Quarter Day and nothing took place but what I expected and as time is very precious with me, could not see what valuable end the loss of two days would answer. However I feel it my duty to give a short epitome of our doings—I have had two meetings with the School party,[1] the first was cheifly to learn thair Spirit, disposition, etc—however, at the close of it, I gave them an invitation to join thair School with ours and for every member to come back to the Society; in this I treated them with all tenderness and meekness, the sequal was a *negative*—— In the second meeting I made them a proposition (and gave them a week to think of it) to let thair School stand (as thair were people to support it) for them to come over to us, at the end of the week a negative—Now, Sir, I dare go no further, neither would it be prudent to do it, neither could I ask either you or the District to let me, for we have the eyes of our best friends upon us, beside I don't think that we have any authority from the word of God to go a *step further*. Notwithstanding all this we are very friendly, they allways come to hear me and I learn by the bye, that they speak of me respectfully——

In my last I hinted that I expected somthing would take place with Mr. Briggs, who was the Deligate to Bristol and so it has come to pass. I foresaw it and told him of it; he thanked me, but his own will being his law did not regard me—On account of his measures, it was thought adviseable to put him back upon trial, upon the Local Preachers' Plan. It was so ordered and I reported the result of that meeting to him, I beged of him to comply; he thanked me for all my kindness to him and his friends, but wished to go off the Plan, *I immediately did it*, for I will not *sneake* to any man, he had all respect shown him, in fact I treated him as a Brother and he acknowledges it, and now for the result and I think it will draw a smile, etc— Mr. Briggs sets up preaching for himself (some think this was the plan why Mr. Harrison's proposition was not complyed with by the School party). Mark the importance of the man expecting I suppose to carry numbers with him, but alass alass *not a Soul has left, nor a Soul went with* him in the Circuit. Amen and Amen—And after trying his new preaching plan for a *fortnight* and no more and then came *personally* to me requesting a Note to go in to the Haslington Circuit; of corse I treated it with *contempt*; however here is: 1st that Mr. Briggs is not of so much importance as he expected. 2d the new plan don't answer 3d a want to get away; and 4 that he is in our hands and now is my *time* and by the help of God I will treat him as he deserves, etc——

---

[1] This letter is the sole trace of one of the obscurer episodes in the struggle of the preachers to control independent Sunday schools linked with Methodism. Cf. no. 85 *infra*.

Thus Sir you see how it is with me, O pray for me, I need *wisdom patience* etc, indeed I need be all out both a Christian and a Minister in the sense of the Apostle—Bless God I continue to rejoice in tribulation and find his work is my delight—Have every reason to believe I am where God would have me. I continue to pirsue the plan named in my former letter. We have an *amazing* Spirit of *hearing*. People are *thirsting* for the Word through the Circuit and souls are coming to Christ. O that the two Sticks may be one. At the last quarterly meeting I was desired to ask the Chirman of the District wheather he would grant an hired Local Preacher to the Bacup Circuit (knowing that we have no claim upon the List of reserve) and I am to make the report to the next Quarter Day——

77. *From Joseph Entwisle*   Birmingham, January 17, 1826

Copy of a letter from Mr. Leppington,[1] dated Wisbeach, December 29, 1825

Rev. and very Dear Sir,

A second Robinson of Beverley having made his appearance in this town, by a pamphlet just published by Edmund Waller of Wisbeach, a leader, Local Preacher and Trustee, (entitled, *Remarks on Sandwith's Apology for the System of Wesleyan Methodism, Also a letter on the character and utility of the Local Preachers, with an Address to the members of the Methodist Societies—To which is added a Short Correspondence with Mr. Stocks of Manchester on the subject of Church Government*) from which much mischief is likely to ensue in this and other circuits around us, I shall be glad to know what steps I am to take relative to the business. Of this author no doubt you have heard already through the medium of Mr. Bunting, into whose hands Mr. Stocks put Mr. Waller's letters to him, etc. some months ago. I would have procured a printed copy, and sent it you, only I did not wish the party concerned to know that I had done so, being determined to take no steps till I had heard from you.

As our Local Preachers' and Quarterly Meetings are on Wednesday next, I shall be much obliged by a line by return of post. . . .

Yours etc.

J. C. Leppington.

Reply to the above:

My Dear Brother,   Birmingham, December 31, 1825

Yours is just come to hand. I fear the enemy is sowing the seeds of discord. Whoever is right or wrong, religion always suffers in what are *called* religious disputes. I am at a loss what to say. As I

---

[1] John C. Leppington (d. 1833), superintendent, Wisbeach circuit, 1825–1827.

do not know the contents of the pamphlet, I cannot say *how far* it may be prudent to notice it *at the present time*. On a general view of the subject, perhaps it will be best to proceed on the Quarter Day in the usual routine of business. Should alterations be proposed in any part of our discipline, it would be well *for you to tell them calmly, that you do not consider yourself authorised to alter any of our rules*.

You have need my dear brother, of wisdom, and prudence, and patience, and love. It would be well to confer with your brethren in the neighbourhood, and also with some of the most experienced and most steady friends in your circuit. *Do nothing in haste. If there be* design to divide *in anyone*, he will take advantage of the circumstances as far as possible. You have need, therefore, of circumspection—and adherence to rule—and great meekness and patience.

May the Lord direct and guide you. I very much wish to hear the result of your Quarterly Meeting—and also, a copy of Mr. W.'s pamphlet. Do all you can consistently with duty, to keep peace. I am your affectionate Brother

Joseph Entwisle.

Copy of a second letter from Mr. Leppington, dated Wisbeach, Jan. 10, 1826

Rev. and very dear Sir,

Your obliging letter I received, and agreeably with your wish stated therein I write to inform you of the proceedings of our Quarter day. At 11 o'clock on the 4th Instant (the time appointed in the Plan 6 weeks before) we had our Local Preachers' Meeting in the chapel—10 of them present out of 19. Agreeably with your advice, after singing and prayer, we commenced the business in the usual way. Our first question was—'Are there objections to any of the brethren, in reference to religious experience, moral conduct, etc., etc.?' We had proceeded but a very little way, before we were interrupted by the coming in of a man from the circuit, who *had been* a Local Preacher, but not having met in class for a considerable length of time, received no ticket in September nor met in class since, I had (acting on the rule 'which requires every Local Preacher to meet in class, and to conform to all our discipline—none to be excused in this respect') left his name out of the new plan which I made in the latter end of November. He became very troublesome to us by his loquaciousness about himself, and frequently interrupted us in our business. We proceeded however as well as we could with the characters till we were called to dinner at half past one o'clock. I then told the brethren, that as the Quarterly Meeting was to commence its business at half past two, we had not time to go any further, and I would adjourn the Local Preachers' Meeting to another time, either to some day in the coming quarter, or to the next Quarter day—of which I would give them timely notice. We accordingly closed our sitting, and went to dinner. At half past two, my colleague, a few stewards, and myself, being met, we sang and prayed, and then entered on the business of the Quarterly Meeting in the regular way, receiving Quarterages, etc. At half past three, we were surprised and interrupted by the rushing into the chapel of a number of persons with Mr. Waller at their head. On seeing them, I immediately said, 'such of you brethren, as are stewards, or representatives of Societies in the Circuit, have a seat here', and requested them to come forward, adding that I was glad to see them. Mr. W. then, as foreman of the party, said, 'Have not Local Preachers and Leaders a seat here and a vote?' I replied *suaviter in modo*, 'No', stating that at one Conference I had asked the President that question, and he said 'No', and the rule says 'No'; and I read the rule to them. I had also said in the former meeting in the morning—'That I did not consider myself authorised to alter any of our rules.' One of the Circuit Stewards asked, 'Could they not stay, and *see* the business done?' But before a reply could be given, the right hand man of Mr. W. (a shoe-maker of the name of Harrison) cried out, 'That is not sufficient, Mr. Friend.' They then all retired. We resumed our business without any further interruption, save only that when the quarterage of the two places (amounting last Qr. to £3. 16. 0) was called for, the persons who had received it from the Societies where they lived, being of Waller's party, had retired with him, and when our messengers had sought them out, and requested them to send the monies, they withheld them; and the result was, on the disbursements being stated, that I had to go from the Quarterly. Meeting without them. The Circuit Stewards here will not advance any money to pay disbursements after the monies received at the Quarterly board have been disposed of. The Meeting closed in peace between six and seven.

At seven, my colleague preached, and we had a watch-night till ten, without Mr. W. or any of his friends affording us any assistance. Indeed this was no *new* thing, having acted in the same way at Michaelmas watchnight. After Mr. W. and his party had retired from the chapel in the afternoon, I found they had associated themselves in the house of Harrison; but I heard nothing of their proceedings there till Saturday morning, when at a distance of 9 miles from Wisbeach, on my return home from the country, *a Brother* told me that W. and his party had entered into an agreement and signed it, not to fulfil their plan; and for a *pretence*, assigned the case of the man above mentioned, who so interrupted us in the Local Preachers' Meeting. Having heard this, I waited the issue of their last Sunday's appointments before I wrote to you. I *now* find that if any such engagement as that stated above was entered into, it was a *rope of sand*, as Waller and others of them attended to their appointments last Lord's Day. From private members I hear they are busily engaged in carrying into execution Waller's advice in his pamphlet to withold their monies, and so injure our finances; and in other ways throw impediments in the way of their prosperity. Nevertheless in Wisbeach our congregations fill the chapel; yea, some go away because there is no room for them; and if my information be correct, all the seats are let. Mr. W. is also busily employed in sending his pamphlet through the circuit by means of disaffected persons like himself. At the last Conference nearly all the congregations in the country were lost. Blessed be the name of the Lord that it is *now otherwise*. Our receipts last Wednesday were larger than any preceding Quarter day in the last year.

With whom to advise here as to the steps I should take I know not. There is no official character with whom I could commune with safety; and to confer with the preachers in the District, the distance is, and the expence would be, so great, I can only do it by letter; and this mode would make the whole business public, and answer no valuable end—besides, I have not *time*, the labours of my circuit are incessant, more so than in the first year of my itinerancy in Norwich. I wish YOU to direct me. I have not yet taken one step respecting Mr. W. or his pamphlet, nor even shewn my opinion. At our Local Preachers' Meeting we did not proceed so far as the examination of characters, as for Mr. W's name to be called. Of course, I was saved from everything referring to it or him and said not a word about it.

I have procured a copy and *now* send it to you. You will be so kind as to write me *again as soon as possible*, as *I* stand still, *till* I hear from you. There is not one of the six class leaders here, but what is more or less disaffected to Methodism, and many of the official men in the country. They are greatly influenced by the Pamphleteer. There has long been an almost entire lack of discipline, and the men in office have just done as they pleased; and of course, at the end of the year, 'No objections to such a one and such a one'. Methodism (if in this Circuit it could deservedly bear that name) has been an *unenclosed* piece of ground. I have seen many circuits in a poor state in my time, without contributing to the poverty of any of them, but never one so low as this. Religious experience is in general very shallow—and Methodist discipline in the last stage of consumption. . . .

J. C. Leppington

My Dear Friend,

The length of my letter will, perhaps, fatigue you. However, I wish you to have all the information that I have received. If you have not seen Waller's pamphlet you may get a copy at Dean's Bookseller, Manchester. *It is so low and scurrilous, that I* think there is little to fear from it. I think upon the whole Mr. L. has acted very prudently hitherto. He does not say whether he used any means to get the Local Preacher to meet in class—whom he left out of the plan. My fear has been that Mr. L. might be precipitate. But you see he waits for direction. I scarcely know what to do. It is difficult to give *specific* directions, when they are to be executed by one in whom one has not entire confidence. I intend to write him by the next post and inform him that I have written you as I find it *needful to* have your opinion. In the meanwhile *I shall advise him to act according to rule and to say with perfect meekness of* temper that he has no authority to alter our rules. Do tell me *without delay, your thoughts.* I have a *bad opinion* of the Pamphleteer.

Since I wrote you last, I have been at Coventry—I met the Local Preachers who remain with us at 10½ a.m., at two the Quarterly Meeting. At both these meetings I explained our entire system. I brought strange things to their ears. They were surprised when I informed them of the Plan of Pacification, and that *that* plan provided for the *trial* of a Travelling Preacher, etc. I could not find *one person* who had ever read the Plan of Pacification.[1] This convinced me *more deeply than ever* that we ought to have a digest of our rules to put into the hands of our people. After evening preaching at Coventry, I met the Local Preachers who had left us, taken a room in Coventry lately occupied by the Ranters, and are forming a party in the Circuit. I spent nearly two hours with them—nine in number. They behaved to me *personally* with all due respect. But it was plain that their plan was fixed. There is *only one* of the whole number that the people will regret to lose. The congregations in Coventry never were *so good as now*—nor the seats so well let. Brother Carter's manner does

---

[1] The Plan of Pacification (1795) enabled a majority of trustees, of stewards and Leaders in a Society, believing their preacher 'immoral, erroneous in doctrines, deficient in abilities, or that he has broken any of the rules' relating mainly to the administration of the sacrament, to put him on trial before the preachers of the District. 'The chairman of the District shall be president of the assembly; and every preacher, trustee, steward and leader shall have a single vote, the chairman possessing also the casting voice.' If the verdict went against the preacher, he was to be considered removed from the circuit, and the District Meeting was to consider how to dispose of him till Conference. What Entwisle seems not to have said is that the context of this provision in the Plan shows that it was originally conceived as a brake upon unilateral action by trustees.

K

not secure to him *much reverence*—yet he is *so laborious* that he is generally beloved. Brother Walker, his colleague, has been laid up and he has done the weekday work of both—in general. Next Monday if God will, I go to open a new chapel near Coventry when I shall see how things are going on.

A few of our Local Preachers here have wished to have a fund for the relief of each other in distress.[1] I advised them to drop it, and they have done so. Have you anything of the kind at Manchester? I was informed that you had.

John Walton[2] is at loggerheads with the leading men at Skipton. He should not have been a Superintendent. He is unwell and has had a hired Local Preacher for 3 months . . .

We are going on well here. . . . It is probable that another chapel will be erected in this town, as nearly £900 is subscribed by less than 30 individuals. . . .

78. *To Joseph Entwisle* (Birmingham) Manchester, January 24, 1826

My fixed opinion of Waller of Wisbeach is that he ought to have been put away from us last year, as soon as his letter to Mr. Stocks was detected. It is plain he cannot be cordial with us, as he is on principle an opponent of our discipline. He ought therefore to leave us; and the *earliest* separation will be the least mischievous. As I have no hope of reclaiming him, I think he should, on the ground of his declared hostility to our system, be immediately renounced, unless he will quietly withdraw. The misfortune is that Mr. L[eppington] is not quite the proper man to manage such a matter with a becoming mixture of firmness and of caution; and indeed if he were to act ever so prudently, his former character for driving would make all *he* did unpopular. I therefore earnestly recommend that you should go to Wisbeach, and officially settle the matter on the spot. If that *cannot* be, could you not request Mr. Reece[3] to go as your Deputy? The distance from London is not great. Such a step might save a large portion of the Society.

I waited till I could consult Mr. Marsden,[4] before I answered your letter. He fully concurs in the opinion I have given. . . .

We have no Local Preachers' Fund here.

---

[1] On this question see Introduction, p. 7.

[2] John Walton, preacher, Skipton circuit, 1824–1825, superintendent, 1825–1826.

[3] Richard Reece (d. 1850, *aet.* 84), superintendent, London (Southwark) circuit, 1824–1827. President 1816, 1835.

[4] George Marsden, superintendent, Manchester (Oldham Street) circuit, 1824–1827.

79. *From Joseph Entwisle*   Birmingham, February, 18, 1826

Copy of a letter from Mr. John Straw, a Preacher in the New Connexion, dated Bury, Lancashire, February 16, 1826.[1]

It is with feelings of respect and humility that I intrude upon your attention—I who am an entire stranger, and yet have to lay before you a subject which in its bearings on my comfort and usefulness is of no little importance. I am a young man, not 25 years of age. I was made nigh unto God by the blood of Jesus in my 15th year—began as a Local Preacher to call sinners to repentance in my 19th year—and was called out as an itinerant minister in my 22nd year. You will by this statement anticipate me in saying that I am at present on ministerial probation in the New Connexion. I have, in this connexion, been brought up from my infancy, and brought up with its almost necessarily attendant prejudices. But from these educational prejudices my mind has for some time been disentangled; and the ecclesiastical polity which I was taught to reverence for its pretended accordance with holy scripture and the rights of man, I believe upon close observation and mature consideration to be at variance with both. Since called to itinerate in the responsible work of the ministry, I have by the people been better treated than many of my colleagues. I have favourably had peace with all. My temporal wants have been far better supplied than I deserve. Moreover I have had no lack of opportunity to publish the everlasting gospel of God our Saviour. These candid declarations will, it is highly probable, lead you to ask, 'Why then this change of sentiment? Why then abandon a mode of church government in which you have been educated?' I will, Revd. Sir, freely answer these inquiries. The kind of government which is prevalent in our connexion I firmly believe to be highly unscriptural and pernicious. The sacred Scriptures vest in the hands of ministers authority in the church: for they are therein represented as having rule over the people. But of such authority to rule our preachers are divested. Instead of ministers having the rule over the people, the people have rule over them. The people are the rulers, and ministers are the ruled. Our system in theory does not

[1] There was a steady trickle of applications from New Connexion preachers to be received into the Old, especially in the indifferent years for the New Connexion, which were also generally indifferent years for the Old (and included the mid-'twenties). The Wesleyan connexion was generally sympathetic to individual secession (M.C.A. MSS. J. Stamp to Jabez Bunting, March 24, 1812) though chary of proposals to strike a bargain on behalf of a group of preachers (the welcome given to such a proposal in M.C.A. MSS. J. Taylor to Jabez Bunting, December 2, 1804 seems to have aroused no official response). John Strawe, became preacher with the Methodist New Connexion 1823, and with the Wesleyan connexion 1826; d. 1841. See also no. 80, *infra*.

assume such an aspect, but it certainly does in operation, and by this it is not unfair to estimate its merits. A system of church polity which so daringly usurps ministerial rights and prerogatives is sure to be productive of effects of a prejudicial character. This is also exhibited in the practical influence of our system. Leaders, stewards, trustees, teachers, and even singers, assume an authority over the preachers; and by denying them all interference with their concerns treat them with contempt. Hereby the high, dignified and authoritative character of the christian ministry is dethroned, and therefore is too powerless to command respectful regard. This is diametrically and necessarily pernicious to the cause of God. For the hearts of ministers and people are alienated from one another; mutual jealousies and dissatisfactions are always existing; ministerial energy is grievously repressed; consequently ministerial comfort and usefulness are mournfully injured. Hence I am, not from passion, but from principle at enmity with the distinguishing mode of government in our connexion; because it robs God's ministers of their scriptural authority and influence—and is necessarily destructive to the unity, zealous cooperation, and prosperity of the churches.

This change of opinions in matters of church discipline places me in a trying situation. I have in our connexion nothing in prospect but that which wounds and pains, because of the baneful influence with which its peculiar mode of administration assails the hearts and labours of ministers. I have also in the world but a cheerless prospect. Were Providence to elevate me unto one of its stations of opulence and honour, I could never enjoy it. I can enjoy nothing in the present state, save God and the ministry. Of all desires this is uppermost in my soul, to live and die a good minister of Jesus Christ.

Being in this dilemma, and having a soul deeply imbued with Wesleyan Methodism—in its grand sciences of theology and polity— I humbly address you, Rev. Sir, as the honoured President of the Conference and most fervently implore your compassion and help. Whether I am to continue ministering to a people whom I cannot now esteem, or whether I am again to devote my energies to the grovelling concerns of the world, or whether you will receive me into the bosom of your connexion; and if you will receive me, how and when you will bestow the favour, are questions which occasionally agitate and depress my mind. . . These things . . . Rev. Sir, through the medium of this paper I carry unto you, beseeching you to deal with me according to those divine graces for which your praise is in all the churches. An answer as soon as convenient will greatly oblige your humble supplicant.

John Straw . . .

My dear Friend, Birmingham February 18, 1826
The preceding letter has made a favourable impression on my mind.
I think if he be pious and orthodox, and of acceptable and useful abilities, he should be encouraged *in a constitutional way*, to look forward to a reception among us. However, I shall defer replying to this letter, which I received this morning, *till I hear from you*. He is your neighbour, and you have an opportunity which I have not of making the necessary enquiries, which I hope you will be enabled to do soon. It is remarkable that while Mr. Robinson and Waller are writing and labouring to promote K[ilhamitis]m, those who have *tried the system* are speaking the truth. . . .
[Is looking forward to receiving the opinion of Bunting Newton and Marsden on the Wisbeach case; Leppington acts most prudently.] . . . There are 13 chapels in the Circuit—most of them deeply in debt—some private property—some unsettled.—In Wisbeach there are *6 leaders and 80 members*. Since receiving his last letter, I am inclined to think that it might answer a good end were I to go over to their next Quarterly Meeting, and explain to *all its* members our *plans and usages, the reasons of them and their utility* etc. This mode was useful at Coventry, it might be so ⟨at Wis⟩beach. So if you and Messrs. M[arsden] and N[ewton] think well of it, I will arrange with Mr. L. accordingly. . . .
I am more and more convinced of the *strong probability, almost certainty*, that Mr. Watson will succeed me in office.[1] Mr. N[ewton] says it is certain. If so he cannot be Secretary to the Missions . . .
. . . John Walton seems to be doing mischief at Skipton. No doubt you have heard of his suspension. . . .

80. *To Joseph Entwisle* (Birmingham) Manchester, February 25, 1826
Your patience, I fear, has been almost exhausted; but really there has been no help for it. You desired me to 'call a Council'. Now our excellent friend, Mr. Newton, is so seldom at home,[2] except on Sundays that I almost find it impossible to engage his attendance for any consultation. At length, however, we have contrived to catch him; Mr. Leppington's case has been reconsidered; and I am again desired to report to you our unaltered and unanimous opinion.
1. That the Wisbeach case cannot with propriety be suffered to go on much longer in its present state; and that Waller should either

---

[1] Richard Watson succeeded Entwisle as President of Conference in 1826.
[2] Robert Newton was largely engaged with fund-raising for the Missionary Society at public meetings. He was said to have raised more money for religious objects than any other man of his day.

promise to behave peaceably, and give up party-making, or be obliged to quit the Society, or, at the very most, be continued only as a private member, and excluded from all office among us.

2. That, from peculiar circumstances, Mr. Leppington, though he appears to act prudently and in a good spirit, is not *the man* to whom the management of this business can be confided alone; and that you, as the President, should therefore go over to Wisbeach and meet the parties, in order to conclude this unpleasant business, and force it to a speedy crisis.

I rejoice to find, from your last letter, that you have adopted the same view, and are inclined to go to the Wisbeach Quarterly Meeting. May God grant you direction and success! . . .

Mr. Watson, I have no doubt, will be, if spared, our next President. But I still think he must stay another year in London; and his election will be an *additional* reason for soliciting him so to do. Remember that, with all his talents, he knows comparatively little of the *business* of the Connexion; and, if President, must have an efficient and practised 'Council' *very near* him. This he will have in London. But what could *he* do, in that respect, if stationed at Birmingham? He cannot, I agree, be *nominally* a Secretary for Missions. But the name of the brother to be appointed as his Assistant in the official correspondence of the Presidency may be published with those of Messrs. Morley and Mason; and Mr. Watson may still do the principal part of the work at the Mission House, only sitting in the chair of the Committee instead of the end of the table. This was the plan adopted in my own case, when I was President. . . .

Mr. Straw's proposal seems to fall under the same principles which you applied to that of the single preacher at Leeds or Dewsbury. I have not been able to learn here anything of his character. Will you ask him to fix a day with Mr. Marsden for coming over privately to Manchester, when he Mr. Newton and I, might converse freely with him? . . .

81. *From Zachary Macaulay*   London, March 13, 1826

[*Written on an Anti-Slavery Society circular, dated March 10, 1826 and signed by Richard Matthews, Secretary, remarking on the great change in sentiment on the slavery question, and demanding that the Imperial Legislature take the question of the legal rights of slaves out of the hands of the local assemblies.*]

I cannot better reply to your letter of Saturday than by sending you the annexed circular wet from the press. It is the first copy which has reached me. So far are we in town from concurring in Mr.

Clarkson's view of the subject,[1] that one and all of us, in Parliament and out of Parliament, conceive that if ever there was occasion of exertion, it is now—now when, on the eve of an election, and immediately after a second delusive reference to the Colonial assemblies, every man in the kingdom seems bound to exert himself to prevent our cause from suffering from silence, or even from delay in the expression of his feelings. I should rejoice to see a thousand more petitions, crowding the table of parliament before Brougham brings on his Bill.[2] As for the postponement of that measure for a single day, it arose from the extraordinary and unheard of mistatement, acting doubtless on misinformation, which Mr. Canning was himself so far misled as to make to parliament.[3] His statement was in substance to this effect. That eight colonies out of thirteen had provided means of religious instructions; had decreed the observance of the Sabbath; had given security to the property of slaves; had modified discretionary punishments by the master; and had abolished the driving whip; that seven colonies had admitted slave evidence and given facilities to manumission; that five had legalized marriage and prohibited the separation of families and that two had established savings banks.

Now in fact ten colonies have done nothing and the other three very little. We were taken by surprize in the first instance; but on enquiry the delusion vanished—and it is not even pretended that the statement was correct.

You do perfectly right to hold your meeting; and if it were only to convince the colonists that the nation was unanimous in enabling Government to redeem their pledge, if not this year yet the next, of forcing the colonies to adopt their measures, should they still decline to do it voluntarily. Instead of anything being gained which our petitions have prayed for, a course the very reverse of what we prayed for has been adopted. Parliament has not taken the work into its own hands, but has again delegated it to those who neither will nor

---

[1] Thomas Clarkson, vice-president with Wilberforce of the Anti-Slavery Society.

[2] Henry Brougham, moved on May 19, 1826, that as the House had had no satisfactory response to its resolutions on the treatment of slaves by colonial legislatures, it should consider early in the next session such measures as might be necessary to effect their purpose. The motion was defeated.

[3] On March 1, 1826, Buxton, presenting a petition from the people of London, urged that so little had been done for the slaves that the House should either abandon its pledge to them, or take the matter into their own hands. Canning replied that this would be hasty and precipitate, and that most of the self-governing colonies had adopted important reforms. Two days later Brougham moved for a return of acts passed since May 15, 1823, which revealed that little had in fact been done. *Parliamentary Debates*, xiv (1826), pp. 975–978, 1082.

can perform it. I will bring your letter before the Committee the day after tomorrow. Brougham and my son are both at Lancaster and they will go thence to York, but I fear the affairs of the Circuit will make their appearance at Manchester impossible—but if any of your friends should be visiting Lancaster he may see Brougham and ascertain his motions. I will write again to Mr. Babington.[1] I will speak to Lord Suffield, etc.[2] and let you know. Mr. G. Phillips[3] is cordially with us and I hope might be induced to attend. I do not know about Stanley.[4] I will write again probably on Wednesday and let you know what farther occurs to me. . . .

82. *From Thomas Salt*   Uttoxeter, July 20, 1826

I told you in my last the Church Wardens had taken a room that would not hold one fourth of the congregation. Yesterday one of the Wardens came to me and said the Bishop[5] had asked, 'Have you applied to the Wesleyan Methodists for the use of their Chapel.' The answer was no; the Bishop said, 'O, why dont you apply to them, they are so nearly allied to the Church that I have no doubt they would accommodate you, and you can get no place so respectable or well in the town.'

And he (the Warden) came at the suggestion of the Bishop to ask if we would accomodate them, and wished to have an answer that night. I immediately went to Mr. Rennison[6] to consult with him, he saw no objection to it and said we might alter our service from half past ten to half past nine and they might go in at eleven. I likewise took counsel of 3 Brother Trustees (all in the Town) and they were of opinion we should accomodate them, so they are to have the Chapel morning and afternoon, and we shall have our evening service at six o'clock as usual. . . .

---

[1] Thomas Babington (1758–1837) of Rothley Temple, Leicestershire, brother-in-law to Zachary Macaulay.

[2] Edward Harbord, 3rd. Baron Suffield (1781–1835), liberal peer, and almost single-handed champion of abolitionism in the upper house at this time.

[3] Perhaps George Richard Philips (1789–1883), M.P. for Steyning, 1820–1832.

[4] Edward George Geoffrey Smith Stanley, later 14th earl of Derby; at this time M.P. for Stockbridge; sympathetic to the views of Canning under whom he became under-secretary for the colonies in 1827.

[5] Henry Ryder, Bishop of Lichfield and Coventry, 1824–1836, the first evangelical bishop, and, as son of the 1st Baron Harrowby of Sandon Hall, a member of an important local family.

[6] William Rennison (d. 1854, *aet.* 69), superintendent, Uttoxeter circuit, 1825–1826.

83. *From John Sumner.*[1]   Sowerby Bridge, July 22, 1826

I hope you will forgive the liberty I have taken to address a few lines to you on a subject in which I know you feel a lively interest, *viz.* the Yearly and July collections made in our Connexion.[2] Ever since I have known Methodism I have always considered the Yearly Collection to be of very great importance in its economy. Perhaps I shall not assert more than the truth if I say Methodism would not at this time have occupied the ground it does, nor furnished its present preachers the comforts they enjoy, but for this Collection. The future spread of Methodism will, I apprehend, depend no less on the efficiency of this collection than in time past. If so, then every exertion should be made to keep (or rather to get) it up to the original standard of 1/– per member. At present it is only half that sum and the Yearly and July together only about 9d per mem[ber]. Every one who earnestly wishes the welfare of the Body, must be pained on looking over the list of the circuits to see how *very far* some large and respectable circuits fall short of their proper quota.

Might not some plan be adopted to improve this branch of our finance? It has been thought by some that we have too many public collections; and certainly it would be more easy and perhaps more advisable to lessen rather than increase their number. Would it be well then to give up the July, as a *Conference* collection, and make a rule requiring each leader to produce 1/– per member for his class, leaving him to choose his own method of collecting it. He might collect it either yearly or quarterly, from his own members entirely, or partly from friends to whom he might have access. Or if this would be thought impracticable let each Circuit be held responsible for the sum of 1/– per member, to be raised either by private subscription in the classes, or aided by a public collection through the Circuit as the Preachers, Stewards, etc, think most advisable. There would be more *equal*, *permanent*, and *efficient* aid to the Contingent Fund for the extension of Methodism by a plan something like this, than can ever be realized on the present plan. Make it a part of the outlay of a

---

[1] John Sumner (d. 1837, *aet.* 46), preacher, Sowerby Bridge circuit, 1825–1827.

[2] On these collections which supported the Contingent Fund see the Introduction, p. 6. The letter illustrates (1) the difficulty which Methodism faced, in common with the independent denominations, of maintaining, in the long run, both a pastoral ministry and genuinely itinerant (i.e. not church-based) evangelism; (2) the impossibility of maintaining both a popular following, and the formal obligations of members to contribute their class-monies, obligations which were hardly anywhere completely met; (3) the impossibility of maintaining the strict theory of Methodist finance that the Society (*i.e.*, the membership) supported the ministry, while the congregation supported the chapel trust. The subject is resumed in no. 84, *infra*.

Circuit, or the duty of each leader individually, and I am sure it will be entered into with more spirit in our Societies than it now is, and will be provided for without much difficulty. At present there is an unjust inequality in the contributions of different circuits to the Contingent Fund. I say *unjust*; because where there is equal ability, there lies in *this case* an obligation to equal contributions. But is this realized? Compare the Districts one with another, and then compare the Circuits in each District, and you will perceive a great difference, which perhaps it will not be easy to reconcile. Is there not reason to fear that *some* of the stronger Circuits, knowing they shall not receive or need help from the Contingent Fund, do not make those exertions they would do if they were in more narrowed circumstances, and which a few are nobly making?

If a plan of this sort were adopted it would prevent the recurrence of a circumstance which has taken place in the Halifax District this year, *viz.*, a very large deduction from the grants to the poor dependant circuits, made at the September Meeting in consequence of the failure of the Yearly Collection. The case is a distressing one: for although at least two of those Circuits exerted themselves to make their Yearly [Collection] equal to last year, and a few other circuits not dependant did the same, yet the deficiency on the District was £73! Which sum was *all* thrown upon the *poor* Circuits *according to the amount of the claims of each*. Who would not feel this to be a grievous hardship if placed in one of those circuits? I mention this because [it is] a case that happened under my own notice; there may have been similar instances in other Districts though I hope not many, and that they will never recur. It would in my judgment have been more just to have required every Circuit to pay the same Yearly as last year, or to have divided the whole deficiency by the number of members in the District, and required each circuit to pay its part. . . .

84. *From Jonathan Barker*[1]   Burslem, September 15, 1826

I suppose you have seen, or heard of what has been published in various provincial papers, but particularly in the *Liverpool Advertiser*, and the *Pottery Mercury*, and I suppose in some of the London papers, viz. amongst many other changes which are to take place in

---

[1] Jonathon Barker (d. 1839, *aet.* 75), superintendent, Burslem circuit, 1826–1828. The question, 'Who have died this year?' is asked at the beginning of the Minutes of each Conference, and the obituaries of preachers and supernumeraries which answer it form a roll of honour of itinerants who have died in the work.

our connexion, we are to have three Bishops, *viz.* Messrs. Bunting, Newton, and Watson; perhaps you can say at what period this is to commence, I hope, not till it is printed in answer to the Question, Who have died this year? Jonathan Barker, who travelled 40 years etc. I believe the whole story is invented by our small friends, if possible, to set us one against the other. And yet, I say it not to flatter you, if we must have Bishops, I would rather that you were one than any other man amongst us, for I believe the God of nature formed you to take the lead, whether in Church or State, in any, or every department; but amongst us the name of Bishop will not sound well, though a man may rule without the name, and to your rule of wisdom, prudence, equity, and love I can cheerfully submit, indeed the whole connexion ought to feel obliged to you for it. . . . But the chief reason of my writing to you, is to give you a little statement of the affairs of this circuit as far as they are come to my knowledge. Mr. Cormie the Circuit Steward has informed me that they are in debt nearly £300, and have no probable means of liquidating it upon the present plan; the bringing in the third preacher has brought them in part into this dilemma;[1] the income of the quarterly board does not now meet their demands, and how is the debt to be paid off, or even reduced? There was no absolute need of a third preacher, unless their funds had been equal to their increased demands. Although this is an old Circuit, yet very few comply with the rules of 1d per week, and 1/- per quarter. Numbers of the societies raise nothing weekly, and give nothing at the quarterly visitation; they raise a little amongst themselves, and send it to the Quarterly board. I shall do all in my power to bring them into the Methodistic plan, but it will require time, patience, and much persuasion, nothing else will do in this hotbed of Kilhamitism, Ran⟨te⟩rism, and every other ism that is subversive ⟨of⟩ all rule and order. It will come to this at the Conference, that the single Preacher *must be droped*, and *two must do the work*; the Circuit will be rather hard, but two may do all the work without any place suffering. I have often thought that most of our embarrassments arise out of the want of prudence, on the part of the Brethren, it will take at least eight years of the greatest economy, care and exertion to bring them to feel that they stand on terra firma. Mr. Cormie and Mr. Machin both declare that they will advance no more money; they declared this at the last quarterly meeting; what am I to do? I will do what I can. Perhaps no Preacher ever entered upon his work under more favourable auspices, amongst all ranks and all temperatures, the boiling hot ones, and the more cool and

---

[1] A third preacher had been appointed to the Burslem circuit in 1823, but was dropped at the next Conference.

dispassionate; I shall endeavour to turn all to the account of Methodist discipline. . . . Our congregations are in general very good; on the Monday evening I have hitherto had from 1000 to 1500 hearers at Burslem.

I thought it right to give you this statement by way of *self-defence*, lest it should be said, that things have been brought to this ruinous state, under my administration. . . .

85. *Jabez Bunting's notes for speech at a Circuit meeting to discuss the Sunday Schools for Children of all Denominations, Manchester, September 20, 1826.*[1]

1. Want of *security* in the present constitution for vital truths. Rules *none*. *Name* worse than none: *pretends* to be latitudinarian. Deeds worse than none, if London Road be a specimen.

2. The *principle* of running schools with the church never to be sacrificed, never concealed. Bad effect on teachers and scholars.

3. The means of this union among Methodists, a lega⟨l⟩ right of ecclesiastical vigilance lodged in the minister and Leaders. These *our* authorities. With these ⟨I⟩ trust, under God, you ⟨should wholly lodge?⟩ Schools.

4. Many of these children the children *of our* people. We have no right, as a church, to abandon them to others. Others have no right to take them from under our care.

5. Methodist money and labour should go to extend Methodist influence. Others act on this ground e.g. Church, Dissenters.

6. Schools under chapels especially should be under a direct Methodist Jurisdiction—else *imperium in imperio*.

---

[1] The identification of this document, the holograph of which is at Duke University, Durham, North Carolina, is made possible by M.C.A. MS. Scrapbook of James Everett, fo. 421, printed in the Appendix, *infra*. The 1826 Conference appointed a committee (*cf.* n. 1, p. 116) to systematize legislation governing Methodist Sunday schools and 'hoped' that those [undenominational] schools, which claim a relation to Methodism, and are supported in part by collections made in our chapels, will be induced as speedily as possible to adopt the same leading principles, and to walk by the same general rules' (S. Warren and J. Stephens, *Chronicles of Wesleyan Methodism* (London, 1827) i, p. 399). Bunting who was a leading member of the committee immediately raised the question in a meeting of the Stewards and Leaders of the Manchester (Grosvenor St.) circuit. Full Wesleyan control was established in the annual general meeting of the Manchester school in 1830. (*A statement of the origin and condition of the Sunday schools for children of all denominations in Manchester* (Manchester, 1836).) The connexional pressure here applied met with mixed success, for there were great secessions among the Sunday schools during the Warrenite and Wesleyan Reform separations. See also no. 87 *infra*.

7. If we bind ourselves once to the All Denomination principle ⟨con⟩trol will be as impossible to us [as] our other friends say it is ⟨to⟩ them.

8. If we bind ourselves to a latitudinarian system we disqualify ourselves for association with Methodist Schools. One such we have. Shall we stigmatize that plan in order to sanction a worse.

9. Duty of guarding our young people from injurious associations.

10. If now settled right, permanent peace; if not, perpetual discussions.

11. Union not desirable, division better, the school too unweildy.

12. We do not like to concur in palming on the town schools which are really to be conducted by Methodists, and to be made in fact subservient to that particular modification of Christianity called Methodism as *Schools equally open to the influence and controul* of all denominations—which the present title means if it mean anything.

86. *From Thomas Galland*   Beverley, October 2, 1826

A favourable opportunity offering, I enclose you a copy of *Mr. [Mark] Robinson's New Constitution;* a mighty apparatus, sure, for the government of some half score or half dozen, the former, I believe, the outside of his present number of members, if indeed there is any membership among them, they are now beginning to contend about *money matters*, and the *Beckside Chapel*, into which they so imperiously introduced their Irishmen, now is a heavy additional weight upon them. It is evident, I think, to all but one or two of themselves, that a *strong hand* presses heavily upon them; they have been *kicking 'against the pricks'*, which now *enter into their soul*.

There is only one point of Mr. Robinson's schemes about which I still feel some apprehension, and that is [h]is obtaining interviews in London and the neighbourhood with the *Home Secretary*, Mr. Peel and other great men. I am fully persuaded that the man is animated by such a spirit in reference to the Body, the preachers especially, that there are no methods at which he would stick, to prejudice the kinds of the great, and array against us the arm of power. The failure of his scheme of setting up a standard against Methodism in Beverley, will doubtless tend to exasperate him still more, and the effect of his 'leprous distilments' into the ears of our *great ones*, may, in various ways operate to our disadvantage, but here the mind finds repose. *The Lord reigneth!* If only we *are true to ourselves*, He who *is King in Jeshurun* will not forsake us. . . .

There have lately been paragraphs extensively diffused amongst the public journals respecting *Methodist Bishops*—to these as having found their way into the Hull papers, Mr. Treffry[1] and myself have given an explicit contradiction, as also to reports respecting a change in our practises respecting service *in church hours* and the *administration of the sacraments.* Mr. Atkinson, the bearer of this letter, and one of our respectable friends and *staunch supporters* here, will probably have a paper in his pocket, should it not be enclosed, containing this. . . .

Our matters here are I hope improving. Indeed I am *sure* they are almost beyond our most sanguine expectations. We have some measure of the power of the Spirit of God, hence conversions are taking place, and congregations are increasing. To God be all the glory. At Hull also I have reason to hope the aspect of things in Methodism is altering for the better. Mr. Treffry is *gaining* with them, I think, and Mr. Isaac[2] and Mr. Beaumont[3] promise fair to fill their pews. . . .

87. *From Thomas Preston*[4]   Bolton, October 6, 1826[5]

A circumstance has arisen in this circuit which has excited in my mind much painful feeling, and which I fear in its results will be some loss to our Society. You know that at Halshaw Moor we have a School Room, where we preach on Sunday evenings and which is occupied as a Sunday School the other parts of the Sabbath. The ground on which the building stands was conveyed to Mr. Holland Senr.[6] and in the deed of conveyance it is stipulated that the Wesleyan Methodists should occupy the building on Sundays for public worship, except in Church hours; and another clause states that the Minister of the Parish shall at any time be at liberty to attend the School, and address the children. No other deed has ever been executed except the deed of conveyance. So that the School is private property, with the exception of the clauses before mentioned.

---

[1] Richard Treffry, sen. (1771–1842), superintendent, Hull circuit, 1825–1827. President 1833. Governor of Theological Institution 1838–1841.

[2] Daniel Isaac, preacher, Hull circuit, 1825–1826, superintendent, 1827–1829.

[3] Joseph Beaumont, M.D. (1794–1855), preacher, Hull circuit, 1825–1828. A prominent spokesman for liberal political views in Methodism.

[4] Thomas Preston, superintendent, Bolton circuit, 1825–1827.

[5] This letter illustrates the fact that not only the Methodists (as in no. 85) but also Churchmen were making forward moves against the informal arrangements which had subsisted with many Sunday schools.

[6] The junior preacher at Bolton in 1821 reported that 'we have no travelling on the Lord's Day excepting once in six weeks in the evening when we go to Mr. Holland's, who are charming people, and their place is a paradise' (M.C.A. MSS. J. Hanwell to James Everett, October 15, 1821). Roger Holland was a trustee of Fletcher St. Chapel, Bolton.

I believe there never has been a public collection made for the School, but by a Methodist Preacher; but these have been discontinued for some years; and the School is now free from debt. For the last twelve years or nearly that time all the teachers have been members of our Society with a few exceptions. Mr. Holland's family has all along given their personal attendance as teachers.

For some years the Leaders and some of the members of Society have been wishful to have more previledges than they had of public worship, for in the School they could only be allowed preaching on Sunday evenings. When I came to this circuit I was convinced we could not extend Methodism much on the present plan, as we could have no Lovefeast, nor Sacrament, nor preaching in the course of the Sabbath, although we have nearly 100 members in Society. We made some efforts to try to rent a room, for afternoon preaching, without success. However things went on as they had done for some years before, until about three weeks ago, when the circumstance transpired which I referred to above, and which is the reason of my writing you.

During the late tour which the Bishop of Chester made through this part of Lancashire, he consecrated a new church at Halshaw Moor. The Sunday after the consecration notice was given in the School that the children would have to attend the church; and that the intention had been communicated to the Bishop, and the clergyman who was to officiate had expressed his anticipated pleasure in seeing the children attend his ministry. It was agreed however that a meeting of the teachers should be held, and the measure considered. One of the Leaders from the place called upon me, and informed me that Mr. Holland Junr. and Mr. Lomas had proposed the children attending the church, and also informed me of the intended meeting of teachers. He also gave me to understand that a great deal of confusion was already excited, and if the measured was carried into effect, it was probable we should have a considerable rent in the Society, as in effect they would have given all their labours to the Church; and that Methodism would have still less chance to spread than it had now. I felt greatly perplexed with the case, and hardly knew what to advise, as I saw difficulties of rather a formidable kind which[ever] way I turned. However for the present I advised that at the meeeting the friends of Methodism should propose an adjournment, and that I should be requested to attend the meeting when the case was considered. A resolution to this effect was proposed and adopted. At the time appointed I attended the meeting of teachers, and Mr. Roger was called to the chair, as he had occupied that situation at the former one. After several persons had expressed their sentiments, I delivered mine. I stated the conviction of my mind that all Sunday Schools should be connected with a place of public worship; but that I wished as a Methodist Preacher to have the same order established at that place, which we had in every other in the circuit, of preaching to the children and teachers of the School: And also remarked that, as there was a sufficiency of inhabitants in the neighbourhood, that it would be well for the friends of the establishment, to begin a new School, that the country might be benifitted by our joint labours. After some further discussion the matter was put to the vote, and there was out of about thirty persons, a majority of twenty against the measure. This decision would, I hoped, have set the matter at rest; but I soon found it had only been like the letting out of water. I have had a pretty long conversation this forenoon with both the Mr. Hollands on the subject, and find they are determined to carry the measure into effect. I stated the reason of the opposition on the part of the Methodists, that we considered it a transfer of the children to the church. To this Mr. Holland replied that was not his attention. I also stated the wishes of the Society was to have preaching at such an hour on the Sabbath as the children could attended, and reminded him that such was my wish before I knew anything of the present plan; but he said that such a step at present would be like opposition to the Church. So that I found I could gain nothing whatever way I turned. Mr. Holland stated his intention of calling another meeting of teachers, to consider the subject again, but their minds are made up, whatever the issue of the meeting may be.

When I was at Manchester the last time, I had an opportunity of mentioning this affair to Mr. Marsden,[1] and he advised the measures so far followed. But how to proceed further, I feel greatly at a loss. I fear I cannot preserve the Society intire in any way I take. If I give any sanction to the children going to Church, I fear the Society will be divided; and on the other hand if I take a decided part against the measure, I am not certain how it will go with Mr. Holland's family. And a middle measure seems impracticable. My judgment seems inclined to abide with the Society, but I know not how we should go on for a place of worship, as I suppose we could not enjoy the School room, or at most we can have no more preaching than we now have. . . .

P.S. Mr. Roger stated to me the schools in Manchester for all denominations who attend the church. But I suppose part attend the Methodist Chapels also . . .

[1] George Marsden succeeded Preston as superintendent of the Bolton circuit, 1827–1830.

88. *From John Mason*   London, January 22, 1827

Since I had the pleasure of seeing you in Town my attention has
of course been directed in no small degree to the subject of my
entrance upon the Book Concerns,[1] and though it is not my intention
to draw an appalling picture, nor do I intend to shrink from the task,
yet I do assure you the more narrowly I inspect the whole system
the worse I find it. In order to form a correct opinion as to the amount
the Book Room should furnish the Conference annually I found it
necessary to go into more minute calculations than those which before
engaged my thoughts (excepting the periodicals) and the result is as
follows.

By our tracts we lose annually not less than £250. [By] the Catechisms, Sunday School Hymn Book and some other Miscellaneous
works our loss is about from 5 to 10 per cent on the year's sales.
The Hymn Books yield us about an average profit of 15 per cent.
The periodicals pay well, but you are aware that the want of a proportionate profit on the above standard works of the Connexion
for which there is great demand is a very heavy drawback upon those
works which yield a good profit. But I am not at all discouraged
because I see or think I see my way now clear and believe it a call
of Providence to go and redeem that concern so intimately connected
with the vitals of Methodism, and the ruin of which must inevitably
have involved us all in the most distressing circumstances. It is in that
state that it must gradually be revolutionized and may be brought
round to become a most important auxiliary in the spread of the
Gospel at home, as well as supporting partially the Widows and
Superannuated Fathers of the Connexion. But at present it is looked
upon as our father's loaf and every child must have a slice. Of that
you are well aware.

The following are the proposals I intend submitting to the Book
Committee but should like your opinion upon them first. The sum
proposed to be allowed each year during the first three years is the
same as last Conference and beyond which I dare not engage to go
and likewise pay the Interest upon the debt and meet all the expences
of salaries, wages, etc, etc, which will be not less than from £2200 to
£2500 *per Annum.*

[1] John Mason became Book Steward at the Conference of 1827. The Book
Room for which the itinerant preachers acted as travelling salesmen, proved less
profitable to the connexion than was generally hoped. Rejecting good advice to
leave the business to a lay professional, (M.C.A. MSS. Robert Lomas to Jabez
Bunting, July 5, 1806; February 16, 1808), Conference kept the office as a place
of dignity for a preacher. As this letter shows, they were still expecting substantial subventions from a publishing house which was itself in debt.

L

Contingent fund	1500
Legalized do.[1]	1000
Irish Brethren	400
Seniors do. 2½ *per cent*	750

1. That at the Conference 1828, 1829, 1830, the Book Steward shall place at the disposal of the Conference out of the profit of the concern £3650 each year to be divided among the several funds (including the Seniors fund) in such proportions as the Conference may appoint.
2. That at the Conference 1831, 1832, and 1833, he shall advance to the Conference £4150 to be disposed of by them as above.
3. That at the Conference 1834, 1835, 1836, he shall advance £4650 each year.
4. That whatever amount the Book Steward may realise more than the sums specified above either from the profit of the current year or from the sale of the stock on hand, such amount shall be appropriated in liquidation of the debt upon the Book Room, and the Conference engage on their part that they will not during any of those years request from the Book Steward a larger sum than what is above specified.
5. That should the Conference become embarrassed in consequence of calling out more Preachers than the regular income of the Connexion together with the above specified sums will meet, they shall not call upon the Book Steward to borrow monies and thereby increase the debt upon the Book Room to meet those claims but the Treasurers of the respective funds shall provide for such deficiencies as the Conference may appoint.
6. That these regulations be entered upon the Journal at the next Conference.

From this you will perceive that at the end of the 4th year I propose to advance £500 and at the end of the 7th £1000 above the present grants to the several funds but beyond that I dare not engage to go, as all I can possibly raise above those sums must go towards liquidating the enormous debt and to make it work well I must have a good capital at my command which may be turned to good account.

The first three years will be the trying time and during those periods if I am favord with health of body, vigour of mind, the prayers of my Brethren, and help from God (for if ever I needed wisdom and discretion I shall need it then) I do not fear but it will be so far brought round as to make the remaining years much more comfortable to me and advantageous to the Connexion at large. . . .

[1] The Legalized Fund was a kind of group insurance scheme by which the preachers made provision for their aged brethren, widows and orphans.

89. *From Josiah Hill*[1]   [Liverpool], July 24, [1827]

. . . It has long appeared to me that something important might be effected in *directing* and *assisting* the studies of our young preachers during *their four years of probation* so as to render their examination at the District Meeting more beneficial to themselves, and more satisfactory to the brethren.

Instead of *merely* requiring from them a list of the books which they have read, in the course of the preceding year, while we remain totally unacquainted with the degree of knowledge they have derived from them, it would be a most essential advantage to them, and ultimately, an unspeakable blessing to the Connexion, were the Conference to propose certain *standard works*, such as would bring the whole system of *Methodist divinity* and *discipline* before them, in a condensed, plain, and as far as possible, in an analytical form, such works to be divided into four parts, judiciously graduated and suited to each successive year of probation, and to be as text-books of examination in the District meeting, such volumes as Mr. Watson's *Christian Institutes*, and others which might be mentioned, would be admirably adapted to such an object.

Some such plan as this would operate not merely in exciting diligent application, but in preventing that diffusive and superficial reading and thinking, which tend neither to improve the understanding, nor to furnish the mind with the principles of Christian doctrine, or useful knowledge.

The young man who with these advantages is found, at the end of his probation, anything less than *well instructed*, both in the doctrines and discipline of Methodism, must surely be deemed, *unfit* for, if not unworthy of, having a part in our ministry.

At such a period as the present, when education is everywhere, exciting an ardent thirst for knowledge, and every means of information, and improvements are brought within the reach of even the lowest class of society, I hope we shall not remain stationary. If our young preachers are not required to be accomplished scholars, our people have at least a right to expect that they shall be sound Methodist divines. . . .

P.S. A reference to this subject will be found in the minutes of the Liverpool District Meeting.

[1] Josiah Hill (1773–1844), preacher, Liverpool circuit, 1825–1826; Liverpool (South) circuit, 1826–1828. The letter exemplifies the pressure which began to build up in the later 'twenties for the more systematic training of the preachers, and which led to the resolution of Conference in 1834 to found a Theological Institution.

90. *From Isaac Turton*[1]   Leeds, October 4, 1827

I expect you will receive a letter by this post from Mr. Grindrod[2] respecting the disturbed state of the Societies in Leeds—and which will make you acquainted with the proposition made to him. But my object in writing is to state my case, and ask your advice how to act. Above twenty local preachers in my circuit have attended the illegal meetings headed by Mr. Johnson, of whom you have heard, and these have resolved to stand or fall with him, in company with about the same number in the East Circuit, and in doing this they have acted in a way which has put them into the greatest perplexity. At our Local Preachers' Meeting everything was perfectly calm and peaceable. The usual business was gone through, apparently to the satisfaction of all. In the Quarterly Meeting it was the same till one, *viz.* J. Yewdall[3] brought forward a resolution relative to the removal of Mr. Haswell[4] and intending to censure the persons concerned in it. This, however, after a long conversation was withdrawn; and all parted in peace. In the same evening, another illegall meeting was called. Persons were in waiting to about our vestry to give notice of it as secretly as possible, and at the meeting, I am told, 49 out of fifty promised not to preach without letting either of the Superintendants know of it, that we might be surprized, and the people, I suppose, excited to espouse their cause.

Now in all this they have acted as [if] there were no Leeds West Circuit, as if it had no Superintendant, and as if not a grain of authority belonged to him, and thus [this?] without any offence, and after apparently pledging themselves to be faithful to me and each other, they have actually overlooked my authority, in neglecting wilfully to do their work. Brother Hollingworth[5] and I have spent two days in running after and reasoning with them, but with two or three exceptions, it has been in vain. When charged with this conduct they were confounded, and said neither I nor my colleagues had displeased them, but they argued that when the circuit was divided it was agreed that the Local Preachers should be considered as *one*, and hence they had a *right* to do as they did, and never notice their proper, in fact their only superintendent. This then is the fact with many, nay

---

[1] Isaac Turton (d. 1851, *aet.* 74), superintendent, Leeds (West) circuit, 1827–1829.

[2] Edmund Grindrod, superintendent, Leeds (East) circuit, 1827–1829.

[3] Matthew Johnson and Josiah Yewdall, two of the leaders of Methodist radicalism in Leeds, and of the campaign against church rates in the Leeds vestry

[4] John Partis Haswell (1790–1870) preacher, Leeds circuit, 1825–1826, Leeds (West) circuit, 1826–1827.

[5] Joseph Hollingworth (d. 1836), preacher, Leeds (West) circuit, 1827–1829.

most of them. They have cut themselves off from me as Local Preachers and now, I have been told by one who is in the secret, that the
best of them would give their ears to get back again, being perfectly
ashamed of what they have done. Now will you favour me with your
advice as to how I am to act in this matter. You will find by Mr.
Grindrod's letter that there is a proposition by which the East
Preachers wish to make the West Preachers a partty, and I fear it is
a trap to ensnare me, and induce me to take back those who have
seceeded. I suspect that if I do anything to recognise their relation
to me as Local Preachers still under me they will turn it against
me . . . Mr. Grindrod is acting most judiciously and firmly. I am
affraid of myself. You know how pliable I am *thought* to be and it is
too truly. . . .

91. *From Thomas Stanley*[1]   Dudley, October 18, 1827

. . . The affairs of Leeds have given me much pain, all that we could
do to prevent the meetings of Local Preachers, Leaders and others
after the Conference produced no effect, and when together their
speaches were of a most inflamatry nature; and all bearing on the
political question of there rights. The Leeds Society has in it a large
number who do not think as we do on national or church government; some of these are Local Preachers and Leaders, whose office
gives them much influence over our people. Our Leaders Meeting
is not composed of those men who ought to fill that important office,
nor can it be till our best friends will acc[e]pt of office, and rally
round the Superintendent, perhaps this day of trial may open their
eyes and convince them of the necessity of the thing.
    The influence of these men also in the Sunday Schools[2] is very
great, the rising generation are in great danger from them, and they
take with them their views into the parish Church (for the vestry will
not hold them) and on every question Johnson, Yewdall, etc., take a
part and then they are cheared by the populos, when opposing the
officers of the Church and Parish.
    The great danger in the present state of things is the loss of our
young and inexperienced members, may the Lord keep them from
harm. . . .

[1] Thomas Stanley (d. 1832, *aet.* 59), superintendent, Dudley circuit, 1827–1830.
[2] The undenominational New Schools of Leeds had been transferred to Methodist control by a majority of two votes at the annual meeting in 1816, but reports of the political aspirations of the teachers continued to cause alarm in
Conference (Leeds City Archives, MS. Sunday School Minute Book 1816–1842;
G. Smith, *History of Wesleyan Methodism* (4th ed., London, 1866), iii, p. 113.

92. *To Thomas Galland* (Leeds)   N. pl. or d. [late 1827]

I learn from Mr. Dawson,[1] who passed through Manchester today, that your Prayer Meeting Leaders are now disposed to take up the fag-end of faction and discord.[2] Their system also needs much reform in Leeds; and I hope the opportunity will be seized to bring them under complete discipline, and reduce them to their proper level. This is tedious and painful work, but it was all necessary and great good will eventually result from it. . . .

93. *From Thomas Galland*   Leeds, n.d. [Post-marked Nov. 20, 1827]

Copy of the Preamble, and Resolutions entered into at the Leaders Meeting, held at the Old Chapel, Leeds, November 12, 1827.

No. 1.

It is the earnest desire of the Superintendent of the Circuit and his colleagues to gratify the wishes of all the people amongst whom they labour in the word and doctrine: nor is any object more desirable than to unite the sentiments and affections of all by promoting their spiritual interests in the most effectual manner. The great object of helping one another forward in the way to the heavenly country will, in their opinion, be best attained by a strict and conscientious regard on the part of all to the long established laws and usages of the Methodist Society. Without an adherence to these, as a matter of principle, and as a proper manifestation of our allegiance to *Him*

---

[1] 'Billy' Dawson of Barnbow (d. 1841), a noted Local Preacher and circuit steward of the Leeds (East) circuit, took the view that both sides were in error; the Trustees ought not to have pushed the organ case beyond the District Meeting, and when an appeal was made to Conference the members of the District Meeting ought not to have changed their minds under pressure from Bunting, and thus set the Leeds radicals aflame; on the other side Sigston was doctrinaire, stubborn and suspicious, and invited disciplinary action by holding weekly meetings at his house under pledge of secrecy (M.C.A. MSS. W. Dawson to R. Pilter, December 10, 1827: W. Dawson to T. Mease, December 17, 1827). On Dawson generally, see J. Everett, *Memoirs of William Dawson* (London, 1842).

[2] Like the Sunday school, the Leeds cottage prayer-meetings were an institution originally independent of circuit constitution, but now affected by the division of the circuit. For over a generation, they had formed a highly organized means of extending Methodist influence at a popular level. (Leeds Central Library. John [should be Thomas] Wray's MS. History of Methodism in Leeds xi, fos. 131–139). As a result of this conflict new *Rules of Leeds Prayer Leaders* (Leeds, 1828) were published, under which no one was to be a prayer leader till he had been a member of Society for a year; he should lose office if he ceased to be a member. All the preachers were to be members of the committee, and the superintendent was to preside.

who is the Lord and Master of us all, there can be amongst us no fellowship of saints, nor any of the inestimable advantages of Christian Communion.

In order to do whatever is possible on his part for the removal of every stumbling-block out of the way, the Superintendent of this Circuit desires freely to express his thoughts before this meeting on all the subjects referred to in the propositions submitted to him a few days ago by certain individuals of this meeting.

First: He is willing to give every assurance that the organ to be erected in the Brunswick Chapel shall be employed in strict accordance with our long-established usages in worship, the end which it is designed to answer being to give every facility to our people in singing 'the high praises of God *with the Spirit and with the understanding also*'. The right of the Leaders Meeting is also gladly acknowledged to offer their advice to the *Superintendent* in respectful terms, on all points connected with the simplicity and spirituality of our worship, whenever they shall judge it needful.

Second: On the same principle it is wished to be understood that the Conference gladly receives communications from all bodies, duly authorized meetings, and even individuals among us, on any matters on which they may imagine themselves to possess cause of complaint [or] of remonstrance. The Superintendent pledges himself and thinks he may pledge his Brethren also, to do what in them lies in bringing their requests, observations and remonstrances before the Conference.

Third: The Local Preachers have of their own accord 'resigned their office'; but they have taken this step, as is now pretty well understood, with very different intentions, some of them being activated by principles which others utterly disclaim. They must therefore be treated with by their different Superintendents *on their individual application.* The circumstances in which they stand towards the connexion are so widely different that any other method of meeting their case is evidently impracticable. Should any of the Local Preachers lately on the *Leeds East Plan* think fit to apply to the Superintendent for restoration to their office, they will be received in the spirit of Christian affection, nor will anything be requested of them, which the principles and rules of the Body, as applying to the particular case of each does not indispensably require.

On the whole case the preachers refer with great pleasure to the Minute of the Conference (1826) which engages them '*readily and cheerfully to protect all our members in the exercise of such functions as belong to them according to our general laws and usages*', at the same time they call upon the Leaders' Meeting to remember that according to our Rules and indeed the great principles of the *New Testament*, the Superintendents in our Connexion, are not 'the mere Chairman of Public Meetings, but the pastors of Christian Societies, put in Trust by the ordinance of God, and by their own voluntary association with us, with the scriptural superintendence of their spiritual affairs, and responsible to the Great Head of the Church for the faithful discharge of the duties of that Trust'.

No. 2.

Having thus entered into a frank exposition of his own sentiments the Superintendent, in the existing posture of our affairs, finds it bound upon his conscience by a solemn sense of duty to seek from the Leaders for an equally frank statement on their part of their adherence to the principles of Wesleyan Methodism in general, and especially of their determination to discharge their duties as leaders of classes in our Connexion, in a cordial and faithful manner. It is directly asserted in certain paragraphs which have appeared from week to week in the *Leeds Mercury* that some of our Leaders have assembled in illegal meetings, which, as holding office in the Methodist Connexion, they were bound to discountenance and denounce to the Superintendant. It is further asserted in the same widely circulating newspaper, that, at one of these meetings, Leaders in our Society did enter into resolutions, binding the parties to withold their weekly monies from the Leaders' Meeting, and engaging them to advise the members of their classes to suspend their contributions. And, although it would seem that this resolution was modified at a subsequent meeting, the *spirit of it* is manifestly still retained; for it is undeniable that some Leaders continue both by *precept* and *example* to countenance their people in *partially* if not *entirely* witholding their accustomed contributions; thus acting in direct opposition to the rule which requires them to receive from their members *what they can afford to give*.

There is no ground for saying that this is an uncalled for or unwarrantable measure. When such representations as those which now agitate the public mind have been circulated on an authority emanating from *this meeting*, when there is unquestionable evidence to connect these paragraphs which have been the cause of such widely spreading mischief with Mr. Joah Mallinson, one of the Society's Stewards, and when this Brother publickly asserts that two thirds of this meeting are of the '*dissatisfied party*', it is manifest that the Superintendent can no longer delay to probe the matter to the bottom, and ascertain who of the present members of the Leaders' Meeting are Methodists on Mr. Wesley's old established principles and who are not? This is now the more absolutely necessary, as it will be needful for this meeting, *properly constituted*, to proceed without delay to assist the Superintendant, under the rules of Pacification, in deciding on the cases of certain members of this meeting which require immediate notice.

Then the meeting was called upon in alphabetical order to sign the following resolutions:—

We the undersigned members of the Leaders Meeting assembling at the Old Chapel in Leeds, taking into consideration the troubles at present existing in the Society, and especially the reports which have been widely circulated in newspapers respecting the proceedings of a part of the members of the Meeting, do feel ourselves called upon to express our cordial attachment to Wesleyan Methodism, and our determination to discharge our proper duties in the office which we hold in the Methodist Society, by freely subscribing our names in token of our cordial assent to the following resolutions.

I: As our regular weekly Leaders' Meetings are sufficient for the transaction of the business of the Society, and our Quarterly Meeting for the business of the Circuit, and as other meetings of Leaders, Local Preachers and others called without the knowledge and consent of the Superintendent, are contrary to the Rules of Pacification, and tend to disunite and divide us, we unreservedly engage not to attend any meetings of that description, but conform ourselves to our existing laws on that subject.

II: As it has been reported, that many of the Leaders of this Meeting, have united in a determination to advise the members of their classes, not to pay their usual contributions, we hereby engage to observe and enforce in our classes our old rule on that subject, not only by receiving what the members are willing to give, but by prudently, and in the spirit of Christian kindness, advising them, as need may require, to contribute as God hath prospered them.

III: We hereby renew the engagements which we either virtually or formally made, when we were first appointed to our offices as Leaders, to act in all things, as God shall give us grace so to do, in conformity with our excellent discipline, which we believe, as a whole, to be agreeable to the word of God; and to seek for ourselves, and press upon the members of our classes, such a heartfelt belief of those essential doctrines of the Gospel which are taught amongst us, as shall produce in our lives and in theirs, all the peaceable fruits of righteousness.

Signed by:

Chas. Turkington	Geo. Crawshaw	Thompson Dean
Wm. Higgins	Judith Hague	John Lawson
Saml. Brown	Joseph Elmsley	Joseph Walton
Jno. S. Barlow	Jno. Jefferson	Thomos Wray
Sarah Barlow	Saml. Jackson	Assenters
W. D. Boothman	Mary Phillips	Elizabeth Brown
Mahala Butterfield	Hannah Slater	Edward Denham
Mary England	Thos. Simpson	Robert Knapton
Benjn. Bray	W. Gilyard Scarth	Joseph Pearson
J. Cundale	James Stead	Nimrod Ramsden
Mary Cullingworth	Wm. Whitely	John Townend
Henry Cullingworth	Mary White	John Wood
	James Crawshaw	Wm. Pickering
	John Simpson	James Simpson
		George Wetherall

N.B. Brother Proctor and various others it is expected will sign.

My Dear Sir,

By request of Mr. Grindrod I address to you the sheet containing these documents, which will themselves almost sufficiently explain the course we are pursuing. We have now been engaged for two successive Monday nights in explanations with the Leaders, and ascertaining their distribution into *three classes*: 1st. *Signers*. 2y. *Assenters* who nevertheless decline to sign. 3y. *Dissentients* who altogether refuse whether to assent or sign, and who particularly object to the *1st Resolution* which pledges to an observance of our Law respecting illegal meetings. These in general say that they have attended such meetings, and will not engage to give up the practise.

The line we have taken is this. Mr. Grindrod declares the *signers* and even the mere assenters competent to render assistance in the exercise of discipline under the Rules of Pacification. But those who dissent from these resolutions (which you observe pledge to *nothing new*, but only declare the intention of those subscribing them to discharge their unquestionable duty) he stated to have thereby *in effect renounced their office as Methodist Leaders;* and he was at perfect liberty to consider them no longer in that capacity; but being disposed to treat the case with all possible forbearance, he was still content that they should be restrained from no functions of Methodist Leaders, but such as by declaring their dissent from important points of our discipline, they were in the nature of things, altogether unfit to discharge. I would add more, but the arduous exertions of last night, preaching and then *Leaders' Meetings* until the solemn hour of *one*, the dead of night, really quite unfit for me enlarging and almost for composition. But Mr. G[rindrod] and Mr. Scarth[1] will I expect be with you on *Friday morning to breakfast* and explain all. . . .

94. From Edmund Grindrod   Leeds, November 28, 1827

The President[2] says, 'I approve of the men and the measure.'[3] He intends being with us on Monday evening next and commissions me most earnestly to request you to meet him on that day, that we may have time to deliberate on the best mode of proceeding. He seems to be in excellent spirits and says he hopes we shall so dispose of the Leeds business as to read a useful and lasting lesson to the whole Connexion. . . .

95. From Thomas Galland   Leeds, December 21, 1827

. . . I forwarded you on Tuesday last a *Patriot*, containing some account of Sigstone[4] and Co.'s meeting on Monday night, and I have given directions for a *Mercury* to be forwarded to you by this night's post, which will contain, I expect, a long account of Sigstone's meeting, and also a pretty long piece consisting of divers particulars, and headed, 'Beverley Methodist *versus* Mr. Mark Robinson'. I thought it needful to occupy for once, an intire column of the *Mercury* in this case, 1st. Because publicly challenged in the same paper by Mr. Robinson. 2y. Because that individual is at present *prowling about* and *very busy* here in Leeds,[5] and his case was by *Matthew Johnson* on Monday night publicly mixed up with their own. 3y. Because Mr. R. has succeeded in gaining the ear of the clergy in this place on the subject of Church Methodism. He harangued them, I understand, for an hour and upwards in a meeting held at the vestry of the *old church* on Tuesday, which meeting adjourned until Thursday, but its deliberations seem to be kept a *profound secret*.

On this ground I have taken occasion in the close of my letter to allude to our feelings as a body of preachers on the subject of

[1] W. Gilyard Scarth, an old friend of Bunting, and Treasurer to the Leeds Brunswick Trustees.

[2] John Stephens, President of Conference, 1827–1828.

[3] *I.e.*, the appointment and composition of the Special District Meeting which met to settle the affairs of the Leeds circuits. Bunting is here summoned to the meeting on the somewhat doubtfully legal title of President's special adviser.

[4] James Sigston, Leeds schoolmaster and revivalsit (see n. 3, p. 46 *supra*). Acted as the constitution-maker for the Leeds Protestant Methodists who separated as a result of this dispute.

[5] Mark Robinson also reappeared at the time of the Warrenite secessions in 1835. M.C.A. MSS. Jabez Bunting to John Beecham, November 16, 1835.

Church Methodism, and would particularly call your attention to those closing remarks, which, I am happy to say, met with the high approbation of such of our brethren as I was able to meet with and submit them to their consideration yesterday evening. . . .

96. *To Joseph Entwisle*[1] (Bristol)   Salford, December 22, 1827

. . . Now about Leeds. By this post, I believe, you will receive a printed letter, containing the Resolutions of the Special District Meeting, which, as you will see, I attended, *at the importunate request of the President* and of the Leeds preachers. Those resolutions will give you a fair and *not exaggerated* or *coloured* statement of the facts, and an account of the views we *unanimously* took of the whole case. The organ is the *mere pretext* among the *heads* of the schism; and would, I believe, be cheerfully abandoned, if there were any ground whatever to believe that such a concession would cure the evil. But the root of it lies much deeper. There was a *radical* faction there, whose meetings had assumed all the fearful characters of a *Methodistical Luddism* (*secret vows or bonds*, etc., included) and of whom it was indispensable to the *permanent peace* of the Society that it should be forthwith purged. A very large portion of the East Leaders was unsound. The case was the most awful and perplexing I ever saw. We at one time had no hope but in dissolving the Society and beginning again, because, though the great mass of the Society, and nearly all our more respectable friends were right, the *poor Leaders, and younger Leaders and Local Preachers* were largely infected with the spirit of revolt against the first principles of our existing Church Government. At last things brightened; and the middle course we adopted, though doubtless some will censure us, is likely to have a good effect. Our President be⟨haved⟩ most nobly, and was surely specially assisted by ⟨the⟩ Lord. The great mass of disaffection is among persons who worship at the *Old Chapel*. *Nine tenths* of the Brunswick Congregation and Society are on one side; and the work in that Chapel prospers amidst all this horrible bustle.[2] The Resolution of the Trustees, and those of the sound local preachers (drawn up by W. Dawson) have done much good in this crisis. They will be published in a pamphlet with the District Resolutions etc. . . .

Through mercy, we are doing well in this now small circuit; small, I mean, as to the number of members, for we found ourselves reduced to 1170; and have hard work to get on, as to finances. However, our

---

[1] Joseph Entwisle, superintendent, Bristol circuit, 1826–1829.
[2] The great losses of membership took place in the Old Chapel at Leeds.

Congregations and Societies are on the increase and we have nothing but peace and love. . . .

97. From Thomas Galland   Leeds, January 4, 1828

By request of Mr. Grindrod, and also in conformity with my own previous design, I address to you a few lines, with an intent to put you in possession of the leading features of our existing situation, as its complexion varies in some hues at least almost from day to day. . . . We held our Quarterly and Local Preachers' Meetings for the East Circuit on Monday last (*Dec. 31st*). Mr. Grindrod, of course, was not able to attend, but both meetings were exceedingly satisfactory to Mr. Close[1] and myself, in the spirit of firm adherence manifested towards *Methodist discipline*, and of *cordial union* both one amongst another, and towards the preachers. An impertinent note was read from Matthew Johnson,[2] in reply to one from Mr. Grindrod requesting the *minute book of the Quarterly Meeting*, in his custody as Recorder, and stating that having as much right to retain it as Mr. Grindrod to withold his ticket, and that *at all events* he should not forward it to this Quarterly Meeting. The reading of this note produced in the Quarterly Meeting *a strong sensation*, much against M.J., but telling very nicely in favour of Methodist rule and order. At the Local Preachers' Meeting, the brethren, *C. Smith, Vickers, Kaye* and *W. Atkinson* were restored to their *former places* on the plan, having satisfied Mr. Grindrod in respect of their unfeigned sorrow for their past conduct, and their unshaken attachment to Methodism and to the Preachers. *Howes* was conditionally restored—*Sanderson* called upon me the morning after the Local Preachers' Meeting; as I saw he was very earnest in his solicitations, I gave him the best advice in my power, and while I told him that he could not possibly be restored on the forthcoming plan, yet, as far as I thought prudence would allow, spoke to him *comfortable words and kind*.

On Wednesday (January 2nd) I attended the West Quarterly Meeting and was present towards the close of the Local Preachers Meeting. Several valuable brethren, *Whalley, B. Rindle* and others were likewise restored to their plan, and a *very good feeling*, with but little drawback, was manifested at the Local Preachers' Meeting in all its proceedings. By the way, however, we seem to have more warmth and energy in *the East* [Circuit] whether for good or evil.

The general state of things with us is certainly improving. We see an open door of hope: . . .

But I must now come to our *Sunday School Meeting* yesterday

[1] Titus Close (d. 1833, *aet.* 37), preacher, Leeds (East) circuit, 1827–1829.

[2] Matthew Johnson was secretary to the Leeds (East) Quarterly Meeting.

evening: it commenced according to advertisement in the *Old Chapel Vestry*, but did not *conclude* there. The thing was on this wise. Mr. Grindrod, having opened the meeting with singing and prayer, stated that his health would not permit him to continue, and therefore that he gave up his post to me as the next preacher in seniority on the Circuit. This was warmly objected to by Matthew Johnson, who rose up in opposition to Mr. Grindrod's assertion that it was our established usage, for preachers to preside in all meetings connected with our Body, and stated that this regulation was only found in the minutes for 1827. Mr. Keeling[1] interposed a few words in reply, and on Mr. Grindrod's leaving the vestry, I took in the midst of no small opposing clamour the seat he vacated; on this *Mr. James Dickenson* of Burley moved and *Mr. Buttery* seconded a proposition that *Mr. Joah Mallinson*[2] be called to the chair. I strongly stated that this motion was quite superfluous, as it was my determination to keep the place to which I had been called; however, there was a show of hands by the party, which Mr. Dickenson declared to be in Mr. Joah Mallinson's favour, and he came up to take the chairman's seat and act in that capacity. On this *Mr. Turkington* proposed that all the friends of good order and Methodism should remove to the *Library Room*, a proposal which was immediately acceded to by numbers of our respectable and warmly attached friends. I took care, on vacating my seat to gather up and pile under my arm, the *reports, books, and papers*, which lay before me, a measure which, I understand, is very obnoxious to the faction. We mustered very strong in the *Library Room*, proceeded with the usual routine of business, and appointed suitable persons to visit and take possession of the schools on Sunday next. I fear there will be much unpleasant striving and opposition on that day. *Mallinson* had gone from their opposition meeting, and got into possession of the keys of the *Bank School* just two or three minutes before some of our friends had arrived on the same errand—*bella, bella, horrida bella.* A *special committee meeting* is appointed for Tuesday evening. Thus we are circumstanced at present. . . .

98. *From William Henshaw*[3]   Sheffield, January 9, 1828

I embrace the opportunity of sending by Brother Harris[4] a copy of

---

[1] Isaac Keeling (1789–1869), preacher, Leeds (West) circuit, 1826–1829. President 1855.

[2] Joah Mallinson, one of the most furious of the Leeds agitators, was a Leader and Circuit Steward.

[3] William Henshaw (1775–1841), superintendent, Sheffield circuit, 1827–1829.

[4] Thomas Harris (1791–1863), preacher, Rochdale circuit, 1824–1827.

the Address which passed at our adjourned Quarterly Meeting, as you desired to see it. I told you of the manner in which that Meeting closed, and we then hoped that all hearts would have been united in the great work. But the spirit of faction is ever restless, and the Resolutions of the London South Circuit were plentifully distributed, and the letters of the London North Secretary[1] sold and given away in abundance, and several Subscriptions to our Schools were withheld according to the system proposed of starving the Preachers into submission, and the Leaders of this miserable party became very jealous lest their dupes should be lulled asleep by our kindness and Christian charity, and at our December Quarterly Meeting we found that the old leaven had fermented afresh, which induced me to treat the Radicals with less respect and ceremony than formerly. I had heard of their intention to oppose at least some of the Preachers staying a third year, and also to refuse the Circuit Steward to be proposed. The Trustees and Town and Circuit Stewards were called together a few days before the meeting for consultation, and unanimously agreed to recommend to the Quarterly Meeting, all the three preachers to continue a third year. Mr. Rawlins was absent. At this Meeting I first proposed Brother Longden to be Circuit Steward instead of Brother Owen who had been two years in that office. This met with warm opposition, and some bad blood manifested itself, but he obtained a majority of seven votes. The Circuit Stewards then proposed myself to superintend them a third year. I counted 28 hands elevated for my continuance and 18 against it, the number of persons present about 70. I had told them before being proposed, that I waited to know the will of God, and that if I had not a very respectable majority I should take it for an intimation of *that* will that I ought to go. After some altercation I was proposed a second time and lost three votes or rather had three more votes against me. But I am thankful I had all the wise and good, and respectable in my favour. Brother Calder had 20 votes for him and 30 against him. Brother Bridgman had 42 votes for, and 4 against him. When this work was done, I told the Meeting I saw it was the will of God I should leave them, and Samuel Jackson was proposed by Longden

---

[1] While disclaiming any connexion with the Leeds separatists, the London (South) circuit Quarterly Meeting showed itself extremely hostile to the proceedings of the Special District Meeting at Leeds, and later printed a 40-page *Address . . . to the Wesleyan Methodist Conference* of 1828 for private distribution among the members, demanding constitutional clarification. See also nos. 99, 113. Robert Eckett (1797–1862), 'the London North Secretary' who was expelled from Wesleyanism for supporting Dr. Warren in 1836, and became the Bunting of the Wesleyan Methodist Association, was the principal agitator in the London (North) circuit.

in my stead, and John Smith in the place of Calder, and Brothers Cubit and Alder[1] intimated some intention of removing, being both grieved by what they saw and heard.

The only important point in the enclosed Address is the petition to have the introduction of organs into our chapels as well as all material alterations in the mode and form of Divine Worship subject to the same regulations as are in force with respect to the Administration of the Lord's Supper, Minutes Vol. 1st, page 322.[2] A compliance with this request I believe would cut off all occasion of animosity in this Circuit, and would generally satisfy our Connexion. And this I think might be complied with, because it is a much less thing to grant the Leaders a veto concerning an organ than concerning the Lord's Supper—The one is of human invention, the other of Divine injunction. Because the reason assigned for one is equally applicable to the other—Qualification to give the sense of the people—and because at all times the Conference itself has shown great jealousy about Organs, but none against the Lord's Supper and I may add the Trustees in general will not oppose this grant—The Sheffield Trustees in particular. . . .

99. *From Thomas Galland*   Leeds, January 12, 1828

. . . from you we would wish to learn both *when to fight and when to fly.*

. . . It appears to me that measures should be adopted to ensure a very efficient President next Conference.[3] *Sheffield* I understand is rather perturbed, the horizon clouds also in the direction of Liverpool. I cannot help thinking of a *marginal note* which occurs in *Bunyan's Holy War 'Look to it, Mansoul'.*

[1] Frederick Calder, preacher, Sheffield circuit, 1827–1829: Thomas Bridgman (d. 1832), preacher, Sheffield circuit, 1827–1829: George Cubitt, preacher, Sheffield circuit, 1828–1831: Samuel Jackson (d. 1861, *aet.* 75), superintendent, Sunderland circuit, 1826–1829. President 1847. Governor of Theological Institution, 1848–1854. An early advocate of a system of Wesleyan day schools: Robert Alder (retired from ministry, 1851), preacher, Sheffield circuit, 1828–1831. Served in Canada till 1828. Missionary secretary 1833–1851: Henry Longden, the circuit steward, whose father (of the same name) had been one of the most famous characters in Sheffield Methodism had, like his father, some revivalist tendencies.

[2] The Plan of Pacification (1795) forbade the administration of the Lord's Supper in any chapel without the prior consent of a majority of its Trustees, of its Stewards and Leaders, and of Conference. Although the very heavy majority of leaders against the Leeds Brunswick organ was obtained in a circuit Leaders' Meeting, it is certain that if this Sheffield proposal had been law, it would have been impossible to proceed with the installation of the organ.

[3] The next President, 1828–1829, was Bunting himself.

I was proposed at the London North Quarterly Meeting, and in case of my failure, Mr. Samuel Jackson, but Mr. Waddy[1] carried it against us, I understand by a *majority of nine*; a majority, however, I understand, not embracing the real respectability of that Circuit. Mr. Anderson[2] further tells me that the men of the South have prevailed *to tear out of their Circuit Minute ⟨Bo⟩ok* the letter of the last Conference! This ⟨I⟩ suppose, *is their burning by the common hangman.* . . .

100. *From Thomas Galland*   Leeds, January 18, 1828

We are still engaged in our Sunday School contest, but our prospects here, I am happy to say, brighten. The firm course of procedure we have adopted, in connection with the moderate temper manifested in *the resolutions* is working well. The violent proceedings, one after another, in which our opponents engage, more and more confirm our existing friends and continually augment their number.

A subcommittee including the preachers on both circuits is now appointed, to modify the existing regulations of the schools, and bring them more efficiently under Methodistical controul. Of course we shall keep in view the excellent *platform* contained in the *Minutes*.

On the whole, we have great reason for gratitude. I fear however, that the sayings and devices of preachers in other places, will keep alive a flame which otherwise would speedily go out, so far as any serious inconvenience might arise from it; and *retard* that blessed calm and prosperity which they should not be able to *prevent*. . . .

N.B. From Mr. Isaac I have a letter *remarkably strong* against our proceedings; but I will thank you at present *not to mention this*. I have however valuable information as to the course in which *the opposition*, if such it may be called, will be likely to shape its proceedings. They say nothing but what you I think anticipated in our meeting, and can say better than themselves.

101. *From Joshua Marsden*[3]   Worcester, January 22, 1828

As I have the highest opinion both of your wisdom and prudence I wish to lay before you a few difficulties on which my mind wants light and on which my opinion has been called for at a Leaders Meeting. You, Sir, are as our Secretary of State, an oracle and an authority in all that concerns our discipline and economy, hence

---

[1] Richard Waddy, preacher, London (City Road) circuit, 1827–1829.

[2] John Anderson (d. 1840, *aet.* 49), preacher, London (City Road) circuit 1827–1830.

[3] Joshua Marsden (d. 1837), superintendent, Worcester circuit, 1827–1829.

M

I consult you rather than the President because in my view it comes more under your peculiar department. Please then to give me your opinion on the following subjects. 1. The legality or illegality in the eye of the law of our baptising children. 2ndly. Whether to your knowledge the late Lord Chancellor ever declared it illegal. 3rdly. Whether being baptised by a Methodist or a Dissenter constitutes a legal disqualification to any office under Government. 4thly. Whether a Methodist Register is inadmissable in a British Court of Judicature.[1] The illegality of our baptisms prevails here to such an extent that though I have now been nearly six months on the Circuit, I have never been applied too to baptise a single child: for myself this is of little moment, but are not the interests of Methodism involved? Will not this alienate the children of our people from the Pastors of their parents? If the Toleration Act do not legalize our baptisms, to what extent does it legalize our ministry? Is it not to invalidate the ordinances administered by us, that that Quixot Mark Robinson has been using all his efforts? Did you not, dear Sir, maintain at the Conference that we are Pastors to all intents and purposes for which that office was instituted? Then why should any of our preachers tell the people (as have their children already baptised by Methodist preachers) to carry them to the Church and have them rebaptised; this looks queer. I hope, dear Sir, that you will shortly give me your opinion on the above points, and also direct me to such sources of information, as may set my mind at rest. . . .

102. *To Joshua Marsden* (Worcester)   Salford, January 28, 1828

It would give me sincere pleasure to render you any assistance in my power, in your investigation of the important points to which your friendly letter of the 22nd instant refers. But really the subjects are too difficult and complex to be advantageously discussed by *letter*. Such a discussion, to answer any good purpose, would almost require a *Treatise*. Besides several of your questions demand much *legal* learning, before they can receive an answer, to which any deference would be due, or on which any reliance whatever ought to be placed for practical purposes. All I can now say, is, that the valuable pamphlet sold at our Book Room, intitled 'The Judgment of Sir John Nichol in the case of "The King *versus* Wickes" '[2] may, if

---

[1] Persistent difficulties in securing recognition of dissenting registers of births or baptisms by the courts of law or departments of state in this decade drove the Protestant Dissenting Deputies in 1826 to consider, and in 1829, to demand, the introduction of state registration of births.

[2] Sir John Nicholl, *The judgment delivered, December 11th, 1809 . . . in a cause*

you have not seen it already, throw some new light on the subject, in *one* of its branches; and that if you have access to any of the religious periodicals, the speeches of Mr. John Wilks at the Annual Meetings of the 'Protestant Society for the protection of religious liberty' will probably be found there for the five or six years past; and include, if I mistake not, some useful and correct notices of the present state of the law as to Dissenters' Registers. There was a paper on the subject by Mr. Wilks in the *Evangelical Magazine*, perhaps seven years ago, which is also worth consulting. But after all, there is in my mind no doubt of the desirableness of obtaining some new legal provision on the subject; and perhaps till that is accomplished, the less *we* say to our people, the better. Those who consider Infant Baptism chiefly as a *secular* thing, and look mainly at the wordly considerations connected with it, may as well take their children to Church as to Chapel, for any ⟨good⟩ that an Ordinance engaged in with such motives can do. And as to those who look at the *religious* advantages of that holy sacrament, *they* will usually be little mindful of the mere appendage of a more or less valid register, and consult their own consciences, rather than their children's secular interests, in making their choice of the administrator. . . .

103. *From Thomas Galland* Leeds, January 25, 1828

. . . The state of our Sunday School disputes up to a recent period you have been already informed of. Since then it has been resolved on our part to take Counsel's opinion—accordingly a full view of our proceedings and of the case in general in all its aspects has been laid before *Mr. Hardy* the Recorder of this borough, on which case he remarks

1st. That Mr. Grindrod was undoubtedly the Chairman of the meeting assembling in the Old Chapel Vestry.

2y. That being obliged to depart from the meeting, he had a right to appoint me to preside in his stead, for this reason specially, that their being no specific provision relating to this case in the rules of the *Sunday School Society* and it being an Institution in connection with the Methodists, the rules of the Connexion are natural guides of proceeding, which are very explicit on this subject.

3y. That therefore the meeting being under the controul of myself as Chairman, was, in consequence of tumultuous proceedings, properly

---

. . . *promoted by Kemp against Wickes, clerk, for refusing to bury an infant child of two of his parishioners who had been baptised by a dissenting minister* (London, 1810, and later edns.).

removed into the Library Room, that the Committees there appointed are the legal Committees of the Sunday Schools, and all the proceedings of the Library Room meeting, legitimate.

4thly. That in case of any resistance by Teachers or others to the authority of these Committees amounting to a breach of the peace, speedy remedy may be had before the magistrates, but as to questions of property in the furniture etc., the only remedy is *in Chancery*, which he does not recommend. On the whole therefore he advises

5thly. A remodelling of the Society to avoid future unpleasantness. Previously to the reception of *his report on the case*, a Subcommittee had been appointed to prepare a revised scheme of government and administration for these schools. This was produced and considered on the evening when we received Mr. Hardy's opinion. It is the same in effect with the plan laid down in the Minutes with the exception of *the partial admission of writing*[1] which is proposed to be continued under the following limitations—

1st. None to learn writing in the Schools, who are taught it on weekdays.

2y. No children newly admitted into the Schools to be permitted to commence writing on Lord's Days, until they shall be able to read tolerably in the Psalms and New Testament, and have learnt the Conference Catechisms, No. 1 and 2.

3y. That, however, all children, well reported of for general proficiency and good behaviour, and having been six months in the Schools, he admitted to learn writing, and if girls, *sewing also*, in institutions to be forthwith provided for these ends connected with each particular school.

Some of our friends think it would be better now to abolish writing on Lord's Days altogether. Many others are of opinion that this would be making the *inclined plane* which leads to this result *too steep*. I adhere to this view of the subject myself, under all the circumstances as they present themselves to my mind. But your explicit opinion reaching us in time for our *Committee Meeting* next *Tuesday* we shall very highly esteem. . . .

---

[1] The lawfulness of Sabbath writing lessons came to be the great bone of contention between the supporters of the undenominational tradition in the Sunday schools and the advocates of full denominational control (*cf.* no. 2, p. 86 *supra*.) Bunting was turned against Sabbath writing by a paper presented to Conference in 1807 by Wm. Hey, a distinguished Leeds surgeon, and fought the question repeatedly until Conference declared against the practice in 1823. Nevertheless, in many parts of the connexion, as here, writing lessons continued as the only way of attracting the attendance of older children. The new *Rules of the Wesleyan Methodist Sunday Schools for Leeds West Circuit* (Leeds, 1828) permitted writing and arithmetic only on weekdays.

My contest with Mark [Robinson], is now I hope terminated; I have the satisfaction of learning that it has done good both in Leeds and Beverley. From the latter place Mr. Hutton writes me, 'Mark was never so cut up as this time, you are rendering us as a Body, a great service, for which we thank you'. . . .

104. *From Thomas Galland*   Leeds, February 6, 1828

I just write a few lines by way of introduction to the accompanying statement [wanting]. It is from Mr. Hillaby,[1] formerly a preacher in our Connexion, but who, being suspended by a sort of minor district meeting held in Driffield in the fall of 1824, was induced to connect himself with Mark Robinson's party. The case appears to those who have looked into it to be one of peculiar hardship, on these grounds. 1st. There does not appear satisfactory proof of the charge brought against him; and the evidence in his favour seems to have been rejected on very unreasonable grounds. 2y. It sems that he was put on his trial very hastily, without having proper time allowed to prepare such materials of his defence as he could otherwise have produced. 3y. He was thrown upon the rash step he took of associating himself with Mr. Robinson's opposition by the despair into which he was thrown by a letter from Mr. Mason informing him that he must not too sanguinely expect that the Conference would hear his appeal; as such a course was perfectly optional with them. Mr. Grindrod does not consider that Mr. M. rightly expounded the law of the Connexion, and if it was an error, the consequences to poor Hillaby have been very serious. 4thly. Mr. Hillaby has that respect to the call which he believes he has received to the full work of the ministry, that he feels it upon his mind to put his affair into a train of further investigation, before he makes definitive arrangements with a view to any secular business. If on a review of the case, you think the Conference will receive an appeal and appoint a Committee, I am persuaded that he will not be dissatisfied even if the result should be against him, but will act with us as a cordial friend and if thought fit, a Local Preacher likewise. However, if you think that the Conference, even on the recommendation of the Hull District, would see no ground for exercising its powers of supervision, your expression of this opinion will determine Mr. Hillaby's course immediately, and settle with him a point of conscience. There is one feature of this case which especially interests me in this

---

[1] Samuel Hilaby, preacher, Swaffham circuit, 1822–1824.

affair; it is the history of Mrs. Hillaby. She is a young person of respectable family formerly settled at Newcastle; there she was brought under serious impressions amongst the Methodists, and, resolving to join them, was on that ground constrained to depart from her father's house. She took a very comfortable situation in a Quaker's family as governess, which she relinquished to go in the same capacity in Mr. Bradnack's family:[1] here she met with Mr. Hillaby at that time travelling in the Swaffham Circuit with Mr. B. and a connection was formed between them, having the sanction of the Missionary Committee, at whose disposal Mr. H. and his concerns were specially placed. She endured with her husband many hardships in Ireland, where he went by way of exchange for one of the Irishmen in Beverley, and since there return, their situation in that town has been far from comfortable.

Neglected by her own family in consequence of her attachment to Methodism, separated from the great body of the Methodists by her husband's connexion with Mr. R., and altogether slighted by that individual, the situation of this aimiable and accomplished young woman, is certainly such as to call forth the sympathies of a feeling heart, and I am persuaded that her character and qualifications would do credit to any of our stations, whether at home or abroad. Before ⟨their⟩ departure from Beverley I invited Mr. and Mrs. ⟨H. t⟩o tea, when the circumstances of being kindly noticed by our Preachers and friends produced an almost overpowering effect upon her spirits. I confess myself moved with the whole case; and if a conformity to the general principles of our administration will admit of it, I should feel great pleasure in her husband's resumption of his situation among us. He has verily been in one of the best of schools for learning attachment to *Wesleyan*, or, as Mr. R[obinson] invidiously but not improperly terms it, *Conference Methodism*. I will thank you to look over the case as drawn of by Mr. Hillaby, and hope you will favour me as early as possible with your opinion upon it. . . .

105. *From Donald Frazer*[2]   Durham, March 14, 1828

. . . Mr. Ward[3] some time ago resigned his office as Leader because the last Conference made the doctrine of the Sonship a test in admit-

---

[1] Isaac Bradnack (1774–1833), superintendent, Swaffham circuit, 1821–1824.
[2] Donald Frazer, preacher, Durham circuit, 1826–1828. Left the ministry to preach in Canada, 1831.
[3] John Ward, prominent Durham Methodist, solicitor, and politician. Author of a MS. tract on the Sonship of Christ. M.C.A. MSS. B. Slater to Jabez Bunting, February 6, 1828.

ting candidates into the Ministry amongst us; and lately he has left the Society, apparently with the impression that honor and wisdom went along with him, on account of a very severe satirical poem which had been written against him by an anonymous author. They tell me that previous to his marriage he had been a remarkably pious and excellent man but that he has been deteriorating ever since, and he is now one of the most imperious and impatient of contradiction of any that I know. For what reasons, I cannot tell, but he has a very strong antipathy to the Conference and to a number of our preachers. The former, in defiance of all decorum and without the smallest provocation he characterized at a Leaders' Meeting which I attended as '*intolerant* and *intolerable*', and at the latter, when opportunity occurs, he throws out his venom. But I must say no more upon a subject on which it is unpleasant, and serves no useless [useful] purpose to write.

The Leeds business has excited some bad feelings amongst us, but I hope it will soon die away. There are restless spirits in every place, which are ready to seize at every thing that presents itself to vent their spleen; but the great body of the people I believe are truly united and attached to us. There is nothing I dread more amongst us both as preachers and people than the spirit of division, if this once get in, like a flood it will bear down all before it. There can be no medium course steered by us now; either we shall be the greatest instruments God ever employed in renovating the world, or we shall fall to pieces and lose what we have gained. May God pour upon us the spirit of love and of a sound mind! God is carrying on His work in this Circuit. In one of our country places we have taken about 140 on trial, in another 30, and the spirit of prayer is pervading our Societies generally. Casson[1] is carrying all before him at Gateshead! The luminaries of New Castle are comparatively unheeded in consequence of the appearance of this extraordinary Comet! The people come in crowds from New Castle to hear him and in the country parts of the Circuit he is received as an Angel from heaven. He opened a little chapel in our Circuit, on which occasion I went to hear him. His mind is but little cultivated, and his discourses are deformed by many quaint and low expressions; but there is an affection and fervor in his manner, and a disposition to labour, I mean by attending prayer meetings to a very late hour, which are productive of very extraordinary effects. There is nothing farther in these parts that I know of deserving of notice. . . .

[1] Hodgson Casson (d. 1851, *aet.* 63), preacher, Gateshead circuit, 1827–1830. Began as a zealous field-preacher, and entered the regular ministry, 1815.

106. *To Edward [mistake for—Edmund] Grindrod* (Leeds)

Salford, May 10, 1828

... I have hastily read the proof just received; and am, generally, delighted with it.[1] It is the very thing wanted, a statement of *facts*, and will do a world of good. It must, by some means, be *freely* circulated among preachers, and all our leading friends in all the Circuits. If properly directed to individuals, and wrapped up in parcels for *each Circuit separately*, and so sent up to Mr. Mason in *very good time*, I should hope he would do you and all of us the common justice to circulate it with his June book-parcels. But lest certain preachers should refuse to deliver them, when received, under the pretence of keeping their circuits quiet, I think that the Committee of Privileges, to whom the Noncon.[2] Circular went, and a few other leading men in different Districts, should be served by post—paying the postage! I wish too that one copy at least could somehow be sent to some one preacher, who would be depended upon to make it known, in each District, before the District Meetings, which will be generally held early in the week after next. It would be well to add a P.S. referring to the District Resolutions, and those of the Trustees, etc. etc. stating that they are sold by Mr. Mason. Excuse these suggestions, and keep them to yourself, or colleagues. Now for some objections.

1. I decidedly recommend the omissi⟨on⟩ of the sentence about the Noncons. being 'generally of the very poorest'. It may ⟨be⟩ misrepresented; and all that is useful in the fact is elsewhere *implied*, especially where their average contribution is specified.

2. Too much honour is, with a kindness which I deeply feel, paid to *me*. When you refer to measures which I have certainly had a principal share in recommending or advocating, I am mentioned much *too individually*. Some clause, recognizing the equally influential and valuable services on those occasions of Brethren who have thought and acted with me, is due to truth and justice and to my own sense of obligation to my *public* friends and coadjutors. This will be *expedient*, too, as well as right. Many would not *bear* such an eulogium on *me*.

3. I think the clause about my offer of a place in the Church should be cancelled;[3] or at least made more general. The proposition made to me at Leeds I consider as *confidential* in a sense though no secresy

---

[1] *Two letters containing a plain account and explanation of various material circumstances of the late separation in the Leeds circuits* . . . (Leeds, 1828).

[2] *I.e.* the Leeds Protestant Methodists.

[3] The nature and source of the offer of Church preferment to Bunting is not known.

was formally enjoined. I much prefer its total omission, unless you see some *strong* reason for retaining it, in a more general phraseology. . . .

107. *From Edmund Grindrod*   Leeds, June 23, 1828

. . . The Leeds Non. Cons. have issued a reply to our late Circular. They call their publication *A Refutation of the false statements and gross misrepresentations of Messrs. Grindrod and Co., etc.*[1] Several of our most material facts they have not even noticed, and those with which they have attempted to grapple remain unrefuted. But their pamphlet abounds with lies and misrepresentations; and in bitterness of spirit and calumny it exceeds all its precursors. You, my dear Sir, as usual, are honoured with the largest share of the reproach of Christ. Nearly one whole page of closely printed letter press is filled with scurrilous abuse of you, such as calls forth expressions of indignation from all whom I have heard speak of it. I hope, however, that they will not succeed in inflicting that pain upon your generous heart at which they aim, and I am fully persuaded they will greatly increase the number of your friends and diminish your foes. I have no doubt the Conference will do you justice. Do not, my dear Sir, persist in objecting to take the Presidency. Your none election to that office will please none but the favourers of faction. Mr. Galland and I intend to meet you at Gomersal on the 9th ult. [proximo?] and then we can more largely converse upon these and other points. In the meantime I will embrace the first opportunity of sending by a private hand, the pamphlet. It will be of considerable advantage to us at the Conference, as it demonstrates that the party in opposition are destitute of veracity and integrity, and invincibly opposed to us and our system. . . .

108. *From Aaron Floyd*[2]   Canterbury, June 27, 1828

We held our Quarterly Meeting on the 26th, and the business of the meeting being nearly finished, one of our Stewards got up and took

---

[1] M. Johnson, W. Rinder, and J. Hodgson, *A reply to various false statements and gross misrepresentations contained in two letters lately published by the Methodist preachers in Leeds* (Leeds, 1828). Bunting figures little in the pamphlet until the last page when the whole responsibility for the Leeds case is laid upon him (p. 15): 'No authority but that which he has usurped, could have induced Conference to give permission to erect an organ against the wishes of the society, and in the very teeth of their own law.'

[2] Aaron Floyd (d. 1836, *aet.* 49), superintendent, Canterbury circuit, 1827–1828.

out of his pocket the *Imperial Magazine*,[1] and said I wish to call the attention of this meeting to the Leeds buisness for I think it is proper to notice the conduct of the Preachers towards our injured brethren. 'I believe' said he, 'it will be brought forward at many Quarterly Meetings at this time'. When he was proceeding to open the leaves to read, I told him as a Steward he could not read such an article in our Quarterly Meeting. Immediately he put it into the hands of a Local Preacher near him, one of the same spirit with himself and said, 'Hear, do you read it, for unfortunately it appears I am a Steward and cannot do it.' I then told him that I was a Methodist Preacher and as such would not preside at a meeting where such a paper was read; our buisness is to do the work of a Quarterly Meeting and not the buisness of the nonconformists at Leeds. He then told me I was just as arbitrary in my measures as you were and the brethren had been at Leeds. I told him if he did not know what was right for him to move, I knew what was for me to put to the vote at a meeting as the Superintendant. I told him if he insisted on reading it that I should conclude the meeting. My colleague thought it right that the paper should be read out of the *Imperial*. I told him if he judged it so then I would conclude the meeting and he might preside. The Steward then said that which they did would not be considered as official but a mere *Cabal* and it would not be regarded by the Conference and that they would be looked upon as the Nonconformists. And said 'When I have anything in future to bring forward here I shall write two or three days before the time to give notice of it'.

He seemed much mortified for he had got up sum kind of a protest to read after he had finished what he designed saying. But he put it into his pocket book, after he had shewn it to the other Steward and my colleague. This will convince you of the anti-Methodistical spirit which is in Kent, as well as in Leeds, and no doubt if they had power and influence [they] would be as bad. Observe we have not lost any members, nor has any thing more been spoken even. Not a word [has] been said or done than what I have here stated to you. But I do think there has been some correspondence with some Stewards and the Nonconformists. And I think as an individual the less there is said at Conference about the Leeds buisness it will be the better. I must say that considering you as a man, a Christian, and a minister

---

[1] The *Imperial Magazine*, edited by Samuel Drew, the official biographer of Thomas Coke, had long been suspect to the Buntingites because of Drew's sympathy with the theological opinions of Adam Clarke (M.C.A. MSS. James Nichols to Jabez Bunting, April 8, 1819). Apparently the *Magazine* carried the appeal of the Leeds Protestant Methodists. M.C.A. MSS. Jabez Bunting to Joshua Marsden, May 6, 1828.

of Jesus Christ, I esteem you, I admire your tallents and decision of
character, and have said that your services to the Connection could
not be estimated.

Praying that you may long live to be made a blessing to us as a
body and that the day may be far distant when the connection shall
know your worth by the want of your invaluable services. . . .
[*P.S.*]
I thought [it] my duty to make you acquainted with this. I believe
it was his intention to send a Protest to Conference.

109. *From Joseph Agar*[1]   York, July 10, 1828

It has often been on my mind to write you since the unhappy division
of our Society at Leeds, the effects of it reached our Quarter Day
last Tuesday. As bad news spreads fast and gets magnifyd I thought
you will have heard of it at Manchester.

It give me and all our principle friends much pain to have our
peaceable Quarter Day interupted by a Local Preacher, a stranger
almost in York, saying we might well be in debt as we give our
Preachers too much for servants and other things. When I wanted to
put him down he said he had as much right to speak as me and would
be heard. Then another moved a resolution against the Conference
respecting granting leave to put up a orgain in Leeds Chapel; this
was done at the conclusion of the meeting when many of the Old
Methodists was gone away. However, it was carried in favour of the
Conference. Mr. Veevers[2] was very ill used by a few, and three held
up their hands for him to leave at the year end. Mr. Crowther[3] had
some time since signifyd his intention of leaving at Conference on
account of his health and his children. The rumer is all our Preachers
is going away. I believe 3 parts of the Society very much wishes tham
all to stay. They the Preachers say they was not supported at the
Quarter Day; the truth was, we have been so happily preserved from
wrangling etc. in all our meetings, the friends did not know what to
say, or do. Leeds and too many other Societys they are too much used
to speachifying in their meetings, besides if they leave us what a

---

[1] Joseph Agar (1761–1847), Sheriff of York, 1812, a leading York Methodist
of long standing.
[2] William Vevers (d. 1850, *aet.* 58), preacher, York circuit, 1827–1829. Vevers
had contributed *Observations on the power possessed and exercised by the Wesleyan
Methodist ministers* (London, 1828) to the Leeds controversy and for the rest
of his life was much in print as a defender of the Methodist constitution and the
Protestant cause.
[3] Jonathan Crowther II (1794–1856), preacher, York circuit, 1826–1829.
Headmaster of Kingswood School, 1823–1826.

president and a rejoicing these few dissatisfied members will have in future they may fancy something against a Preacher or Preachers bring it forward at Quarter day.[1] We will set them off as we did before at the end of the first year. I believe we shall pet[i]tion for all to stay again, for we have not asked one Preacher: *should they leave us*, we shall be on the float. I know you will make no bad use of those hints. Their is one great evil in our Societys, spreading false reports. I wish some one would show the evil of it in our *Magazine*; ⟨it is⟩ mostly done for want of thought, they hear a thing ⟨said⟩ and it's repeated to other's not considering the consequences; of late I have thought the Lord has a controversy with us and permitted all this trash to be circulated round the kingdom to humble us—to induce us to pray more to the Lord to heel our backslidings and revive us again, that our wills may be lost in his will and our hearts given more to the Lord and that we may again love one another with a pure heart fervently.

I have always said what will the Methodist Body be if we loose the cementing Bond LOVE.

May the Lord bless you and direct you in your ardious situation. . . .

P.S.

. . . I call'd upon a friend day after Quarter Day. He went with me to talk to the Local Preacher and pointed out the great evil he heard us patiently, said he sees his error and from that day would try to mend. . . .

110. *From James Blackett*[2]   St. Austell, September 12, 1828

As you have been much engaged in the affairs of the Leeds business, I think it right to send you a few lines stating that the decisions of the Conference are generally highly approved in this county on that subject. I am really thankful to God that you were engaged by the Ex-President to attend the Extra-District Meeting at Leeds, and that the meeting came to the opinions and resolutions to which they did, for had the standards of Methodism been lowered at that meeting, the Conference had they been disposed, could hardly have been able with all their strength to raise it up again to its proper position. I am also thankful to the Head of the Church for the full investigation of the affair at the last Conference, and for the firm stand which was made there in properly recognizing the constitution of Methodism, I can assure you from my own personal knowledge of the opinions and

---

[1] All three of the York preachers left the circuit at the Conference of 1829.
[2] James Blackett (d. 1848), superintendent, St. Austell circuit, 1828–1830.

sentiments of nearly all the influential men in this District (I know not an exception) that the Conference has risen higher in their esteem and a tone is given to Methodism far superior to what it had,[1] and also those who were inclined to call irregular meetings, either through ignorance of our economy, or out of opposition to our rules, are put upon their gaurd, and not only so, but such persons will be watched and gaurded against by the most judicious of our people. We have general peace and unity in this part of the Kingdom. Praise the Lord for it! We have nothing to fear but to go . . . on in the name of the Lord, attending to all our economy, temporately, judiciously, and firmly, and the God of peace and love will be with us. I should not have troubled you with any observations from myself, had it not been that I thought it would give you pleasure to know that we are all in peace, and looking up in expectation of a greater outpouring of the Holy Spirit of God. As to the seceding party at Leeds, they will not do any good to themselves nor to the cause of God. *Their opposition originates in settled contempt of good methodistic order* and it is supported by a continued unwillingness of controul. Not one person can continue a member [in] the Methodist Society without being under controul, and very properly so, or how could we have any system, or order? But those people think every person and thing in Methodism must bend to them and their schemes; yet they themselves are determined they will not be under any controul, but will walk after their own plans. But what is likely to be the result of all this? Confusion and every evil work. What has been the case before with persons who have seceded from Methodism? Have not many fallen and become a prey to infidelity? See the results of the Kilhamitish division, of Thorsby's division[2] etc. etc. How many souls 'walked no more with Jesus' in consequence of them? Shall we not (notwithstanding the oppositions of those who oppose themselves) lift up our hands and voices to save such strangely infatuated individuals, even striving to pluck them from the fire? But are we to

[1] Cornish Methodism had expanded so rapidly in the previous decade that it bore less resemblance to the official administrative model than that of any other part of the country. Despite the opinion here expressed it not only continued for many years in its irregular ways, but suffered a serious secession in 1835.

[2] Alexander Kilham was expelled by Conference in 1796, and his Methodist New Connexion was founded in 1797. Francis Thoresby, preacher in the Leeds circuit, 1794–1795, and an active promoter of the administration of the sacraments in Methodism, was 'suspended by the District Meeting for his indecent behaviour to sundry girls, chiefly servants' (M.C.A. Tyerman MSS, i, fo. 140). In 1796 it was reported that Thoresby was very popular, and that Benson's opposition to administering the sacrament was enabling him to get a chapel built. M.C.A. Tyerman MSS, iii, fos. 273, 278, 279.

risk the cause of God and give up any of the vital principles of Methodism to save such persons? NO, VERILY, for that would be to sacrifice our trust in a twofold sence, first to betray that cause committed to us by the Head of the Church and secondly to sacrifice those people we design to save. Methodism must be preserved *inviolate*, and people should be taught to study it as connected with the revealed will of God. It is in my opinion the nearest in doctrine and discipline to the Primitive Church of any other system; but those persons at Leeds would introduce the greatest disorder in our Body. They would set the feet against the head, and the hands against the eyes. I know you have been assailed, and you may be again by those people, and also it is possible your feelings may be harrowed up by some of our brethren making injudicious remarks, and it is possible for *you even* to tire in keeping your head up in the torrent of abuse, which you have had, or may have to stem, therefore, I have thought I would venture to show my opinion on this subject for your encouragement, 'least you grow weary and faint in your mind'. Go on, my dear Sir, and take courage, the Lord is with you, and with his cause. I now fear I have not sufficiently kept in view the high office you sustain, but have written to you with too great familiarity; but if I have offended in this respect, I have so good an opinion of your urbanity, that I hope you will pardon me. I can only say it is the regard I have for you and Methodism, which has induced me to address you for the first time to encourage you in your great work and in the *support of Wesleyan Methodism*. . . .
P.S.

I think this Circuit will now be capable of being well worked by three preachers. The division of Truro and Redruth Circuit[1] I think will answer well, and they will be a great blessing to Cornwall, for when large masses of people are together they are difficult to manage. Last year I had in the Redruth Circuit, 4 travelling preachers, 30 Local Preachers, about 4000 children in the Sunday Schools, 400 teachers, 22 chapels, about 3000 members of Society, and 10,000 hearers on a Sabbath. These are too much for one person to manage well. . . .

111. *From William Henshaw*   Sheffield, September 15, 1828

As the Lord has placed you at the head of our Connexion I think it right to acquaint you with whatever occurs of importance in that

---

[1] Truro had been divided from the Redruth circuit in 1799; in 1828 the St. Agnes and Gwennap Circuits were carved from Truro, and the Camborne circuit from Redruth.

part of the Body over which I am more especially placed. Brother Hanwell[1] rode over from Barn[s]ley in great alarm with tidings of a rent about to be made in his own Circuit. Two Agents had come from Leeds to stir up the people to revolt. The Theatre had been hired to preach in, and he expected about 20 out of 28 Local Preachers would leave him, and 400 of the people. And there was to be a great Meeting that evening. I advised him to return, and persuade two or three tried men to go amongst them, as David sent Hushai to defeat the counsel of Ahithophel; and inform me of the result. I enclose you his letter, which will give you to see that although great mischief is doing, yet the breach is not so alarming as was apprehended. Brother Banwell[2] is prudent, active, and affectionate, and will prevent all the evil that can be prevented.

We are yet very quiet in Sheffield. The people who signed the Memorial to Conference,[3] are much dissatisfied with the reply. Mr. Sigston has also been over to feel the pulse of some of the leading men, and to learn what they think of the Resolutions of Conference. I understand nothing will be attempted before the Quarter Day, but that if I determinately keep out the business from the Quarterly Meeting *that* will be a signal for revolt. All my Brethren think, and several of the leading friends here concur with them that it will be better to allow of a free conversation, and to hear all that the dissatisfied party have to say, and fearlessly and good temperedly to meet their objections. I do not anticipate a division amongst us, I fancy the people have more sense. And yet it is marvellous how some good men delight in exciting commotions, and making mischief in the Churches, and do it so piously. If anything important occur I will write you. . . .

[*Enclosed*:]—*John Hanwell to William Henshaw*, September 10, 1828. I sit down with the intention of giving you an outline of what has been going on among us here since I had the pleasure of an interview with you.

Agreeably to your advice I rode home with all prudent expedition and prevailed upon Mr. Cocker to attend the Non-Cons. meeting. He made the attempt and was refused admission. I understand from 60 to 70 persons were present among whom were eight or ten Local Preachers or Leaders who after hear[ing] various addresses consented to have their names put down so being willing to join the new community. On my return home I learned that on Tuesday evening in last week Mr. Methley and two others, all of them very warm men in this division, had called a meeting of the Society in *Burton*, a

[1] John Hanwell (d. 1854), superintendent, Barnsley circuit, 1827–1829.
[2] Error for Hanwell.   [3] *Cf*. nos. 98, 114.

village two miles from Barnsley, and where Mr. Methley resides, had harangued them in their own way and closed with saying, 'Now all of you who are resolved to sink or swim with us let us have your names': all present excepting one pious young woman and two old women, of whom it is said they were so ignorant that they could not make them understand what they meant, complied; in number not fewer than fifty. On Thursday I wrote a note to Mr. William Smith of Cudworth, who is one of the Burton Leaders, requesting him to meet me at Burton at two o'clock, and we spent four hours and a half in visiting the persons who had left us at their own houses. They assigned reasons for so doing of the weakest and in some instances of the most foolish kind. I preached there in the evening and gave tickets to as many as would receive them and eight persons did so. I informed them that Brother Smith would meet his class as usual. In the forenoon of this day Mr. Methley sent in his resignation. He was steward of Burton Society. I called at his house and as he was from home requested he would give me an early call. He did so on Friday forenoon and we conversed for two hours. As might be expected we differed at all points, for he's a thorough Non. Con., but we kept temper though both sides spoke very freely. This evening, Friday, my Colleague went to preach and give tickets at a monthly place called Carlton where [we] had eight or ten members. But the Leader, an old man aged 82, who had been in Society more than 50 years, informed him that they had made up their minds to receive no more tickets. Mr. Lomas[1] reasoned with him, but in vain, and the old gentleman said in future they should receive the Non. Con. preachers; the preaching was in the old man's house. I can easily account for this act as one of the hottest in opposition, *viz.* the man who preached at Leeds in the Radical Chapel, lives at Carlton and has considerable influence.

In existing circumstances I judged it proper to convene as many of the Local Preachers, Stewards, Leaders, etc. as could be got together for the purpose of rectif⟨y⟩ing mistakes, exhorting to peace, etc., etc. and we me⟨t⟩ for this purpose on Saturday night. Many of the disaffected were present and I took take [care] that our staunch friends should not be absent who in the meeting expressed their firm attachment to Methodism, and their reasons for that attachment. The unprejudiced were much satisfied, and those of an opposite mind received information on points unknown to them before. This meeting I am persuaded will have its use.

Two of the Non. Con. preachers preached in Barnsley on Sunday, and took up two hours in a public assembly on Monday night in

[1] John A. Lomas, preacher, Barnsley circuit, 1827–1829.

stating their objections against Methodism and its preachers. At the close of the public meeting [they] requested all those Local Preachers and Leaders who intended to unite with them to stay. How many did so I have not heard. Hearing there was to be the meeting I have just mentioned I judged it prudent to pay another visit to those Preachers and Leaders who were disaffected. I did so on Monday forenoon, and entreated them to take time, not to pledge themselves to anything that night. Some of them were much affected with what I said. I prayed with most of them. How they acted I have not yet learned. I was inclined to take this step out of love to them, and that I may have the satisfaction to reflect that I have done everything in my power to save them. Six of the Local Preachers have resigned, two of them were Leaders, and two class Leaders. More I suppose will do so. Still the majority of both Leaders and Local Preachers stand firm. and I hope the division will be neither so serious nor extensive as I at first apprehended. Pray for us and be free to suggest any advice you deem necessary. . . .

P.S. My aim is to act with *mildness, firmness* and *prudence*. If they will leave, I let it be their own act. . . .

112. *From R. Wood*[1]   York, September 23, 1828

. . . Through mercy, we have peace and a prospect of its continuance, in this city and circuit. The Leeds Noncons. or 'Wesleyan Protestant Methodists' have visited Harrogate; and two Leaders and one Local Preacher, *at least*, are expected to join them. These Brother Harrison[2] states he shall 'take no pains to keep; they are *unworthy men*'—but he is doing the best to preserve the simple-hearted from being led astray. I do not hear that they are likely to gain a footing in any other Circuit in this District. May the Lord keep his vineyard night and day! . . .

113. *From John Mason*   London, October 1, 1828

Your sermon on Justification[3] has long been out of print and is very frequently asked for. I wish you would print a new edition of it without delay, or if you choose I will print it for you and the Book Room and you divide the profit; perhaps the latter will be the better plan and if you consent I will put 1500 to press forthwith. I

---

[1] Robert Wood (*c.* 1788–1851), superintendent, York circuit, 1827–1829.

[2] William Harrison, senr., superintendent, Knaresborough circuit, 1828–1829.

[3] Bunting's most famous sermon, *Justification by faith. A sermon preached in Albion Street Chapel at Leeds* (Leeds, 1813). *Cf.* nos. 124, 144 *infra.*

N

have intended writing to you some time, for we are not doing right to let that sermon remain out of print and I hope you will not object to one or other of my proposals.

The disturbers of the peace in the South[1] made a resolute attempt at the Quarterly Meeting to cause a division, but happily they could not succeed. The preachers allowed every man to have his say (and they did not curtail their speeches) after which McNicoll[2] replied in a very powerful, eloquent, and constitutional speech which must have told upon some of them very sensibly, after which Dixon took up the business in a way that did credit to his judgment and piety and he brought many of them to tears after which they prayed and retired and a long list of Resolutions which were to have been proposed found refuge in the pocket of one of the authors and framers.

Mr. Eckett[3] brought forward the business at Queen Street Quarterly Meeting, where Mr. Reece[4] allowed him to go on as long as he thought fit and then laid his hand upon it and that also died away, and now I hope we shall have peace and prosperity. They are much pleased with their appointment in the South. . . .

114. *From William Henshaw*   Sheffield [postmarked October 8, 1828]

Resolutions prepared for the Sheffield Quarterly ⟨Meeting⟩
I beg leave to move:
That from events which have recently transpired, and their momentous bearing on the whole Connexion, this Meeting deeply deplores the existing necessity of distinctly adverting to the same. Previous to the Meeting of Conference, many of us were under the influence of an expectation that measures would be adopted by that Assembly, which in their operations and tendency, would counteract the painful effects produced by the exercise of an authority, altogether at varience with existing law, and also entirely destructive and subversive of the great principles forming the Constitution of Wesleyan Methodism. But in the hope thus entertained we have been grievously disap-

---

[1] London (Southwark) circuit. *Cf.* nos. 98, 99, 140–143.

[2] David McNicoll, assistant London (Southwark) circuit, 1828–1829.

[3] Robert Eckett (*cf.* n. 1, p. 167 *supra*) had already published *A letter to the Rev. John Gaulter on the late occurrences at Leeds* (London, 1828), and took advantage of ruffled feelings in the London North circuit, where conference had appointed preachers rejected by the trustees in 1827, and where it had been impossible to replace circuit stewards who had resigned in March 1828; James Leach, *Wesleyan Methodism* (London, 1828).

[4] Richard Reece, superintendent, London (Great Queen Street) circuit, 1827–1830.

pointed, and instead of the adoption of plans founded in justice and equity, the illegal acts of the then executive authorities have received the highest sanction of Conference, and the individuals immediately concerned in those acts of aggression, have obtained the unbounded approbation, and unqualified thanks of that Body.

That this Meeting has viewed with feelings of utter astonishment, and decided disapprobation, the conduct of the preachers towards our worthy Brethren at Leeds, who by their opposition to the arbitrary and unwarranted assumption of power by the Preachers, and in defence of the just rights and privileges of the people, have incurred the resentment of the Conference, and thereby subjected themselves to the 'thunder-bolts of ecclesiastical censure' which have been so unjustly hurled against them.

We complain specifically, 1st. That the Law of 1820 was violated by the Conference of 1827 ⟨hav⟩ing granted leave for the erection of an organ, not only without the sanction of, but in opposition to, the decisions of the regular District Meeting, and also in direct opposition to the known and declared will and wish of the majorities of the Leaders' and Quarterly Meetings.

2nd. That the Special District Meeting, convened at Leeds was altogether unconstitutional and illegal, inasmuch as several individuals, and those of the greatest influence and known to be decidedly in favour of the obnoxious measure, were called in, who had no right whatever to be present.[1]

3rd. That the proceedings of the said meeting were equally unwarrantable, cruel, and unjust, especially in that of the proposing of *Tests* as ordeal,[2] till then unheard of in Methodism, and the consequent unjust expulsion of official members from our Body.

4th. That the late decision of Conference, in sanctioning, and thereby adopting the proceedings of the Preachers in the Leeds Circuits, and of the Special District Meeting, is a most wanton and outrageous violation of the solemn compact made with the people in 1797, and will, if suffered to pass into law, deprive the members of Society of their rights, as Englishmen, as Methodists, and as Christians.— This Meeting therefore hereby enters its most solemn protest against the whole of these unrighteous, and unhallowed proceedings.

5th. That this Meeting expresses its warmest approbation of the conduct of the few amongst the Preachers in Conference, who so nobly stood forward in the defence and support of the just rights

---

[1] Especially Jabez Bunting (summoned as President's special adviser) who had moved Conference to over-rule the District Meeting and grant the application for the organ.

[2] See no. 93 *supra*.

and privileges of the people, and to them we most cordially present our sincere and unfeigned thanks.

From William Henshaw

I think it right, as a gracious Providence ⟨has⟩ placed you at the head of our Connexion, to acquaint you with every important occurrence connected with the Sheffield Circuit. On my return from the Conference I found a spirit of general dissatisfaction and even rebellion had spread itself through every part of the Circuit. The Resolutions contained in the [Conference] Minutes were reprobated, the Annual Address was scouted, threatenings were held out, and a correspondence kept up with the Leeds and Barnsley Non. Cons.— and it was said the Music Hall was to be the place of general meeting, taken at a considerable expence. The Trustees were our pillars of support. The approach of the Quarterly Meeting was dreaded by our friends, and prayer was made. The day arrived and we met the Local Preachers from 9 to one o'clock, about 60 of them. We got through the business well. Read a letter in the *Leeds Mercury*, purporting to be written by a Sheffi⟨eld⟩ Local Preacher, and said the man who had written that le⟨tter⟩ could not be continued on the plan. Many who were most ⟨sus⟩pected disow⟨ned⟩ it, and no one had courage to adopt it—after dinner, and the regular business transacted, the battle begun. ⟨I⟩ had previously agreed with the Preachers to allow every ma⟨n⟩ the full use of his tongue, and begged them to prepare for war, and to combat with our opponents every inch of ground. The obnoxious Resolutions, which I send you the original copy of on the other side of this sheet, were read, and hotly supported by eight-tenths of the people, and the memorial to the Conference, and the letter from the Conference in answer to the memorial were read also. To put those Resolutions from the Chair, on the certainty of their passing by a vast majority, you will see were impossible. We disputed until after midnight and then appointed a Committee to draw up other Resolutions, and adjourned the Meeting until seven o'clock on the Friday following. Much good was done at the first meeting, and more at the committee meeting, which ended with good Brotherly feeling, there being an equal number of leading men chosen from both parties. Friday evening meeting was crowded. People came from all parts of the Circuit. Two strings of Resolutions were read and argued upon, both of them much more moderate than the one adjoined. After some time Mr. Bronson, an Attorney, and Circuit Steward, produced an address which he had shown to no one, embodying the Resolutions in respectful terms, which I *could* put without affecting my conscience, and ending with a *petition* to

Conference, that the Leaders Meeting might hav⟨e a⟩ veto in respect to Organs, *as* of the Lord's Supper. The other Resolutions were withd⟨rawn⟩ and this address unanimously adopted. Then there followed such an ⟨affecting⟩ scene as I never before witnessed. As if the Lord had descended visibly in the mi⟨dst⟩. Floods of tears from most eyes, sobs, praises, singing, 'Praise God', Halle⟨lujah⟩, confessions of sin, mighty prayers, loud shouts, hearty shaking of h⟨ands just like?⟩ a Band Meeting!! A vote of thanks proposed to the Chairman for his pati⟨ent conduct th⟩ro' the whole of that painful business. The next day friends con⟨gratula⟩ting each other, and telling from house to house, how great things ⟨God⟩ had done for them. All is now perfect amity and likely to ⟨remain so⟩. The Leeds Radicals fully reckoned on powerful support from Sheffield, and there never was a more complete change effected by God's grace on the furious passions of men. It will much paralyze the efforts of all the radical parties around us. I received great assistance in this struggle from the talents and address of Brother Cubitt and Calder, and Alder and Mr. Longden, and even Brother Bridgman behaved better than you would have supposed his principles would have allowed him to do. Good men here deeply interested for the welfare of Zion feel a gratitude to God, like one who has most providentially escaped from the edge of a precipice over which he was in imminent danger of falling. An eminent outpouring of the Holy Spirit for which we are praying, would now be a very glorious thing for the Sheffield Circuit. . . .

P.S.

It had been anticipated that I should not allow of any discussion in the Quarterly Meeting on the Resolutions of Conference, and which non-allowance was to have been the signal for separation— yet there was a general dread on men's minds as to the consequences of separation, which may in some measure account for the extraordinary feeling produced by an amicable adjustment of differences. . . .

115. *From R. Wood*   York, October 11, 1828

. . . When I last wrote, I had heard that some of our Leaders, etc., who professed themselves dissatisfied with the decisions of Conference on the Leeds question, were thinking of withdrawing from us—and that there was reason to fear a serious rent would follow. What to do to prevent this, I scarcely knew. At first, I proposed a friendly interview with the dissatisfied—but soon found that would not be an effectual remedy, as several were ashamed to own their disaffection; and would not, in compliance with such an invitation, come to have such explanations given as might remove it. Some of them wished to introduce the business into the York Leaders' Meeting—but this I resolutely refused to allow. Under the exigencies of the case, my colleagues, Brother Joseph Agar, and myself, risked a somewhat hazardous experiment. We invited all our official men, Trustees, Stewards, Leaders, and Local Preachers, to meet us—that we might, in a *free* and *friendly* conversation, talk over the grounds of their complaints. This, they gladly accepted—and we met them on Thursday evening last at seven o'clock—and continued with them three hours and a half. The result, as far as I could gather it from their expressions and apparent feelings (for we allowed no moving, seconding, or voting), was, that they were *generally, satisfied.* There was, indeed, only one point on which a few held fast their discontent to the last—*viz.* that some expression of disapprobation of Brother I. Keeling's first pamphlet,[1] and of what they thought its unconciliating and unchristian spirit, had not been made by Conference. The meeting, I believe, has done much good. The gathering storm seems to have been driven back. And I have now no fear of losing a single Leader, Steward, or Local Preacher—or half-a-dozen members, on this account. My mind is lightened of a heavy load—and I now rejoice. But, with the experience I have had of the combustible nature of the members of the York Society, I rejoice 'with trembling'. . . .

116. *To Joseph Entwisle* (Bristol)   Salford, October 24, 1828

[The Exeter trustees should apply for a grant from the Chapel Fund] . . . We saw so much at the last Chapel Fund Committee of the shameless selfishness of some lay-members of that committee, that one hardly dares count with certainty upon the decisions of a body so composed. But London is the only place where we have witnessed such a want of disinterestedness and I think our Sheffield friends, though a little tainted with the London Radicalism, are likely to send to that Committee in 1829 men more generally accessible to reason; so that I hope there is no great doubt of our success. At all events, I, for one, if spared to that period, shall feel it a duty to you, and to Exeter, to give your plan all the support in my power. Mr. Marsden, to whom I have shewn your last letter is quite of our mind. . . .

All here is perfect peace; and w⟨e are⟩ blessed with some prosperity. *Our* Societies at Leeds are doing well, both temporally and

[1] I. Keeling, *A letter to the editors of the Leeds Mercury on the present unhappy dissensions of the Methodists in Leeds* (Leeds, 1827).

spiritually. The disturbances at Sheffield are *for the present* over, and they are hoping for a revival of religion which will prevent the revival of faction. The separation at Barnsley is not so formidable as was at first reported. The Southwark Protest is, I should think, *too bad*, and too plainly rebellious against the first principles of Methodist union and government, to do any very extensive injury. But the *spirit* of the thing is horrible, and shews a cool, and deliberate malignity towards the Conference. We should be much better without the *ring-leaders* in that schism, than with them. The more I see and hear and think and pray, the more decided I am against *increasing* the power or multiplying the *administrative* functions, of Leaders' Meetings. A government carried on by endless debates and majorities would ruin the real work of God among us. . . .

117. From Joseph Entwisle

N. pl. or d. [*Postmarked*: Bristol, November 8, 1828]
. . . I am surprised at what has been done in Southwark! A number of copies have been sent to our friends here. Some have returned them. *None* that I know of approve of the Circular—or its design. Surely many of those persons whose names appear to the '*Resolution.*' must *have been drawn* to sign, and will regret that they have done so.
We enjoy perfect peace here. . . . We have three of the largest congregations in the City: largest by far, and the 4th, Portland, is good. . . .

118. From Isaac Turton Leeds, December 7, 1828

. . . You would probably hear while in Leeds that there is likely to be a general remove of 5 out of 7 preachers. I have intended it all along, as my place has not been the most comfortable because of several who have remained among us, who have held up the hands of those who have left us. My fear is that they will try to influence our successors to the injure of the cause for which we have suffered. I trust however that Conference will do its very best as to an appointment for Leeds.
We have just lost one of our Leaders by death, whose class has been disaffected, and now I find they talk of their right to choose their own Leader. We shall probably lose one half. Such is the doctrine on church government they have imbibed, which would soon fill our Leaders' Meetings with men the very opposite to what they ought to be. But I trust the Lord will interpose to save our Connexion from such ⟨doct⟩rines, and the men who hold and defuse them. . . .

119. *From Isaac Turton*   Leeds, December 22, 1828

... There are very few pleasing inducements to the Brethren to come to Leeds, even on the *brightest side* of our *affairs*. I sincerely wish that the view you gave the Conference on [the] whole Leeds affair from the beginning to end, could be given in print for the illumination both of preachers and people. I think it would do immense good to our connexion at this time. And yet, *in this matter*, I have seen *so much* the *balefull influence* of *prejudice*, I have scarcely *any confidence* in the *clearest* statements, or most *forceable* reasonings. I sometimes have very gloomy ideas concerning the *future peace* and *prosperity* of our great body. However, the Lord loves it infinitely better than we do; and knows best *when* and *how* to rescue it out of the hands of men whose proceedings tend to its ruin. *May He graciously interpose* at this *eventfull crisis*. I shall not live to witness the events of many more years. But I hope and pray that *you* and *others* I could name, may be spared for many years as the *guides and guardians under God* of the Methodist Connexion. ...

120. *From Joseph Sutcliffe*[1]   Bath, December 26, 1828

... I named in the Stationing Committee as also in Conference, that it would not do to let our Yearly Collection remain stationary while our wants swell and increase. You verbally recommended to the Conference. But I would suggest, that a circular should go with the February books to every preacher, pressing, that in no Circuit the Yearly Collection should be less than *eightpence* per member. The Bath District averages but 6d. though Bath reached 8d. so that in some places it did not exceed 4d. I am sure the brethren can make it sixpence in the poorest circuits. Many Circuits are now suffering for want of an additional preacher, and Ranters occupy the neglected ground, and want of money seems the sole cause. The circuits that give pledges should be forced to keep their pledge, at least with a £24—in the worst cases for the first year.

I hope, ere I die, to see the embryo of a Methodist Colledge. All our people in trade now give a boarding school education to their children and an unlettered pastor with a provincial dialect sounds but ungracious on their ear. The evangelical clergy, the polish and good learning of many dissenters, place Methodism in a contest very different from former years. What should we do against these opponents if Lord S[idmou]th should once stop the itinerant plan,[2] a

---

[1] Joseph Sutcliffe, superintendent, Bath circuit, 1827–1829.

[2] In 1811 Lord Sidmouth had unsuccessfully moved a bill in the House of Lords to restrict itinerant preaching, urging that many itinerants were too unlettered to perform ministerial functions.

scheme that would rejoice the dissenters? The Methodists could in one year give a present of ten thousand books, besides a cabinet of natural history. Such a seminary out of weakness would wax strong. As to the local agitations of the connection, if managed with prudence, they will all die away. It is radicals among the Local Preachers who may give the greatest trouble. Any quarterly meetings who may contend for their charter; it is, in fact what all corporate bodies will do; and all will end in peace unless fresh feuds should be excited. I believe all is peace in the West of England. But certainly some preachers do not look at consequences. Mr. At[mor]e[1] (now in heaven) did not act prudently in Southwark when he placed Leach over such men as Shepherd, Knight, Higgs, etc. He had paid about 1/– or perhaps but 6d. in the pound just before at St. George's in the east. The Knights have been with us for eighty years in various branch[es] of their family and have many estates in Yorkshire, under the name of Laverick, Dealtry, etc. Their cousin at Clapham rises high in the church.[2] In Bristol, 2 were put into office by H.M.[3] without speaking to his colleagues, and John Ball and John Irving driven from the Leaders' meeting! Men have feelings, . . .

121. From William Constable[4]   Lane End, December 30, 1828

Will you pardon my intrusion in laying before you the following case and asking counsel at your hands upon a subject which is of some importance to myself as an individual, and to the public interest with which I stand connected.

Many years ago the Superintendant of this circuit used to form his Sunday Plan *in* the quarterly meeting of the Local Preachers under their immediate co-operation, and subject to their control. But as this practice was considered too great an infringement upon the time and business of that meeting it was proposed that the Superintendant

---

[1] Charles Atmore (d. 1826, *aet.* 66), preacher, London (Great Queen Street) circuit (from which the Southwark circuit was formed in 1822), 1821–1823. President 1811.

[2] William Dealtry (1775–1847), Professor of Mathematics, East India College, Haileybury, 1805–1813. Rector of Clapham, 1813–1843. Chancellor of diocese of Winchester, 1830–1845. Correspondent and friend of Thomas Allan, the Methodist connexional solicitor.

[3] Henry Moore, superintendent, Bristol circuit, 1820–1823, while Sutcliffe was preacher.

[4] William Constable (d. 1845), superintendent, Lane End (or Longton) circuit, 1828–1829. For a brief autobiography see M.C.A. MSS. W. Constable to Jabez Bunting, June 13, 1844.

bring 'an outline of the plan' and read distinctly every mans appointment when the meeting should make any alteration that was deemed requisite. From that time, up to last June, the circuit plan has been regularly presented to, and read in the quarterly meeting of the Local preachers, subject to their revision.

In the Quarterly Meeting held last September the first after my coming upon the circuit, the plan was called for according to the long established custom. I stated that as the present plan had 7 weeks to run, I had not yet formed a new one. I stated also that the act of presenting a plan to the Quarterly Meeting for inspection and revision was a practice I had never witnessed during the 20 years of my itinerancy; they therefore found in my 'ignorance of their customs' an apology for no plan being forthcoming at *that* meeting but hoped I should be fully prepared in this particular by the Christmas Quarterday.

Now Sir, the minute (Vol. 3, page 223) which directs that every Superintendant shall take care that the plans for the Local and Travelling Preachers be made by himself or his colleagues, I do consider as standing directly opposed to the above practice, and therefore at the Christmas Quarterly Meeting held yesterday I endeavored again to evade the subject—and stated that I would take instruction, either then or privately from every preacher in the circuit as to his appointments—that no man should be planned against his will—and that I would spare no pains in meeting every man's wishes during my stay among them, which certainly would not extend beyond the next Conference. Aiming at and laboring to exercise the meekness of wisdom, peace and good temper were supported through the meeting, with a determination however on the part of the Local Preachers, amounting to 28 in number, to adopt those measures that will bring the manuscript plan under their correction, as they will 'never consent to work a plan they have not had a hand in forming'. Should the plan still be witheld, I foresee a gathering storm. Will you therefore oblige me, my dear Sir, with your opinion on the subject? Will the minutes of Conference and the usages of the Body justify my treading in the steps of my predecessors? Or am I right in the view I take of the business, *viz.* that every Preacher may state his wishes to the Superintendant and those wishes as far as possible be met, but that no one but a travelling Preacher has to do with the plan itself? . . .

122. *From John Shipman*[1]   Lynn, January 3, 1829

[*Assistance from the list of reserve is urgently needed in the Walsingham circuit owing to the illness of the preachers*]

P.S

Please excuse me for troubling you with a question on a point of discipline. Is it customary to propose the question of competant ability in reference to accredited Local Preachers? and can a charge of want of preaching abilities be preferred against any one whose talents, etc., are equal to what they were, when he was first admitted? I can easily conceive of a case of this kind, of a man having suffered loss in his soul and with it his talents of usefulness to the Church, and of the propriety of bringing forward a charge grounded on this principle, but I should suppose that he must have previous notice of such a charge: irrespective however of this charge I can hardly bring my mind to perceive the propriety of the question. As the subject has been aggitated among us in a way I thought calculated to disturb the peace of the Society, provided I had yielded to the suggestion, I thought you would favour me with your opinion upon it.

I am sorry to say that disaffected persons in other places by letters, etc., are attempting to disturb our quiet in reference to matters connected with the Leeds question. At our last Quarterly Meeting a powerful attempt was made to introduce the subject but after making the best stand we could against it we succeeded in keeping it out of the Meeting, and we had one of the happiest meetings I have witnessed since I came to the circuit. . . .

123. *To John Shipman* (King's Lynn)   Salford, January 9, 1829

[*Is sending Edward Nye to Walsingham*]

. . . I believe it is our universal custom to propose the question of *competent ability*, concerning every brother on the Plan, at every Quarterly Meeting of the Local Preachers; and that a charge may be brought on that ground at any time. This is the case as to Travelling Preachers and why not as to Local Preachers also? Of course, previous *notice* of any such *charge* should be given, as in all other cases; and everything litigious or captious or personally offensive should be discountenanced. But the usage, rightly administered, is of great importance, and should on no account be abandoned.

I am glad you kept the radical resolutions etc. out of your meeting.

[1] John Shipman (1788–1853), superintendent, Lynn circuit, 1827–1829. Served 11 years in West Indies.

Mr. Watson's very able pamphlet on that subject,[1] in answer to the Southwark resolutions, will do us much service, in the maintenance of sound methodistical principles against the innovations of independency. . . .

124. *From John Mason*   London, January 8, 1829

I should not have troubled you with another letter so soon only I have a request to make which is that you will allow me to reprint your sermon on Justification. You really are not doing the thing that is right in allowing that sermon to remain out of print. . . . [London Southwark] Circuit is in a sad state of Rebellion. They had quite a cabal at their Quarterly Meeting and brought forward another resolution of the old cast which Mr. Treffry[2] refused to have submitted to the meeting until he had seen it and when it was shewn him, he refused to allow it to be proposed. This was of course a very galling measure and they rebelled most resolutely, but he was firm and they gave way. . . .

125. *From William Henshaw*   Sheffield, January 19, 1829

. . . I sent you by Mr. Harris, a copy of the intended Sheffield Address to the next Conference, which I hope you received. It is respectfully worded, and free from bitterness, but whether the prayer of it can be granted I know not. Something to conciliate I think will be requisite. Our Radicals are exceedingly active. Local Preachers and Leaders have gone about to obtain guinea subscriptions in support of that lying pestiferous publication, *The Wesleyan Protestant Methodist Magazine*, 70 copies of which have been already sold in this town. I have felt it my duty to caution our people from the pulpit against this work, and to recommend as a good antidote Mr. Watson's *Affectionate Address, etc.*, of which able address I have sold about 70 Copies. How vainly does this magazine boast of numbers having fallen off from us to them in Barnsley, Preston, York and Newark. At this latter place it turns out to be a division of the Ranters fr⟨om⟩ their Mother Church, who have invited the Non. Con.

---

[1] Richard Watson, *An affectionate address to those trustees, stewards, local preachers and leaders of the London (South) Circuit, whose names are affixed to certain resolutions* (London, 1829). Of this pamphlet Henry Moore remarked, 'Mr. Watson has made one grand mistake. He has taken it for granted that men may be guided by *argument*'. M.C.A. MSS. R. Wood to Jabez Bunting, April 23, 1829.

[2] Richard Treffry, senr., superintendent, London (Southwark) circuit, 1827–1829.

Preachers; and not one Methodist has j⟨oined⟩ them; yet any human being who read the accou⟨nt⟩ in connexion with the former, would suppose it was a division from our Society who had invited them. Oh if they could have got a thousand members from Sheffield to have united with them, they would have triumphed, as when men divide the spoil. And this was confidently anticipated by many. If a few of the leading Radicals were to leave us, it would prove a blessing to this Circuit. But the great body of our people here have no disposition to leave us. . . .

126. *From John Scott*[1]   Liverpool, January 23, 1829

I saw Mr. Newton the Monday morning after our Quarter Day, and he engaged to inform you of the result of that Meeting, otherwise I would have written you word as I had promised. You have felt, I doubt not, a desire to know what we have been doing since. I have delayed a few days to write, that I might the better inform you of the effect of our meeting.

Ever since I saw you in Manchester, our malcontents have been most industrious in circulating the Southwark Address and Protest, and in calling upon the official men afterwards, to learn the effect and to deepen it if favourable to their wishes, and sometime ago I learned that they ensured a majority on their side. I found that almost all who had read the pamphlets were puzzled, and some were quite set wrong; this brought me to regard it as my duty to try to set right the honest part. I did not receive their 'resolutions' until about three days before the meeting, when I found them seven in number (a perfect number!) and all supporting or hanging upon the third, which was as follows:

'That a fundamental and universally understood part of Methodism is that the local government of every circuit is vested in the Leaders, Local Preachers, and Quarterly Meetings with the Superintendant at their head; and that such regularly constituted authorities are amply sufficient for all purposes connected with the just and lawful government of the lay officers and members of Society, and regards the interference of any other power as not only highly improper, but *absolutely illegal*, and calculated to produce the most extensive mischief to the Connexion.'

You will perceive that the rogues go farther than their Southwark leaders and make out Methodism in the circuits *to be* a parish vestry government—this the Southwarkers only *want to make it*. I allowed

---

[1] John Scott (1792–1868), superintendent, Liverpool North circuit, 1827–1830. President 1843, 1852. Principal of Normal Institution, Westminster, 1851–1867.

them to introduce their resolutions at the Meeting, and I then told them that I considered them altogether foreign to the proper business of a Quarterly Meeting, which is to 'inquire into the temporal and spiritual state of each society' in the circuit. The minute of '96, expressing a desire on the part of the Conference to receive information, etc., from Leaders' and Quarterly Meetings etc., and the passage in the Ex-President's[1] speech at Leeds on the subject, were quoted against me. I argued that the terms of the minute were *'information'*, *'intelligence* on whatever concerns ourselves or our people', and could not be fairly construed to mean more than 1.A representation to Conference of any maladministration of Methodism *in their own circuit*, or, 2. A representation to the Conference of the injurious effect upon the work of God, *also in their own circuit*, of some principle or rule of the system, though the system had not been improperly administered, that certainly the Conference did not intend to render Leaders and Quarterly Meetings debating societies, nor seek *opinion* on matters of law and general government, for then there could be no end of debate in our meetings, nor of interuption to the necessary business of Conference by the replies which could be required. Was I right in this construction? Does this restrict the freedom of our people too much? Jacob Stanley,[2] in a letter lately, says, 'Our people have a right to discuss the *acts* of Conference, and no place so fit as a Quarterly Meeting.' I differ from him, except in the case of a *new law*—who is right? I told our Meeting however that as methods had been so dilligently taken to set them wrong, I felt desirous of trying to set them right; and also, I wished for an opportunity to express my opinion of those methods themselves. For that purpose, and to allow our friends who were not with the movers in the matter time to consider what was moved, we appointed to meet that evening fortnight. I then knew nothing of Mr. Watson's pamphlet, but soon found that it was out; so I sent for 60 and put them into the hands of most of our official men. Had I received this in time I should have felt relieved from the work which I undertook and from obligation to undertake it, by referring them to it for satisfaction; I even hoped, as it was, that it might induce them to give up their scheme; but I soon found that, as I stood pledged, I must meet the matter after all.

We met last Friday evening at six o'clock—a crowded meeting, and Webster Morgan as before brought forward the subject, saying that Mr. Watson granted what they contended for, except in extraordinary cases, which he (W.M.) allowed might arise; but that those

---

[1] John Stephens.
[2] Jacob Stanley, preacher, Dudley circuit, 1827–1830.

cases were unprovided for by the law as it now stands, no such provision being contained in the letter sent out from Leeds in '97.
Ashlin, D. Rowland and young Pooley, supported Webster—miserable doings all! I was surprised at Rowland. His speech was without
argument; a bold, impudent attempt to run down Mr. Watson's
pamphlet, and carry the meeting by an harangue—the lion certainly
had been painted more formidable than he appeared. Mr. Sands
made a manly speech against the Leeds radicals (he is cured of
radicalism!) and by the time that three or four of *us* had spoken it
was 12 o'clock. Of course I refused to put the motion, assigning for
my reason that the jurisdiction of District Committees in such cases
as that at Leeds was as fundamental to Methodism, as settled in '97,
as the things conceeded to the people; and that, though I could not
put their motion to vote, so neither could I put to vote those concessions, were their repeal made the subject of a motion. The temper
of the meeting was good throughout; but D. Rowland expressed his
bitter mortification at my refusal to put the question—our friends say
it was because they made so poorly out. The end of the meeting has
been answered to some extent. Most if not all of those whom I had
in my mind, and who had been misled or unsettled, have been set
right, and several have thanked me with great affection for my pains.
A radical however is a radical still, for all that we may speak or
Mr. Watson may write. We have plenty of such on the Leeds Street
side; of convincing them I entertained no hope and so have suffered
no disappointment. They are get[t]ing their *document* signed for
Conference, when, if spared, you may most likely see it—they had
previously intended, if it were not put, to print it; but perhaps they
will take warning from the show made of the Southwarkers. Our
friends here have wonderfully recovered heart; they seem to regard
our meeting as a defeat of radicalism; and pretty sure I am that the
cause of radicalism in this town has gained nothing by this grand
movement. I trust it has fallen with many, as with Mr. Sands, into
greater disrepute. The signers are a respectable set of men, except in
the eyes of the whole society and the town. I mean they are of great
consideration in their own account—they are indeed a paltry faction.
I trust however God will preserve his work among us which prospers
I believe a little, and, but for this, would prosper more. May I
request the favour (and a great one it will be knowing how you are
occupied) of a letter, telling me your opinion of my views and conduct, and giving me any advice which may appear suitable. I have
felt my situation somewhat trying; but I have never been afraid
throughout. I have seen the cause too good to be lost even in hands
not the most skilful. I still trust in God that these clouds will soon

blow over, and leave us with heavens as serene as in our brightest and happiest periods. . . .

[*P.S.*]

Our friends here wish to go to Conference with a protest against the sentiments and proceedings of the others. Had we not better allow them to do so?

127. *From James Gill*[1]   Northampton, February 13, 1829

. . . I feel fully sensible that our rules need a revision, and should be happy to see it effected, as there are also a few obsolete circumstances, necessarily so in consequence of the extended condition of the Connexion, of a prudential nature at the time of their enactment, which our enemies, such as the Leeds dissentients, never fail to make a bad use of: instance in 1793, 'The title of *Reverend* shall not be used by us towards each other'. . . .

It is gratifying to me to hear that in Manchester, and Lancashire generally, peace reigns. We have peace and prosperity in this Circuit, and through the District. It is a great mercy that neither the Leeds, nor Southwark dissentients have hitherto disturbed our harmony, though it has been attempted by the Southwark addresses having been sent to several persons here. Some of local preachers here, however, have gotten that scurrilous, and mischievous publication, the *Leeds Protestant Magazine*. I hope it will not do much harm. Having heard of it, I requested one of the Local Preachers to lend it to me. He spoke to another of them on the subject, who observed, 'I would not for ever so much that Mr. Gill should see it.' I have heard that they intend to *desist* taking it. However I intend calmly and prudentially to watch it. Their recommendation in the February Number to form a Local Preachers' Fund, is a malignant stratagem. I observe, notwithstanding all their sanguine expectations of dividing the body, and their extensive trumpeting, they number only a few in Barnsley, Preston, York and Newark. I trust that the scurrility of their magazine, with the malevolent attempts to divide our body, so prominent in their pages, will ultimately counteract their design, and sink the publication into a state of insignificancy. . . .

128. *From James Miller*[2]

Newcastle-[under]-Lyme, February 19, 1829

Will thank you to give me your opinion on the following questions.

---

[1] James Gill, superintendent, Northampton circuit, 1826–1829.

[2] James Miller (d. 1853, *aet.* 60), superintendent, Newcastle-under-Lyme circuit, 1828–1830.

Has a Circuit Steward a right to vote in a Leaders Meeting by virtue of his office?

If two Travelling Preachers are present at a Leaders Meeting in their own circuit, have both a right to vote or only the Superintendant[?] I can find no rule either directly or indirectly to support the former—nor to deny the latter.

Your early reply will oblige. . . .

[*Endorsed*]—[*To James Miller*]
Answered February 20.

A circuit steward, as such, is not a member of a Leaders' Meeting and therefore cannot by virtue of that office have any right to vote in it. Travelling Preachers, Leaders and Society Stewards compose what is called the Leaders' Meeting.

Every Travelling Preacher present at a Leaders' Meeting in his circuit is a member of that meeting to all intents and purposes. But *Travelling* Preachers are more than *Members*; they are all [present?] as the pastors and ministers of the people; the superintendant is chief pastor; the others are his helpers and fellow labourers in the ministerial and pastoral care. It is perhaps seldom expedient that they should act in the character of *mere* members, by voting; but their right is unquestionable.

I have much objection to giving this kind of opinion on *abstract points of Rule*, because the application and administration of law to particular cases, often constitute the real difficulty. And of *that* one cannot judge unless the cases themselves were fully stated.

It is usually a sign of a wrong state of things when such abstract questions come to be much discussed in a Christian community. Where there is a proper degree of the mind that was in Christ, our people will think more of their duties, than of their abstract rights: and one of those duties is, to 'submit themselves one to another, in the fear of the Lord' . . . .

129. *From John Aikenhead*[1]

N. pl. or d. [postmarked Devonport, February 21, 1829]

You will pardon the liberty I now take in addressing you on a subject in which I doubt not you have as lively a feeling of interest as myself or any individual of that great body at the head of which on various grounds divine Providence has now placed you. I mean the subject of Catholic emancipation falsely so called.[2] I have been

---

[1] John Aikenhead (1768–1835), superintendent, Devonport circuit, 1826–1829.

[2] For Bunting's attitude and his understanding that emancipation would be carried, see no. 130. Persistent reports from Irish Methodists about the evils of

spoken to by some friends warm in the Protestant cause to send petitions to both houses of Parliament from this Circuit against the granting power to Roman Catholics. I am sure from the generally expressed sentiments of our friends the thing can be done and in a way that I hope will do no disgrace to ourselves or to the body of which we are a part. I have said to our friends that it is my duty to consult you on the subject that I may learn whether there be any intention of petitioning the legislature on the subject as a body or whether it would be adviseable to do it rather by Circuits or should opportunity offer only in conjunction with others or be altogether silent on the subject. I am aware that in God is the refuge and strength of Protestantism which I call genuine Christianity, but I feel anxious to know whether we have anything to do beyond praying and waiting on him in the present awful crisis.

You will oblige by a speedy answer and excuse this hasty scrawl. . . .

130. *To Matthew Tobias*[1] (Limerick)   Salford, February 23, 1829

. . . It did not seem to me, though I am always unfeignedly disposed to pay great deference to any opinion or suggestion from *you*, that I could with propriety interfere with our preachers in Ireland, in the way you wished. Of their speaking at Brunswick Clubs, or taking any public part in political discussions, I disapprove as decidedly as yourself. No good can come of it, and much injury to the permanent interests, character, and usefulness, of our Connexion is reasonably to be apprehended, if such a procedure were frequent. But considering that I am not an Irishman; and that it is not altogether unknown that my personal opinion has long been decided in favour of a wise and reasonable concession, under proper guards, such as I think may be provided by an honest and able ministry, of further political privileges to the Catholics,—I deemed it likely that my advice would not have a good effect on the Irish preachers, who I believe are generally very hot anti-concessionists. And I felt too, that such an extra-official act, during my official year, would expose me to the assaults of certain persons in our English Itinerancy, who, I fear,

popery, and their own dangers and suffering (*cf.* no. 53 *supra*) built up considerable Protestant spirit in Methodism. Lord Eldon and the Protestant constitutionists were anxious for a demonstration by the Methodists, but, though in a minority of one on the Committee of Privileges, Bunting blocked any corporate action (M.C.A. Thos. Allan's MSS. Thos. Allan to Thomas R. Allan, March 9, March 19, April 25, 1829). A decade later he was in active alliance with the Merseyside Orangemen.

[1] Matthew Tobias (1770–1845), one of the leading preachers and evangelists of the Irish Methodist Connexion.

somewhat anxiously watch for an occasion against me. I think that if
the evil still exist, and be likely to spread, a kind and temperate
expostulation from yourself and three or four other senior and influential Brethren in your own island, would be the best way of
arresting its progress.

I am *now* exceedingly glad that the Government have taken up this
agitating question. Violent attempts are made in England to excite
a fanatic opposition; but, if the King be steadfast in support of this
recommendation and be not, by back-door influence, induced to try
a dissolution of Parliament the measure will be carried. Many of our
preachers and people are goading each other to petition against it
as Methodists. Private and public appeals are made to me, as the
President, to originate or countenance such petitions, which of
course I must refuse to do. I am sure incalculable mischief would
result from it. We *as a body* never have petitioned *separately*; nor
should we now, on a question so decidedly political in its aspect.

The Leeds Noncons. took away from ⟨our⟩ two circuits about a
thousand members—who are very little missed. Our cause there goes
on as well as can be expected; and the Societies are in a better state
of discipline and spiritual order than for a dozen years past. The
division there has been on the whole a blessing. In the Barnsley
Circuit about 200 have left us; and in York about 20. At Newark the
Ranters have formed a coalition with the Noncons. In Southwark,
Liverpool and Sheffield, there are a considerable number of radically
unsound and disaffected men, who annoy the preachers and our best
friends by violent speeches and by occasionally circulating insur-
rectionary pamphlets, but will not leave us. This I believe is the extent of the evil; and it is not growing either in character or influence.
The Connexion, with the exception of some half dozen circuits is
peaceable, and, I think, prosperous. Watson has published a good
pamphlet against the Southwark Resolutions. London North
Circuit is *particularly* loyal. Manchester is perfectly quiet. So are
most of the Circuits in all the great manufacturing districts. The Leeds
Noncons. publish a monthly Magazine, and have engaged Samuel
Tucker, late of Belfast, to be its editor for £100 per annum. He is
advertizing a work containing very heterodox notions on the
Trinity.[1] What is that man's true character? . . .

---

[1] In *An expostulatory letter addressed to the Wesleyan Methodist Conference,
assembled at Liverpool in July 1832, charging that body with maintaining and enforcing irrational and anti-scriptural dogmata as fundamental principles in their
system of theology* . . . (Liverpool, 1832) Samuel Tucker, an experienced Local
Preacher in England and Ireland, declared that he had left the old connexion
solely because of the aggressiveness of the preachers at Leeds. But he also held

131. *From Edmund Grindrod*   Leeds, March 4, 1829

. . . I can assure you, [from] what I see of the spirit of some of the men who were connected with the Noncons. up to a certain period, and to whom I showed all possible kindness when they professed to be convinced of their errors, I am led to anticipate a removal from this Circuit with no small degree of pleasure; at the same time I feel every disposition to do my best to get them an eligible supply of preachers for next year. . . . The Noncons' magazine for this month is more bitter in its spirit towards us than any of their ⟨former⟩ publications, and it abounds with falshood, slander and religious democracy. It contains a letter from a Churchman addressed to you, and a review of Mr. Watson's pamphlet. You will probably get a sight of it whilst you are in London. I believe it will rather serve our cause than injure it. . . .

132. *From Edmund Grindrod*   Leeds, March 9, 1829

. . . Since I saw you I have not heard much relating to next year's President; but I understand that Mr. Newton[1] favours Dr. Townley's election. On the whole I should have preferred Mr. Marsden;[2] but rather than the Rad[ical]s should gain the advantage of us by a division of our votes, I should readily give my vote and little influence in favour of Dr. T. I have thought on what you said concerning issuing a Circular Declaration on the month of June, and am persuaded that it will be a wise and beneficial measure. In the critical posture of affairs in which our Connexion seems likely to be placed for some time to come, it seems to me a matter of great importance whom we appoint as ⟨Jack⟩son's successor in the Editor⟨ship⟩ at the Conference [of] 1830, should we all be spared so long. I incline to think that that office should again devolve upon you, if you will accept of it: and in that case would it not be well for Mr. [Richard] Watson to go to London North next year and you remain in Salford? . . .

133. *From William Vevers*   York, March 16, 1829

I have written, and sent to the press, during the last week, *Observations on the Members of the Church of Rome giving security to a*

---

that Conference was infringing the freedom of speculative judgment which Wesley had guaranteed his preachers, by insisting on 'the *Unitrinitarian* system, gratuitously but falsely styled "orthodoxy", [which had] . . . driven thousands of upright men into the awful and destructive heresies of Sabellianism, Arianism, and Socinianism'. *Op. cit.*, pp. ii, v.

[1] Robert Newton, superintendent, Liverpool (South) circuit, 1826–1829.
[2] George Marsden, superintendent, Bolton circuit, 1827–1830.

Protestant State.[1] My purpose was formed on Monday last, by reading Mr. Peel's speech; and on Wednesday I sent the first pages to the press, and I expect the whole will be out on Thursday next. I shall forward a copy to you without delay, of which I beg your kind acceptance. The former part is chiefly documentary evidence. It is to the latter pages that I solicit your attention. My avowed object is to produce that feeling which will show itself by addresses to the Throne against the bill now before the House, which I most deeply and solemnly deprecate. If I have the misfortune to differ in opinion with you, and any of my Brethren on this subject, which however *I hope is not the case*, I flatter myself that the spirit of the pamphlet will be no discredit either to me, or the Christian Ministers with whom I have the honour to be united; as I am not conscious that I have written a line, not even the last paragraph in which I refer to Mr. Peel, which 'dying I would wish to blot'.

It has been to me, and I believe to others, a subject of surprise, and regret, that our Committee of Privileges has hitherto been, as far as I can learn, inactive at this important crisis. If the disaffection in 1817 and Lord Sidmouth's Act justified the prompt and decisive steps that were then taken,[2] I humbly think that the present measure demands our immediate, determined, and simultaneous opposition. Let us Address the Throne; and either on the day of presentation, or when the bill is to be read a 2nd time in the House of Peers, let us have a day of solemn fasting and prayer, and thus show that we possess the spirit of our illustrious Founder; and I doubt not but it will be acknowledged by the Protestant Church, and recorded in the pages of our national history, that Methodism has been the salvation of Britain.

I persuade myself that I need not assure you that in *our* late struggles I ascribe our deliverance from a democratical and unscriptural domination, under God, to your christian firmness and manly decision. I alluded you in print in May last as the only man among us capable of taking the management of our helm; and I have regarded your elevation to the Presidential Chair, at that portentous crisis, as our proof that God has not forsaken us. But, if on this occasion I differ in opinion with you, I still have a peculiar pleasure in addressing myself to one, to whose judgement, more than that of any one man among us, I shall always pay the most respectful deference, and from whom I will cheerfully receive instruction and correction.

[1] Leeds, 1829.
[2] *I.e.* the address against disaffection adopted at the time of the Pentridge rebellion, February 6, 1817, and the resistance to Lord Sidmouth's bill to restrict the Toleration Act, 1811.

If in any part of this letter I have used language which, even by implication, is disrespectful, you must forgive me. I have thought much, and I feel exquisitely respecting this deprecated Bill; and therefore, I now write, as I have written in the pamphlet, freely and boldly, though I hope, not disrespectfully or intemperately.

My highly esteemed and intelligent friends Messrs Wood and Crowther, have read and approve of my pamphlet. . . .

134. From John Beecham[1]

Liverpool, Mount Pleasant, March 30, 1829[2]

Mr. Wade, the bearer of this, has kindly engaged to call on you for my manuscript. I have this morning seen a copy of the resolutions which John Russell is intending to introduce at our Quarterly Meeting on Thursday; and I find that, after all, we shall have the constitutional question to go into. The number of resolutions is seven. The following is a copy of the third.

'That this meeting particularly objects to a new test[3] then introduced by the preachers, a refusal to sign which was considered sufficient to deprive a leader or officer of the exercise of his right to vote; and also the 5th resolution of their report which assumes for the district-meeting "The right and power to exclude from office or membership as the case might appear to them to require", both these proceedings being directly subversive of the act of 1797 which declares "That no person shall be appointed a leader or steward, or be removed from his office, but in conjunction with a leaders' meeting" '.

I do not know whether this resolution is intended to deny the interference of the Special District meeting altogether. From what I recollect of the conversation I had with John Russell he admitted the principle, that the District meeting might, in cases of emergency, interfere in Society business. But however he may admit the principle in words, he certainly denies it now as a practical principle. If, as I expect they will argue, that the District cannot do anything but by means of the Leaders' Meeting, it appears to me a useless provision. A factious Leaders' Meeting might as successfully resist the District Meeting as the Superintendent. The District Meeting must of course, have a discretionary power to make the best application of constitutional resources which the case will admit, otherwise I cannot see

---

[1] John Beecham (1797–1856), preacher, Liverpool (South) circuit, 1828–1831. President 1850.

[2] The date is established by Bunting's reply, April 7, 1829, printed almost completely in *Life of Bunting*, ii, pp. 256–258.   [3] See no. 93 *supra*.

what more it can do than the Superintendent might have done.[1] I make these observations in haste to crave the favour of your opinion along with the other observations you kindly promised me. I fear taking any position on the question which is not tenable. We have proof in these resolutions that they are ready to take any advantage. One of the longest resolutions is a protest against Mr. Scott's interpretation of the rule relative to the expulsion of members.

P.S. I may add that Hanson told me last night, that he hopes they are prepared to submit to the majority of the meeting; so that if they are allowed an opportunity to speak their mind on the subject, I think, if they are overthrown, they will refrain from printing.

135. *From William Dawson and Benjamin Stocks*
Leeds, March 31, 1829

At the Quarter Day held yesterday at the Old Chapel vestry in Leeds, it was unanimously agreed 'that the Stewards should write to *Mr. Bunting as President* and *urgently request* him to take the state of the Leeds East Circuit into his *most serious consideration*; and use his *valuable influence* in our behalf the next Conference; and the meeting assures him, that it would confer upon us the greatest favour if he would take *upon himself the Superintendence of our Circuit next year*; but if he cannot do this, that he would use his utmost ability to secure for us Mr. Watson, or Mr. Lessey,[2] or Mr. Newton. Such attention to our wishes would be felt as conferring unspeakable obligations upon the Leeds East Circuit.[3] To this request we cordially agree; and beg leave to enter into more minute particulars than could with propriety be stated openly at the Meeting. You know, Sir, our case at Leeds has for the last two years been most painfully interesting, and the present circumstances in which we are still placed demand the most serious consideration, as it regards the Circuit, our

---

[1] At the Christmas Quarterly Meeting Beecham had stated the official view of the Methodist constitution in opposition to the radicals' emphasis on circuit rights. The manuscript referred to in this letter was a draft of a full-scale development of his speech, one of the first and most important statements of the high Wesleyan doctrine of the ministry, which he published soon afterwards, *An essay on the constitution of Wesleyan Methodism* (London, 1829). As President, 1850–1851, Beecham bore responsibility for the stern enforcement of the doctrine it embodied, at a cost of the rapid loss of one-third of the membership.

[2] Theophilus Lessey (d. 1841), superintendent, Stockport circuit, 1827–1829; Manchester (Grosvenor St.) circuit, 1829–1832.

[3] Though disregarding this prayer for the most distinguished preachers in the connexion, conference appointed an experienced superintendent, Richard Treffry, senr., who came straight from his contests with the radicals in the London (Southwark) circuit, 1827–1829 (*cf.* nos. 140–143 *infra*).

Finances, the Trustees and the approaching Conference to be held in Leeds. The loss of nearly 700 members must have made a serious impression upon our financial concerns, as well as upon our congregations in the East Circuit. The old Chapel congregation has suffered materially, also Albion Street Chapel and Wesley have experienced some diminution, by the secession, and the erection of Brunswick Chapel; and the difference may be a little increased when the seceders open their new chapel which they are erecting in the West end of the Town.

The state in which our Trustees are now placed, is indeed *most deeply interesting*, as the income at present does not meet the expenditure by a serious sum of money. A new Trust will soon have to be created, and regulated, and unless we have preachers of superior talent and influence we must sink (so far as human aid is concerned) and Leeds, which has been the Garden of Methodism will be in danger of losing its fertility, its beauty, and its glory.

As the Conference is approaching, it will require an affectionate active and influential Superintendent to attend to the various duties connected with that important event: so that with those subjects before our eyes, you will not be surprized that we beg most affectionately and earnestly that you would interest yourself in our behalf. . . .

Signed by the sanction of the Quarterly Meeting. . . .

136. *From William Henshaw*   Sheffield, June 6, 1829

[They are trying to find Conference lodgings for 400 preachers] . . . But it is no easy task. For several who received preachers six years since are now dead, several removed, still more are reduced in their circumstances, and two or three only are disaffected, and although the Society has increased in number about 500 members, yet these almost wholly consist of poor persons. The rich flock to the Churches. Two new ones have been opened and a third is nearly finished. All supplied by what are called evangelical clergymen, chiefly young, active and zealous men, who strive to equal us in every good work. And then, they are of the Establishment! The people of the New Connexion have also erected and opened two new chapels and new houses for their Preachers since I came to Sheffield, and are about to hold their Conference here. The Dissenters are all jealous of us. It is also reported that the Non Cons. will hold their first Conference here, at the time we hold ours, will endeavour to trouble our now smooth waters, and then fish in them to catch the unwary. After all, we have nothing to fear, if we live rightly towards God and man. The Lord of Hosts is with us, and the God of Jacob is our refuge. Our Chapel Fund Collection has increased ten pounds. Will thank you not to delay making a return from your District, as we wish to appoint the Preachers to their houses, and also to make a printed plan of what they must do, to be sanctioned by yourself.

137. *From William Leach*[1]   Bristol, July 17, 1829
[Regrets that personal differences among the circuit staff prevented his attendance at Conference]

... There are [a] few little things which I have felt, and which I would have mentioned to you in a friendly way had I been at Sheffield. The division of this circuit[2] as it is proposed to be done will be natural and geographical; but *not equitable*. All the distant country places to which a horse is necessary will fall to our end with a mass of very poor people. The other will be the Metropolitan Circuit, suited to the state of some venerable father in the connection and his favoured helpers. Such a one I hope you will send this year to follow Mr. Entwisle.[3] A man who can take the chair of the District, and Mr. Wesley's chair at Kingswood School.[4] I respect age and standing in the Church of God if connected with piety and faithfulness. Allow me to say that I think too much attention has been paid to junior brethren for some years past. I hope it is not from envious motives that I say the method of electing very junior members for the Hundred has been carried too far.[5] Some of your important

---

[1] William Leach (d. 1846, *aet.* 67), preacher, Bristol circuit, 1828–9, superintendent, Bristol (Langton Street, circuit, 1829–1831.
[2] The Bristol circuit was divided at this Conference.
[3] Entwisle was succeeded in Bristol by ex-President Jonathan Edmondson.
[4] The original Kingswood School near Bath was created by Wesley in 1740 for the education of colliers' children. The school here mentioned was an additional institution created in 1748 for the education of sons of itinerant preachers and other Methodists.
[5] The age structure of the Wesleyan ministry had been greatly altered by the rapid recruitment of young men in the early years of the century. Bunting had risen to power by the support of the young men, their resentment at the caucus politics of some of the seniors (M.C.A. MSS. Joseph Entwisle to Jabez Bunting, June 2, 1809), and their exclusion from the Legal Hundred whose consent gave legal force to the work of Conference, and who elected the President and Secretary. In 1814, Bunting carried a proposal that every fourth vacancy in the Legal Hundred be filled by a preacher of only fourteen years standing, was immediately elected and installed Secretary of Conference. It had been complained at the Conference of 1820 that 'we are coming under the government of rich men who think more of the *young* than the *old* preachers' (M.C.A. MS. Conference Journal 1820). In Bunting's later years irritation at the deadweight of seniority made itself felt again. C. H. Kelly, *Memories* (London, 1910), p. 171.

committees have very junior members in them. Instance your Book Committee for the last year. I have endeavoured to serve Methodism, and have under God done it in some important stations, and have served the Book concern in various ways as your Book Stewards can testify, yet in thirty years I have never once been on that Committee. However, my love of Methodism as a whole increases every year. I can say it is more and more profitable to my soul. And I am hoping to overtake those who are gone before. Though I write thus dont think me a *Croaker*, or *a Conference radical*. No, I hate radicalism in Church and State, as I hate the works of the devil. Yet I have felt a little from the views I have had on the above subjects. I would not say these things or write them to another individual. . . .

138. *From David McNicoll*   Lambeth, July 17 [Postmarked 1829]

The proposed division of our Circuit, of which we have sent you some account,[1] has confounded and mortified the opposition party. And this the more as it is the direct consequence of their own obstinacy. If we are not greatly mistaken, providence has graciously interfered to break, at least in a great degree, this most destructive coalition. They are still striving to oppose the measure, by throwing in every objection they can think of, without regarding the truth of the facts which they state, or the justness of the reasons which they urge.

They are promising to be at peace for the future. For my own part I place no dependance on them. As a proof of their sincerity, since they made that promise, a book has been made public against Mr. Watson[2] and the Conference, signed it appears by a great number of their names. If they were sincere they would have recalled this book. We have not yet seen it, but we are told it is a very bad one.

I thought that as the party are now likely to be conquered, it might perhaps be well if the Conference would overlook the Resolutions, and all that had passed during the year. This might have tended to complete our triumph and to restore peace. But I am afraid this new book will interfere. It perhaps will not be possible, in justice, to pass by such overt acts of injurious hostility to our system. If so, I should, notwithstanding their present promises, expect them still to agitate the circuit and the connexion. They will therefore need to be watched and managed by some very suitable superintendant.

[1] Lambeth circuit was separated from Southwark at the Conference immediately following; the letter referred to has not survived.

[2] *Reply to the affectionate address of the Rev. R. W. . . . , being a defence of the concessions and code of laws of 1797 and of the constitution of Wesleyan Methodism against the modern assumption of ministerial power* (2nd edn., London, 1829).

Mr. Treffry took his leave of them at the Quarter Day, and told them he had fully made up his mind to remove. Since that time, they have applied to him to consent to remain. He seems inclined to change his mind, as indeed he has done several times before on the same subject. If he should remove, I know no person more fit to subdue the party than Mr. Stephens[1] of City Road, supposing that the rule of 8 years, absence from a circuit could in this case be dispensed with. And he is quite willing to go if the Conference appoint him. Ingle[2] would make a good firm colleague for him.

On the Lambeth side we are all at peace and are likely to be. We have had nothing else the whole year. But what is to be done with the Southwark people, I declare I can't tell. Our meetings lately have been worse and worse; would have disgraced a tavern. Mr. Dixon[3] acknowledged to the District Meeting that he now perceived he had been a fool in suffering it with so much silence and that he was determined to be silent no longer. . . .

P.S. The Circuit is at this moment in so hostile a state that we don't know whether it would be prudent for three of us to be absent from it during Conference. There is no mischief which those men are not prepared to do if opportunity occurred. I hear they have had another raging meeting last night at Southwark. Mr. Dixon threatens to leave entirely or look out for another circuit. But we cannot spare him from Lambeth. He would be of essential use to us in commencing our new circuit.

139. *From John Hodgson*[4]   Wolverhampton, July 25, 1829

As I am informed that an appeal will be made to the Conference by six Local Preachers in this Circuit who have been *suspended* for 'holding opinions', and speaking and acting upon them contrary to the acknowledged doctrines of Methodism, *on the subject of Faith*, I take the liberty of presenting to your acceptance a sermon I preached on the general question, in which, I hope I have stated the views of Faith it includes in accordance with the Wesleyan doctrine. The grand point upon which they defend themselves is that their views are '*but* private opinions.' The fact, however, is that they have

---

[1] John Stephens, President 1827–1828; superintendent, London (City Road) circuit, 1827–1829. He had been the first superintendent of the London (Southwark) circuit, 1822–1824. On the eight years' rule, see n. 1, p. 87 *supra*.

[2] Timothy C. Ingle (1792–1851), preacher, London (Southwark) circuit, 1829–1831.

[3] James Dixon (d. 1871), preacher, London (Southwark) circuit, 1828–1829, London (Lambeth) circuit, 1829–1830.

[4] John Hodgson (d. 1853), superintendent, Wolverhampton circuit, 1828–1830.

so much brought those opinions into the general strain of their preaching, conversation, and prayers; and such *unguarded* expressions, and statements have been given respecting man's free agency to believe in Christ unto pardon and sanctification '*at any moment*' or '*whenever he pleases*', as has produced a most painful sensation among our people and hearers: and the enquiry has gone from one person to another, 'Who are we to believe, the man that preached in the morning or him at night?'. With the above brethren it is a main point, that 'because Faith is the act of man therefore it is not a matter for prayer'. The above views have produced such a complete system of Ranterism in our prayer meetings, etc., as induced our last Local Preachers' Quarterly Meeting to take up the subject by a *friendly conversation with the brethren.* We sat, on the subject, from first to last, nearly eight hours, when at past ten at night, (as no arguments were found to prevail) the Local Preachers *unanimously* passed a Resolution but with great tenderness of spirit that unless they 'would admit the *importance* of directing penitent sinners to pray for faith, as well as to believe in Christ that they be suspended untill that pledge be given'.[1]

Your excellent sermon on Justification by faith has been pressed into the service of unguarded sentiment!! And appeals have been made to Dr. Clarke, etc., but with what reason, your and his judgment would easily decide. *If it be necessary* that (in case of their appeal) *I should be called up to the Conference,* I shall give a full statement of the case; *if not,* I will send it in writing. In the meantime, it has given me pleasure to find that not one of our *elder members* has been drawn from their simplicity in Christ by the above doctrines. I know of no spirit of resentment or disapprobation by any of our people, at the decision of the Local Preachers' Meeting. But, I know this that such is the strong attachment of our preachers and people to our doctrines that were I to allow the suspended to preach at all, the far greater part of our Local Preachers, if not *all,* would send in their Plans. I need not add more than that any instructions which you or the Conference see good to communicate shall be sacredly complied with. . . .

P.S. Private. Only one person has as yet left us, a Leader of the name of Powell, who has promised God never more to pray for faith!!

---

[1] The views here described seem to be akin to those which led to the expulsion of the 'Derby Faith people' in 1832, the loss of nearly half the membership of the Derby circuit, and the creation of a small new connexion of midland circuits. The practical upshot, renewed revivalism, was certainly the same. Cf. George Browne Macdonald, *Facts against fiction* (2nd edn. Derby, 1832); J. Hackett, *Arminian Methodism miscalled 'Derby Faith'* (Derby, n.d. [1832]).

and asserted (for he confirmed it to me on enquiry at our last Leaders' Meeting) he should as soon think of going down on his knees to curse God as to pray for faith!!! He now, however, says, 'it would be a sin to curse God but an error to pray for faith'. A pious person will take his class, who in the main are all orthodox.

140. *From David McNicoll*[1]   Lambeth, September 17, 1829

We have not yet ascertained the full extent of our revolt, especially in Southwark. But probably you will not think it an intrusion if I state to you the facts so far as at present we can learn them; for there is a good deal of secrecy in the party, and what may yet follow through their influence it is not easy to say. But we hope the worst is over.

They had held secret meetings, had corresponded with the Leeds Nonconformists, and had actually engaged several chapels, the Scotch Church in particular, near the Elephant and Castle, on a lease at £60 a year, before we had the least suspicion that such a purpose was at all in existence. They first declared their intention to Mr. Treffry at the breakfast meeting on Sunday the 23rd. He was astonished, and asked what he had done to deserve such treatment from them. They said they had designed to postpone all active measures till he had left the circuit, but finding that through Mrs. T's illness he was to remain beyond his time they could wait no longer. But they assured him they would use no influence to take our people with them. How strictly they have kept to this let their consciences declare. The reasons for separation, as alledged in their private meetings, we have been credibly informed were the division of the Circuit; the appointment of a young man, which keeps them out of the principal chapels;[2] and the demur of some of our circuit meetings about the expence of their Sunday breakfasts. In contradiction to this, we had heard some of the leading ones among them publickly avow their satisfaction with the whole of the present arrangements, including the division, which they admitted they once objected to, and at the same [time] they promised to double their subscriptions for the support of the young preacher.

The local preachers who have left are Messrs. Jones, Longridge, Carley, Moorhouse, Plucknett, Moore, Smith, Stubly, Robinson, and Williams; 5 from each circuit. We have 10 remaining on the Lambeth side, and 3 continue in Southwark. We have still more preachers in both than we have full work for. We regret not the loss

---

[1] David McNicoll, superintendent, London (Lambeth) circuit, 1829–1831.

[2] A fourth preacher had been appointed to Southwark circuit in 1825, thus reducing the number of appointments for local preachers.

of such men, but we do lament that many poor people have been led away by them. Five leaders have seceded at Walworth, and taken their classes with them, and as they meet in their own houses they have refused to let us in to speak to the people. We got the addresses of some of them to visit them separately at their homes, but the prejudice excited was such that little good was done by an attempt to reason with them. We have lost one leader at Lambeth and another at Broadwall, but the classes have been saved. We have lost about 60 in all at Walworth, but scarcely an individual in any other place.

It is not the kind of division that we could have wished; for the worst ones remain, and seem determined not to leave, such as Spicer, Griffith, Sutcliffe. The influence of their system has been such that I have lost much of my confidence even in our soundest men. We have not been supported and encouraged by them since Conference as we expected. The spirit that has gone forth against the principles and persons of Methodist preachers in their collective character as a Conference, is, I fear, a very injurious one, and has probably affected a great many people who will not speak out. The mischief which it may occasion to the younger branches of their families it is more easy to dread than to calculate.

We have found that the less this subject is mentioned to our people generally, the better. This will not always apply to leading men at Quarter Days, etc., but as to others I am convinced the rule is good. As the knowledge of a separation soon spread among our people we thought it might be right to warn them at the society meetings against giving heed to the statements of the party, but though this was done in the fairest and most candid manner possible, we found it produced evil rather than good. We could not answer all the falsehoods in circulation; suspicions were excited among them that all was not right in Methodism; they began to make enquiries, and the revolters made an impression where we could make none. The truth is the mooting of the Leeds question awakes the slumbering corruption of the heart and prepares the mind to believe the worst side of things, while a satisfactory answer is rendered extremely difficult from the multitude of the details, the plausibility of the objections, the abstract nature of the principles upon which rules of legislation must always more or less be founded, and the mental contactedness and dullness of the people in regard to such speculations. Many of them are as little able to discuss such matters as a number of stragglers in a barber's shop would be to settle the question of the justice or policy of a nation going to war. We Methodists are peculiarly in danger here from the multitudes of poor connected with us, the freedoms they are accustomed to take with their preachers, and the popular nature of Circuit government among us; for the people of a Circuit are taught to believe that they do almost everything in the management of a Circuit, and that the preachers are and ought to be their mere servants. They suspect both us and our rules. When I first heard that Mr. Watson was replying to the Resolutions I felt a sort of instinctive astonishment, for I had never once imagined that any body would do so. I immediately began to suspect my own judgement in this matter. When the pamphlets appeared I prized them highly, considered in themselves, but not as at all calculated to settle the great question. I believed they would have a contrary effect, not only as being unsatisfactory to ignorant and prejudiced minds, and so far confirmatory of the evil; but particularly as calling for the bold and bitter rejoinders which *would be* believed. The triumph occasioned by the *Reply* to Mr. Watson is very great. I lament to think of the mischief it has done, and that in quarters where one could hardly have expected it. But if writing is still to be defended as a proper mode of meeting the case, I repeat that your own plain and pointed comments on the facts of the Leeds case, and your replies to the weak objections of the party would be most likely to obtain success. But if other writings had not been already published, I should not have even wished for yours.

Mr. Treffry had better perhaps have had a separation at the first by refusing to put the address. Mr. Dixon himself, (for he is somewhat changeable) though he used to say that Mr. Treffry had saved the Circuit, by putting the address, now traces all our evils to that source. He says if there had been no address put there would have been no mortifying reply from Conference,[1] of course no Resolutions, then no pamphlet from Mr. Watson, then no book from Sutcliffe,[2] and in all probability, no such degree of dissatisfaction as to occasion either a division of the circuit, or a revolt.

Those who have left us at Walworth are the perfection party. Mr. Dixon thinks, I believe justly, that Ranterism has been the ruin of that society by preparing them for this revolt. They have a great advantage over us in the private methods they are using to injure us, and in the use of popular slang and falsehood in their writings. We cannot adopt the same measures. They have persons at the end of streets on Sundays to decoy our people away as they are coming to our chapels. Yet strange to say, even at Walworth, our congregations don't seem to be lessened in the least. The party profess that 20 were set at liberty on the first Sunday evening after they had left us.

[1] The 1829 Conference gave its view of the disputed constitutional issues in *Minutes of the Methodist Conferences*, vi, pp. 512–513.
[2] This seems to be the anonymous pamphlet described in n. 2, p. 210.

They have endeavoured to take Gainsford Street Chapel from us. It was taken at a yearly rent for the use of the society. The leaders called a secret meeting, and prepared resolutions for giving it over to the Protestants. Messrs Gill[1] and Ingle got to hear of it, and attended, and with difficulty got a majority against the project, and by these means saved the society; for the people, not understanding the question, would have gone with the chapel. I have just been at Mr. Gill's, who say[s] they have had a meeting the night before last by which he thinks they have quite secured it. Two leaders have left us at Gainsford Street but the classes are saved, and two at Southwark (Bowler and Hiscock), the classes chiefly saved. I don't hear of much evil in the other circuits. Mr. Ford at Kentish Town has sent Mr. Reece some very insulting letters, and has left society, and Mr. Eckett grumbles but I suppose he wont leave.

Our societies generally dislike this separation, and seem inclined to keep the closer together on account of it. I think we have already suffered the greatest shock. We need not much fear the flaming zeal of our enemies. Yet we could like to see a more loyal and hearty feeling towards Methodism among our people. Mr. Dixon says they have not a drop of real unadulterated friendship for Methodist preachers. He is little mistaken. We have a few drops, and but a few. This is the more remarkable as this circuit was many years ago just the contrary. But several causes operated unfavourably before the Leeds question was heard of. My dear Sir, you will I hope forgive the longwindedness of these observations. They are mere opinions of my own, and will of course not be taken for more than they are worth. I am sometimes much distressed and it relieves me to write. . . .

141. *From James Gill*   Southwark, September 21, 1829

Agreeably to my promise, I transmit some account of the affairs connected with the Southwark Circuit. It is, as I observed, a post of honour, or difficulty, and trial. August 18 I received a letter from Mr. Treffry informing me, in consequence of Mr. Grindrod's affliction,[2] he could not leave the house in Southwark until Tuesday 1st September. August 29th I received a second letter from Mr. Treffry, in which he informed me a revolt had taken place of the Local Preachers in the Southwark and Lambeth Circuits—that ten of the local preachers, five in each Circuit had formally resigned,

---

[1] James Gill, superintendent, London (Southwark) circuit, 1829–1831.

[2] Grindrod had had much ill-health during his appointment at Leeds, and was now unable to vacate his manse so that Treffry could take up his new appointment.

opened a communication with the men at Leeds—and purchased one chapel and rented two others.

The Local Preachers had formed the design of letting Mr. T. go quietly off the ground, and as soon as I came to send in their plans to me, but as Mr. T. stayed longer than they expected, and as their plans were formed to commence operations at a certain period, they sent their resignation to Mr. T. This delay of Mr. Treffry was to me a peculiar Providence, as the explosion took place before my arrival, and prevented the perplexity I must have experienced on my first arrival, by receiving the resignation of these unprincipled men.

I arrived here on Tuesday 1st September and immediately commenced my work. I found considerable dissatisfaction prevailed in respecting the division of the Circuit, and because Messrs. Treffry and Dixon were not appointed for Southwark. Various representations were made respecting the division of the Circuit, and animadversions on the Conference. Alarms, and agitation prevailed respecting what might be the extent of the seperation and the people appeared moved like a forest by a violent wind. The sound part seemed scarcely to know in whom to place confidence.

On the 5th or 6th September Matthew Johnson of Leeds arrived in Town, and advertisements were issued and posted in the streets for him and other of the revolted local preachers to preach the following Lord's Day at Horsley Street Chapel, Walworth, Albion Street Chapel and Rosemary Terrace, Peckham—and that the Scotch Church, Prospect Place, would be opened in a fortnight. One of the posters was fixed up near Southwark Chapel, another sent into the vestry, and in the Mint, they stuck two up inside the little place. The place taken in Albion Street is very near us. They did not however do much harm to our congregations.

At the Leaders Meeting Monday night, September 7th, Mr. Bowler brought his class book and delivered it up and H. Hiscock sent in his resignation. I had heard of Hiscock's intention on Saturday and visited him, reasoned with him but without any good effect. He is gone to a Baptist Chapel. I remonstrated with Mr. Bowler in the meeting, but he was obstinate and determined to leave. New Leaders were appointed on whom, we could depend for piety, and attachment to our discipline. I exhorted the Leaders to peace and union. The meeting was as peaceable and orderly as any Leaders meeting I ever attended. One of the Leaders observed to me after the meeting broke up, that they had not had so peaceable a Leaders Meeting for eighteen months.

Thursday September 10th I appointed for meeting the three remaining local preachers, and to take two on trial, men of sound

P

principles. Just before the meeting, about five o'clock, I received notice of a secret meeting called by a circular of the Leaders and Stewards at Gainsford Street. The following is a copy. 'Sir, you are requested to meet the Leaders and Stewards of Gainsford Street Chapel this evening at 8 o'Clock in the vestry on important business. September 10th, 1829.'

This circular was without signature. When I heard of it, I determined to hasten through the business of the Local Preacher's meeting and give them the meeting at Gainsford Street. Mr. Ingle and I went, arrived there by eight o'clock, and surprised them by our presence. We appeared to them unwelcome guests. I sang, prayed, and then enquired the object of the meeting, but could obtain nothing but evasions from them. They asked explanation on the Leeds business etc., etc., I thought it right to explain, and several of them expressed themselves satisfied, saying they had never before had such views of the subject. For upwards of two hours I could not learn the object of their meeting. At last rather accident[al]ly, we obtained the knowledge of the object. The agent in the business, Dowson, I believe intending to shew me an extract from Mr. Wrothall's letter, pulled out of his pocket several papers and the one which came into my hand was the intended concluding resolution of their illegal meeting, and immediately I obtained another paper of the business of the meeting. The following are copies.

'Business of the Meeting.

1. What is the sense of the Meeting on the measures of Conference
   1. In their conduct of the Leeds case generally.
   2. In the case of the address and resolution of this circuit.
   3. In the power claimed for the Preachers as set forth in Mr. Watson's address.
   4. In the division of this Circuit when the appeals sent to Conference against were not noticed.

2ndly 1. Is it desirable to seperate from the Conference Connexion and join the Protestant Methodists.
   2. If it be desirable to join the Protestant Methodists let a requisition be signed requesting Mr. Wrothall to give up the Chapel to the Leaders Meeting.
   3. Appoint a deputation to meet the Committee of the Protestant Methodists tomorrow evening.

We the undersigned Leaders and Stewards of Gainsford ⟨St⟩ Chapel having determined on leaving the Conference connexion and uniting ourselves to the Protestant Methodists, being of opinion that it is desirable to retain the chapel which was taken on the responsibility of the Leaders Meeting and not by the Quarterly Meeting, present our thanks to Mr. Wrothall for his management of the temporal affairs of the same and request that he will deliver it up to the Leaders Meeting. At the same time we earnestly request that if agreeable to himself he will again take it under his care for the use of the Protestant Methodists.'

Mr. Wrothall is Steward of the chapel. The chapel is rented. We now saw the object was to take away the chapel, congregation, and society alltogether, and from the temper of the men when we first came in, there can be no doubt but that they would have revolted and taken the chapel as Mr. Wrothall favoured their views. Mr. Ingle moved that the chapel belongs to the Circuit and not the Leaders Meeting and that Mr. W. is Steward for the Circuit. After explanations given, the resolution was carried by a majority of 2, being 6 for and 4 against. Mr. Ingle moved that all the Leaders continue in connexion with us, and lay themselves out to promote the work of God among us—to this there was a demur, and an attempt was made to negative it by an amendment which I could not put to the vote. Being determined to bring the business to a decision I asked them individually whether they would continue with us. When five declared they would continue—two resigned their office—and three declared they were neuter. Thus we broke up near eleven o'clock, having providentially preserved the chapel and congregation and the great part of the society. It appears they had communications with the seceders on the business and they hoped to have obtained the chapel. More in my next. . . .

142. *From James Gill*   Southwark, October 10, 1829

In continuation of my last letter, I observe that we had thoughts of calling a Special Leaders Meeting at Gainsford Street to appoint two new Leaders in the place of the seceders, but calling at Mr. Wrothall's and finding that he would not be at home till after the regular time of the next Leaders Meeting we let the business lie over till that period, in the mean time looking out for two Leaders of sound principles to fill up the places necessary, and appointing persons to lead the classes till the new Leaders were appointed.

At Albion Street Bradshaw and Edwards resigned their office as Leaders, but their classes did not go with them, and we filled up their places with men of sound principles.

In the *Liberal Times* Sunday Paper on the 6th and 13th September a piece was inserted against the Conference, and preachers, stating the Leeds and Southwark cases, filled with calumny and gross fals[e]hoods, bearing a family likeness to the *Leeds Protestant Magazine.*

On Tuesday 15th September after preaching, we held our Leaders Meeting at Gainsford Street, and elected two new Leaders which strengthened the sound part. The neuters did not appear. I observed the neuters must declare themselves soon, and finding the Leaders in tolerably good temper, determined to exercise discipline on Dowson, who had been the agent in calling the illegal meeting to take the chapel from us; hence the members of the meeting were summoned for this pu[r]pose at the next Leaders' Meeting. I thought that exercising discipline on Dowson might have a salutary effect on the minds of others.

Friday 18th, hearing rumours that *a great push* would be made yet, to obtain a chapel for the revolters, and as Mr. Wrothall was come home, Mr. Ingle and myself waited on him, to know his mind on the subject. Mr. W. considered, he did not hold the Chapel as Steward for the Circuit, but said he would give it up to us, as the Quarterly Meeting, if we would pay the debt upon it. After a long conversation, he came to the following conclusion, that if the Quarterly Meeting would pay the debt upon it they should have it, that he would balance the accounts by the next Tuesday and send them to me, that I might appoint a committee to audit the accounts and confer with him respecting them, and that he should expect an answer to his proposal within three days after the Quarterly Meeting, *viz.* Oct. 9th, and that if the Quarterly Meeting would not receive the chapel on these conditions, he should consider himself justified in applying the chapel to any purpose he thought proper.

Today, we learned that Smith, a seceded local preacher, had collected the Mint class, which he had before lead, half an hour before the time of the meeting, and had induced seven of the members to leave. When the Leader Mr. Harvey came to lead the class he found Smith with them.

On Wednesday papers were distributed at the chapel door to the people when they left the preaching at Southwark called a Report, specifying reasons for the seperation of the revolters, which is written in the usual style of seceders. There still appeared considerable agitation and suspicion in many persons, and one scarcely seemed to know how to place confidence in another.

Mr. Spicer still remains. He is a man of weak mind, destitute of decision of character, and carried hither and thither, as he may be addressed by persons of different sentiments. He has but little influence.

Monday Sept. 21 I received the following letter from Mr. Wrothall. 'Rev. Sir, I beg to inform you my accounts for Gainsford Street Chapel will be submitted to the Leaders Meeting of Gainsford Street tomorrow evening. You will please to appoint a committee as agreed immediately, as I wish to have a definitive answer previous to Quarter Day September 29, that I may not come under liabilities for the coming quarter. I am, Rev. Sir, Yours etc., W. Wrothall.'

I was surprised at receiving this note, in which Mr. W. shifts the ground of his former proposals. He shifts the business from the Quarterly Meeting of the Circuit to the Gainsford Street Leaders Meeting, and the time from the 9th October to before 29th September. I wrote him a note objecting to it; however, he brought them into the Leaders Meeting.

I learnt that the seceders were about taking a place near us in the Mint. They have since accomplished it, and on the day of opening their place, Smith at 7 o'clock Sunday morning preached out of doors close to our place, while one of the fraternity stood at the door of our place to turn the people to Smith, as they came to the prayer meeting. These acts, similar ones, and the scurrilous pieces in the newspaper have opened the eyes of many of our people and have attached other[s] more firmly to us. The Leaders Meeting at Southwark, continues very peaceable. I keep out of the Leaders Meeting every subject that does not belong to it. It seems they have been accustomed to discuss all kinds of subjects which may have taken place in their own circuit or others, by which means the wheel had gotten out of its place. However they are now come into good temper. We have several new leaders made, men of sound principle, and I trust we shall get right after a while.

On Tuesday 22nd September after preaching, the Leaders Meeting was held at Gainsford St. We ordered it so that Mr. Ingle might be there with me. Mr. Wrothall produced his accounts, with a debt of £71, which had accumulated the last four years. Mr. W. denied a part of the proposal he had made to Mr. Ingle and myself. We affirmed he made the proposal as we stated; however, he consented to let the business lie over to the Quarterly Meeting. We then entered upon the business of trying Dowson for his base conduct in calling an illegal meeting to take away the chapel, and observed he had violated his trusts as a Leader and Steward. After he had spoken for himself and as well as he could alleviated his offence, I observed, I did not wish to carry things to extremities, but could not suffer such an offence to be passed by without being visited by an act of discipline, and that he should be suspended from his office of Steward. Mr. Wrothall observed he did not see any evil in calling such a meeting, and that he would call one if he deemed it necessary—I informed him, if he did, he might depend on it, he should be visited with discipline. Mr. W. then moderated very much, and pleaded for Dowson that he *might be forgiven*, as others were guilty as well as he, etc. I observed, I did not wish to push the matter to extremes, and that if Mr. Dowson acknowledged his fault, it should be remitted. He acknowledged it was wrong and I passed it by. The meeting was exceedingly solemn and temperate and the clement act produced much satisfaction. . . .

143. *From James Gill*   Southwark, October 30, 1829

I commence with this at the point where in my last I concluded. I appointed Messrs. Shipton, Day and Holland to examine the accounts of the Gainsford Street Chapel, and on Friday evening September 25, they met Mr. Wrothall, and after examination found a debt of £71 of which the Sunday School was £38 in arrears.

Not knowing the temper of the Quarterly Meeting, and hearing hints that it would not accede to take the chapel with such a heavy debt, at the same time believing that if we lost the chapel it would shake this and the Lambeth Circuit to their centre, with the advice of a few friends, fourteen persons were invited to meet and consult together on the business. Accordingly on Wednesday evening September 30th, the meeting took place and after consultation, we agreed to advance £5 each, to be lent without interest if necessary, to pay off the debt, to take the chapel for the Southwark circuit, and to send a deputation to wait on Mr. Wrothall to know when he would require the money. The deputation that waited on Mr. W., after explanations, agreed with Mr. W. to pay the money by three instalments, one at three months, a second at six months, and the third at nine months. On Friday October 2nd the Committee met to receive the report of the deputation, drew out the bills for payment, and directed the deputation to wait on Mr. W. give him the bills, and receive from him the authority of possessing the chapel. The Treasurer, seat Stewards, tenants, were all appointed and it was determined that the chapel accounts should be regularly audited in the Quarterly Meeting. The deputation waited on Mr. W. on Saturday Oct. 3, but Mr. W. refused to settle the business, unless his book was signed by the auditors. He would not permit Mr. Day to take his book home, and as the accounts for four years had been made up from memory, the Auditors would not sign them. On Monday 5th Messrs, Day and Langley waited on Mr. W., went through the accounts examined the vouchers, and signed them.

Sunday October 4. The Scotch Church was opened some of the Leeds men Johnson and Baraclough were published to take a part. Their congregations were numerous, and collections were made at the three services, which amounted to £26. Messrs. Shepherd and Bowler were collectors. On Monday evening they had a full house at which they gave their reasons for seperation but formed their congregations into a religious meeting to prevent any persons replying to their statements. They expressed their thankfulness for their delivery from tyranny, and for the great things the Lord had done for them; stating what powerful manifestations they had in their meetings; money was in great plenty with them, and they were raised up to be reformers. A very favourite expression with the speakers was, 'we are all of a height'. However notwithstanding they are all of a height, they have made Mr. Jones a presiding Elder. I am not aware that the meeting has done us any injury, nor that it is likely to do us any.

On Monday October 6th[5th], we held our Quarterly Meeting, which was very peaceable, except being disturbed by three persons, Messrs. Stubly, E. Wilson and Hewitt. There had been whispers that an attack would be made on our allowances, and that a specific sum would be proposed instead of board, quarterage, etc., and I had prepared to meet it; but not a word of the kind was dropped, and had it not been for the three above-mentioned persons we should have been very happy.

Stubbly, one of the revolted Local Preachers, came and took his seat in the meeting under pretence of being a trustee for Peckham chapel, a rented place, with a debt of about £27. I observed that when any person relinquished his membership, of course his offices in the society ceased, and as the case of the Peckham Chapel did not constitute him a Trustee in the Methodistical sense, I begged him to withdraw. Mr. Frid observed, as he had his signature with Mr. Frid's for the money, he (Mr. Frid) would take all the responsibility on himself. Several times I desired him to withdraw, but he impudently kept his post. At last he said he would leave if he might address the meeting, but the meeting would not hear him, and we got rid of him after three quarters of an hour altercation. This gave Eli Wilson a fine opportunity for exercising his powers. Hewitt also was troublesome. Once a reference was made to Leeds by Hewitt, but I instantly called him to order. However no indecent reflections were offered on the proceedings of Conference though the men animadverted on the division of Circuit, etc. I was under the necessity of curbing both of them, and the meeting passed off very well. There has not been a Quarterly Meeting so peacable for some time. Our numbers are 968; we have a debt of £34, which is not great, as £20 has been paid for removals. I introduced the Gainsford Street Chapel business, but guarded myself against touching any points which might produce altercation and it was approved. Mr. Hewitt however, rose to defend Mr. Wrothall, and as no person had reflected on him, Mr. Day was provoked to say, 'that the less that was said about the business the better'. I invited Mr. Reece to our Quarterly Meeting but being unwell he could not attend.

On Tuesday the deputation waited again on Mr. Wrothall to settle the business, but he said he would not settle it at present, as reflections had been made in his character at the Quarterly Meeting, nor did he approve of so formal a deputation. After some explanations, and Mr. Day's observation that he was the only person who had said anything like reflection, he became friendly, and he said he would call upon Mr. Day tomorrow and settle it. He called upon Mr. Day Wednesday, but would not receive the money, saying, let it be till next week, I am now in a hurry.

Yesterday October 11, Lord's Day, at Southwark our evening's congregation was more than usual and we had a very excellent Love Feast, numerously attended and very blessed testimony delivered of the operations of the Divine grace. It was very lively, and such was the disposition of the people to speak, that when I concluded two or three were on their legs to speak. This I consider as a prelude of good.

We may have lost about thirty members including five local preachers, and six leaders. The people do not appear disposed to leave us, and but few members have gone with their Leaders. We do not suffer in our congregations from the revolt. Our Quarterly collection at Southwark was £14. 14s, which was something more than the preceding quarter, and I hope and trust through the blessing of God peace will be restored and prosperity ⟨with⟩ it. The Leaders Meetings have all been peaceable.

October 12. Monday evening. I examined the characters of the Leaders, according to the *Minutes of Conference* 1811 Vol. 3 p.[222] and gave them advice how to lead their classes to advantage, so as to promote piety, and holiness in the minds of the people. The Leaders were very attentive and serious, and I believe most of them were thankful for instruction. I have since heard of their satisfaction being expressed.

On Thursday October 22 Mr. Wrothall received £72, and delivered up the Gainsford Street Chapel to us, so that our fears in that business are over. He continues as a Leader, and perhaps may come into a better mind. There is a moving by the influence of grace in the people and congregation of Gainsford Street. Congregations good. At Albion Street we have a gracious prospect of good work. At

Southwark there is a blessed influence in some classes, the bands are increasing with much life, prayer meetings better attended, and the people generally I trust becoming more spiritually minded.

On Tuesday 20th Mr. Charles Jones, and his wife sent me their class books, resigning their office as Leaders, but determining to continue members. Mr. Jones was one of our most troublesome men. I called at his house to converse with him. He professed great respect for me, but I did not offer him his class book nor his wife. The next Leaders Meeting October 26, Mr. Wilson came, began to speak, I stopped him, not being a member of the meeting; he said Mr. Treffry and the friends had given him liberty to attend. I then permitted him to speak. He related Mr. Jones's excellencies and the necessity of offering him his office. Spicer and Davies spoke on the same side; but I was prudently determined not to acquiesce. Many of the leaders are glad he is out of the meeting. . . .

[*P.S.*] The storm has very considerably subsided, and a calm I trust is succeeding which will terminate in prosperity. . . .

144. *From John Mason*   London, October 30, 1829

I have sent you the slips of your valuable sermon upon Justification by Faith, which has been under God rendered a blessing to many and would have been a still greater blessing had you not suffered it to remain so long out of print. . . .

The dissentients in the South [Circuit] will not be able to effect much. They make a noise for the present and some of the dissatisfied in the other London Circuits may join them but not I believe to any extent that needs excite alarm. A leader has left in the East and joined them and and has taken away a considerable portion of his classes, but that is all at present. Mr. Eckett has been preaching for the dissentients but I do not know how Mr. Reece will act in the affair. There is a considerable feeling of dissatisfaction in that Circuit but no open breach, tho' it would not surprize me if there was. I hear the cause is reviving in Leeds after the sharp struggle and there is a cheering prospect of good in both the Circuits. The Sheffield *expected* division turns out quite a failure and they also will see good days I doubt not. . . .

145. *From Samuel Jackson*[1]   Sheffield, November 26, 1829

[Will Bunting preach the annual sermons on behalf of the Benevolent Society?]

[1] Samuel Jackson, superintendent, Sheffield circuit, 1829–1831; Sheffield (Carver Street) circuit, 1831–1832.

. . . I have hitherto opposed their wishes, being reluctant to trouble you with this application, knowing the multiplicity and the weight of your cares, and labours, in connection with Methodism. Several peculiar circumstances, however, appear to render a visit from you, at this time, specially desirable, if within the compass of a reasonable possibility.

1. James Sigstone and Co. have lately visited Sheffield. A meeting was called by public advertisement, and during four hours, they libelled the Methodist Conference, and preachers generally. It is said the man Jabez Bunting on that occasion came in for his full share of abuse. I know no measure more likely to undo any mischief which may then have been done, than for you to meet each of our congregations, as the advocate of the afflicted poor.

2. We have chosen a new secretary to the Benevolent Society in the place of Mr. Rawlins, who has thought proper, in various ways, to connect himself with Sigstone and his cause. This circumstance though trivial in itself, under our peculiar circumstances is a point gained. It has given some little umbrage. I am therefore wishful that something spirited, popular and efficient, be done for the Society.

I should also like a good collection. We have had much distress in the town. I wish old Methodism (God bless it) to preserve all its glory.

3. We have had a division in the Society, which although paltry in itself, is yet attended with circumstances, which are perplexing to us, and injurious in their operation on Methodism. Your presence, counsel, and ministerial influence would materially help us.

4. There [are] evident tokens of a return to better feelings, and more sober views on the part of our principal men. Our public meetings, so far, have given me entire satisfaction. I do not despair of seeing, by the blessing of God, a new chapel in the Park, a division of the Circuit,[1] and an end to those miserable bickerings, which, for some time, have agitated this large and fine society. This revived, hallowed, and important feeling, your visit, will, I am sure, tend greatly to strengthen.

5. Mr. Cubitt has volunteered to take your places, and to do anything that is to be done. I need not say that he is an efficient man. His coming can be announced, and thus all feeling of disappointment prevented. . . .

P.S. Mr. Rawlins, in compliance with a summons, has appeared before the Leaders Meeting. We told him, very plainly, of several things in

---

[1] Sheffield Park chapel, planned from 1827 and opened in 1831. At the 1831 Conference the Sheffield circuit was divided into the Carver Street and Norfolk Street circuits.

his conduct which were unsatisfactory, and inconsistent with his duty as a Methodist class leader—and that he had lost the confidence of his brethren—that we must have a free, and full, and brotherly conversation with him—and that the result of this conversation must be either the restoration of confidence or a dissolution of partnership. His replies were mere shuffles. The feeling produced was that of deep and general dissatisfaction with his proceedings. No man defended him. He has a month to consider the matter. He must either be deprived of his office, or continued in it as *an act of mercy.* Come and see us.

APPENDIX

Bunting's speech to the Stewards and Leaders of the Manchester (Grosvenor Street) Circuit on the management of Sunday Schools, September 20, 1826. M.C.A. MS. Scrapbook of James Everett, fo. 421.

Mr. Bunting, who spoke three hours on the question, stated: 1. That there had been a great deal of private talk—that he wished to be honest and bring it to the light. 2. That the preachers were charged with being at the bottom of it, which he denied. 3. That several of the friends had called upon [him] for the last year and [a] half, requesting him to have Methodist Sunday Schools, that so far back as a year and [a] half ago, he told them it was not the time of agitating the question, that he dissuaded them from touching it, intimating that they were about to have two chapels, and two schools attached to them, they might then determine. 4. That out of 24 of the Trustees of those chapels, there were 18 who were against the schools for all denominations of children being introduced into them. 5. That he was not without his reasons for the measure, since it was adopted though he had not hastened it: and (1) There was no *security*, either by *creed*, or in the *deeds* of those schools, that pure Christianity should be perpetuated in them; for the deeds in particular did not promote this. (2) They were unconnected with any church, perfectly independent of any, and might become Roman Catholic, Calvinistic, Socinian, or any other schools. (3) He objected to children of Methodists belonging to them, for they were given to the body in baptism, the subjects of Methodistical labour from the pulpit. It was proper that every chapel should have its school, etc.

Mr. B. was frequently interrupted—was very impassioned and argumentative—insisted on going on.

The friends of the schools for all denominations urged, on the other hand, 1. That their deeds bound them to . . . [*sheet pasted over the next line*] at liberty to alter. 2. That the generality of the teachers were Methodists and friends of Methodism. 3. That the schools had been gradually verging towards Methodism from their commencement. 4. That they were so far Methodistical that classes were formed, and the children were gradually introduced as members of the Society, to which Society they had become auxiliary. 5. That they were the fruits of general subscription obtained from the public specifically for the purpose of supporting the schools under the present name and in their present form, and that they were not at liberty, as servants and stewards of that public to make any alteration.

INDEX